D1500274

c E

The Myths of Antitrust

THE MYTHS

OF ANTITRUST

Economic Theory and Legal Cases

D. T. ARMENTANO, Ph.D.

ARLINGTON HOUSE   *New Rochelle, N.Y.*

348892

HD
2791
.A76
1972

Library of Congress Catalog Card Number 73-189376

ISBN 0-87000-159-0

MANUFACTURED IN THE UNITED STATES OF AMERICA

To Rose Alta

Contents

Acknowledgments

RATHER than acknowledge assistance, let me explicitly absolve all my former professors at the University of Connecticut and my present colleagues at the University of Hartford from any errors of theory or fact discovered in this volume. Although they have done their best to set me straight along the path of economic righteousness, I have, for the most part, resisted their experience, council, and good advise. Instead, in a typically stubborn fashion, I have gone ahead and written precisely what I believe to be the truth in each instance. Each reader will have to evaluate the correctness of that decision for himself. The plan of the book is as follows. Chapter 1, the introduction, outlines the operations of a free market system. Chapter 2 discusses the theoretical tools that economists employ to "measure" competition and monopoly. Chapter 3 details the important sections of the antitrust laws, some philosophical rationalizations for government intervention, and two early antitrust cases. Chapter 4 is an account of the petroleum industry between 1859 and 1911, Standard Oil of New Jersey's role in that industry, and the famous antitrust action against the Standard Oil Company. Chapters 5 and 6 are detailed histories and accounts of antitrust actions against the American Tobacco Company, the United States Steel Company, the Aluminum Company of America (Alcoa), and the United Shoe Machinery Corporation, respectively. Chapter 7 critically examines the theory of price fixing and some of the classic price-fixing antitrust cases, including the electrical equipment conspiracy of the late 1950s. Chapter 8 details the theory of price discrimination and some famous price discrimination cases under the antitrust laws. Chapter 9 is devoted to an examination of the theory of tying agreements and to a critical review of some classic tying agreement antitrust cases. Chapter 10 reviews merger theory and discusses in detail some of the most important merger cases of the 1960s. And, finally, Chapter 11 criticizes both the supporters and critics of antitrust, and concludes with some suggestions in the area of monopoly and antitrust.

Preface

THIS book attacks an American sacred cow—the antitrust laws of the United States. Like all sacred cows, antitrust laws are shrouded with an aura of authenticity. The prevailing view is that without these laws, a free, competitive economic system could not long endure, and that these laws protect the public from potentially exploitative business monopolies.

Economists, for the most part, have created, nurtured, and sustained the above view. Two generations of economists, both liberal and conservative, have accepted antitrust laws as important bulwarks against the abuses of "monopoly power." Although some economists have disapproved of particular sections of the laws, and although many more have argued for tougher enforcement, few have suggested that a competitive market system could or would do better without them. Antitrust laws are part of the conventional wisdom.

The widespread public impression created by this professional consensus is that economists know what they are talking about. From this premise several "safe" assumptions are made: 1) that there is an operational and reality-oriented definition of "monopoly power"; 2) that there is an economic model which proves that "monopoly power" misallocates scarce economic resources and spoils consumer welfare; 3) that there is an impressive body of empirical data—gleaned from the classic antitrust cases, presumably—that tends to confirm the misallocations suggested by the theory. This book argues that *no such* plausible theory of monopoly power and *no such* impressive body of empirical data *exist*.

This work differs from others on antitrust in two fundamental ways. Firstly, almost all volumes in this area rely heavily on the so-called classical theories of competition and monopoly, thereby reducing serious criticism of these theories to marginal dimensions. The impression from these works is that the criticisms are less impressive than the general theories themselves and therefore do not subtract substantially from the latter's policy implications. Secondly, almost all volumes on the subject present a welter of antitrust cases, void of relevant empirical data. Consequently, any economic evaluation of the conduct and performance of the firms involved is conspicuously absent. Apparently, we are to assume that the firms indicted and convicted under the antitrust laws actually raised prices, reduced outputs, produced shoddy products, colluded with competitors, drove rivals from the market through predatory practices, and abused their presumed monopoly power.

This book reverses the two arbitrary positions outlined above. In this work, the criticisms are more significant than the so-called general theories. Moreover, the antitrust cases examined—the classic cases only—are presented in a context that makes the conduct and performance of the firms involved comprehensible.

Finally, the overall purpose of this book is to provide students and interested citizens with a convenient guide to a comprehensive body of dissenting thought concerning antitrust theory and policy. In the light of this intention, the following volume is not a balanced set of contrasting opinions. It advances an extreme position, buttressed with specific facts and arguments that, hopefully, will encourage serious readers to rethink critically the antitrust policies of the United States.

The Myths of Antitrust

CHAPTER 1

Introduction:
The Theory of the Market System

ANTITRUST legislation did not develop and does not exist in a vacuum. Its context is the American capitalistic business system, and it developed in response to some rather fundamental changes in the market structure and economic philosophy of that system. But certainly a capitalistic enterprise system with or without antitrust is not an axiom of existence. What *is* a capitalistic economic system, and why do men *use* such a system? Theoretically, *how* is such a system supposed to function? And what, ultimately, is a society attempting to accomplish with an economic system? It is these fundamental questions that we shall consider.[1]

Economics is the science of scarcity. It begins with the assumption that man is a rational animal who must sustain himself through pro-

---

[1]The following exposition is a brutally brief description of the "economic problem" faced by all men and the methods by which a capitalistic system attempts to solve that "problem." It is intended only as an intellectual refresher, and to allow a more logical and comprehensible discussion of "competition" in Chapter 2. For readers desiring substantially more detail on these matters, or for those readers unfamiliar with the logic of the free enterprise system, see Ludwig von Mises, *Human Action* (New Haven: Yale University Press, 1963); Murray N. Rothbard, *Man, Economy and the State*, 2 v., (Princeton: D. Van Nostrand Company, 1962); and Armen A. Alchian and William R. Allen, *University Economics* (3rd ed.; Belmont, Calif.: Wadsworth Publishing Company, 1972).

ductive work. Rationality implies that man can order and adapt means to chosen ends and that he is willing to correct errors. Productivity recognizes that existence-sustaining goods are not freely provided by nature but produced by man through the intelligent and consistent human effort. In sum, the nature of man's existence requires that he produce the goods necessary for sustaining and extending life.

Men create goods, utilities, or satisfactions by combining their own energies—mental or physical—with the nonhuman material of nature in a process termed "production." Their self-interest clearly lies in discovering specific techniques of production that use the least valued factors and/or produce the greatest "output" of chosen goods. This desire to maximize the consequences of effort or minimize the effort associated with some produced good is called efficiency. Therefore, in trying to sustain and extend their existence, men seek and apply techniques of production that efficiently combine scarce factors in the production of desired commodities.

Focusing on *one* man will illustrate the basic economic principles involved here. Assume a Mr. X in the context of a deserted wilderness. X is unquestionably faced with the problem of economic survival and with the fact that life-sustaining commodities are not "free"; he must somehow transform the land and its natural resources into consumable goods. And it is clearly in his interest to make efficient use of himself such that he can generate as many goods and services as possible.

Before X begins his struggle for commodities he must determine the relative order of his desires. If food production is the most pressing aspect of his survival, its solution will be attempted first. If it is raining and cold, and if X is unprotected, shelter will also be of prime importance. Rescue, defense, and even recreation are additional alternatives. X must rank his most important ends in relation to their relative value to him and then rationally proceed to achieve them.

Assuming that X has ranked his ends, he must then proceed to discover and apply efficiently the proper techniques of production: he must put goods together. Simple reasoning and movements may allow him to pick ripe berries from a nearby bush without much difficulty. Much more complicated mental and physical effort may be required to construct a lance capable of felling an animal, or a shelter capable of withstanding the extremes of weather. X's ability to satisfy his desires and survive will depend directly on the quality of the factors at his disposal and the efficiency of his techniques. He will survive in good fashion if resources are plentiful and if he is willing and able to discover and apply production techniques efficiently. If his resources are poor, or if he is lazy, injured, or mentally incapable of production, then he will probably perish.

Assuming that X does not perish, it is likely that he will soon reason that the creation of "helping goods" (capital goods) will allow him to increase his present efficiency in many ways. For example, there are several alternative methods of picking edible berries off a high tree. X might first with much difficulty climb the tree, secure the berries, climb back down the tree, and consume the berries. A desire for more berries would require repeating that production process. Or, as an alternative, he might attempt to shake the tree and catch the falling consumer goods. Or he might throw rocks in an effort to dislodge the potential goods from nature. All such efforts are direct methods of production; all such methods attempt to achieve consumer goods by combining labor with nature directly; and all (depending on the skill of the laborer) may be somewhat successful.

Obviously, it will be more efficient in the long run for X to begin the construction of a good he does not directly consume but which helps him produce berries. For example, X might decide to construct a simple ladder for easier climbing or a pole with a hook on the end for shaking berries from the tree more efficiently. The successful construction and application of either capital good will greatly increase the efficiency of his food production. In fact, since the efficient production of berries will economize on other scarce factors of production—notably, labor time—the use of a capital good here will increase X's overall capacity to generate more of *all* goods. Capital goods will certainly lead to an increase in X's standard of living.

Capital formation is possible, however, only if X had already put aside enough consumer goods to tide him through the capital goods construction period. The building of capital goods always requires the use of a reservoir of saved commodities and the temporary lowering of present direct production. X must first save and then "invest." Once capital goods are produced and put to work, their increase in efficiency generates additional outputs (berries) for consumption, thereby creating additional potential reserves that buy time for future capital formation or capital replacement. Additional capital goods imply additional increases in efficiency, additional increases in outputs relative to inputs, the satisfaction of an increasing number of different ends, and a rising standard of overall existence. X is now on his way toward sustained "economic development," and he has earned it.

Although the micro-model just used is admittedly simplified, the economic principles it illustrates can be employed with minor qualifications to highlight the operations of a complex society. Every society faces the great economic fact of scarcity. Creativity and human knowledge must be applied to produce as many goods as possible. Likewise, before production is attempted, ends must be ranked in descending importance, and the formulas for achieving those ends must be devised and correctly employed. Furthermore, a society must make the same decisions and face the same difficulties with respect to accumulating savings and allowing for crucial capital formation. Finally, the consequences of the efforts will be the same: a society that can efficiently exploit its economic resources will become wealthy in consumer goods; and if it cannot, it will not.

There are, of course, differences between a self-sufficient economic situation and a complex society. If the value of trade and exchange are recognized, and if trade and exchange are possible, a society can benefit immeasurably from an organizational technique known as "specialization" or "division of labor." Instead of one man attempting to produce fish nets, saw trees, plow the soil, make bricks, shoe horses, and educate the young, it is more beneficial if *each* man specializes in that aspect of production that he accomplishes best. When all men specialize and exchange their specialized outputs for the specialized outputs of others, the total amount of goods available to all increases many times. Through production and exchange traders are able to enjoy other trader's particular talents and proficiencies. The range, complexity, and variety of the exchanged goods become almost limitless. Men buy and enjoy goods that they could never have created themselves. The net result of specialization and exchange is a substantial increase in the quality of man's standard of existence.

This beneficial difference, however, produces its share of additional complexities. The most general way of expressing these complexities is to note that in an exchange society, producers and traders must *interdependently* solve questions X, for better or worse, solved alone. For example, X ranked his desired ends *himself;* he selected what he believed were the most efficient techniques of producing his chosen ends *himself.* Furthermore, he consumed or refrained from consuming his own production and, consequently, made the appropriate investment decision *himself*. Obviously, a society must develop "mechanisms" for translating demands into exchangeable commodities, for selecting the most efficient techniques of production (and the groups of persons to employ those techniques), and for converting a society's "savings" into capital goods formation. The particular set of economic institutional arrangements that men adopt to help solve these three aspects of the problem of scarcity can be called "economic systems."

For purposes of this discussion economic systems are differentiated according to the respective rules or legal relationships that societies institutionalize concerning the ownership and use of *property*. Pure *capitalism* (*laissez-faire*) holds that all property must be private and all production and trade of that property must not be regulated. *Mixed capitalism* holds that private property and competitive production are useful conventions that governments sanction because these relationships are usually efficient. Accordingly, in a mixed economic system, most property would be private (common exceptions: public schools, roads, bridges, post offices) and most production and trade would be free (common exceptions: regulation of drugs, railroads, interest rates, minimum wage rates). *Corporatism* or *fascism* holds that the state, not the individual, has inalienable rights and that private ownership and free trade should only be permitted when it is in the state's interest. Accordingly, in a fascistic economic system pseudo-private property relationships would be allowed, but almost all important production and trade would be regulated by the state in its own interests. *Socialism* accepts neither private property nor free production and trade as inalienable or desirable. Accordingly, a socialist economic system would employ the public ownership of all the essential means of production (property) and some form of state planning to direct and allocate those resources.

CAPITALISM

In this work we are concerned with only one economic system—capitalism. We shall assume a free market system operating without any government ownership, regulation, spending, or taxation. Yet (and this is the point) how does this free market system "operate," i.e., how does it solve the crucial problems of economic scarcity?

Let us return to our societal situation and assume that men reason or discover that production and exchange would be mutually beneficial. In the absence (initially) of a universal medium of exchange, resource owners and goods owners would likely exchange privately owned property with each other—to mutual advantage—through a "bartering" arrangement; that is, they would exchange specific units of land, labor or capital, or finished goods and services, for units of land, labor, and capital or other finished goods and services. The rates of exchange or terms agreed to by the trading parties would be the *prices* of the exchange. As an example, if a maker of bread or an owner of bread voluntarily decided to accept five labor hours in exchange for one loaf, the terms of exchange would be one loaf of bread for five labor hours and the price of the bread would be in units of labor hours given up. If the loaf of bread were traded instead for two pencils, the price of the bread would be in terms of the pencils given up in exchange. And so it would go for the exchange of all factors, goods, and services.

However, barter as a method of trade and exchange is a cumbersome and extremely inflexible device. It assumes (indeed, requires) an identical "coincidence of wants" on the parts of the trading parties before actual exchange can occur. It makes capital good production almost impossible since few labor factors or landowners would desire to exchange their services for parts of some capital good. It limits and stifles the division of labor and hence holds down potential production and consumption. It is a thoroughly cumbersome system of "exchange," and it is doubtful whether such a system could raise living standards beyond subsistence levels.

Because a market system using barter is relatively inefficient we would expect it to be replaced by something better. In a market economy, over time, it is more than likely that one commodity will become more "acceptable" in trade than any other. This generally accepted medium of exchange or "money" would be a commodity that could be used to purchase any other good or factor. If, for example, "ounces of silver" became the acceptable trading medium, trades and exchanges would take place in terms of "units (weights) of silver given up." When a laborer exchanges five hours of his labor time for (let's assume) an ounce of silver, he could use that ounce to buy any other commodity or factor in the market at any set of mutually agreeable terms. Thus, the acceptable money could act as a claim on an infinite number of economic goods and extend the range of production and consumption fantastically.

The range of production and consumption is also extended in a more fundamental way since a generally accepted medium of exchange makes the prices of all goods and the costs of all factors directly comparable. It thus allows rational economic calculation. It permits producers to seek out the least cost combinations of factors to produce exchangeable commodities. Since all factor and good trades will be in terms of units (weights) of silver, producers will be able to compare the real cost of one factor with another; the entire factor mix with some alternative; and the entire expenditure on factors with the exchangeable value (in silver) of the commodity being produced and sold. They can, therefore, seek to maximize their production, given factor cost, or minimize their use of scarce, relatively expensive factors, given some output level. Thus, rational economic calculation and economic efficiency become possible when all prices and all costs are computed in terms of some homogenous medium of exchange. The free market economic system can now become a functioning *price system.*

The terms of voluntary exchange, though set by mutual agreement by the trading parties, are not *arbitrary* rates of exchange. They are, instead, a consequence of the respective self-interests of both buyer and seller to get the most in exchange for the least sacrifice and a direct function of the demand for and supply of commodities or factors in the market at that time. For example, assume that a potential buyer and seller have come together to negotiate the terms of exchange. Each party wants to achieve the most favorable rate of exchange from his particular point of view. The buyer desires to pay the lowest possible price to obtain the desired units of product or factor. He would be more willing, other things being equal, to purchase a particular commodity (or batch of commodities) if its exchange rate were lower than if it were higher. Sellers of goods or factors, on the other hand, want to exchange their "output" at the highest rates possible. They would, other things being equal, be more anxious to sell a commodity (or batch of commodities) at higher rates than at lower ones. Thus, the willingness of traders to exchange private property is a function of the respective anticipated exchange rates in the market for the commodities or factors under consideration.

These anticipated exchange rates are the context within which trading *may* proceed. If the highest rate potential buyers are willing to pay does not exceed the lowest rate that sellers are willing to accept for some commodity (or batch of commodities), then no trade and, accordingly, no exchange rate is possible. If the rate buyers are willing to pay does meet or exceed the rate sellers will accept, a mutually agreeable price, and hence exchange, is possible. If demand is strong (if the number of monetary units given up per unit of commodity is high), the exchange rate will be high. If demand is low —but still higher than the minimum supply price—the exchange rate will be low. Either way, once both parties reach agreement, an equilibrium price is made that clears and ends the market situation. If new "supplies" and "demands" appear, they can be "cleared" through the same process, providing, of course, the parties agree to negotiate.

A host of scarcity-related problems become solvable once the exchange rates are mutually determined by voluntary trade in a free market. For example, the kinds and numbers of commodities that get continuously supplied in a pure capitalistic economic system will ultimately be determined by the demand and rate of exchange decisions that buyers make. Buyers—in a kind of representation election —select particular products with their money votes. If the prices buyers are willing to pay exceed all the costs of supplying that commodity, then it will be supplied. In short, the goods that get produced in a market economy are those that return a profit. Therefore, in this context, the market system ranks society's demands, translates that demand information to potential suppliers, and clears factor and commodity markets.

"How" the commodities will be produced in an exchange economy is also a function of prices and a consequence of the price mechanism. Much controversy, however, surrounds the particular conditions and assumptions necessary for complete economic efficiency or optimum resource and commodity satisfaction. As a general rule (leaving the exceptions and particular conditions to the next chapter), in a free-market system competition forces firms to adopt efficient techniques of production in order to remain in business. Profits attract new suppliers, and a new supply tends to influence market prices, thereby forcing firms to curb costs or innovate new products. Those suppliers unable to reduce cost or innovate are driven from the market; those that remain are efficient, relative to the prices that buyers are willing to pay for products. Hence a price system, in this context, is the mechanism through which society selects those firms that are to produce goods efficiently.

Finally, personal goods accumulation is also determined through the market system. The amounts of commodities that men gather through exchange will be a function of their money income and the prices of commodities. Their money incomes, in turn, will be a direct function of the demand for and the supply of factors that they own and sell. If an individual sells or rents high-priced land, labor, or capital factors, he can accumulate a great wealth of commodities. Accordingly, if he has little to sell or trade, he will be poor in income and goods. Consequently, in a free market, it is ownership and prices of traded factors (neglecting gifts) that determine the pattern of commodity distribution. Production determines consumption.

A capitalistic economic system allows market-clearing rates of exchange to be determined by negotiation, and profits to accrue to those parties able to keep their costs below the exchange rates of their output. Profits, in turn, key investment decisions and help determine, along with the rate of savings, the pace and direction of capital accumulation. Hence an economic system employing private property and free trade should be able to solve efficiently a society's scarcity problems.

CHAPTER 2

The Controversy Over Competition

COMPETITION

While the American economy in the twentieth century still primarily employs the institutions of private property and free exchange, it certainly does not operate according to *laissez-faire* principles. The decline of *laissez-faire* as an acceptable economic doctrine began with the rise of industrialism in the post-Civil War years.[1] At that time, spokesmen for labor, business, government, and even some economists,[2] began arguing that some federal regulatory control over big business was necessary to protect the public interest. These spokesmen openly attacked *laissez-faire* economics as indefensible, irrational—even immoral; government, they argued, could

[1]There had never been an explicit *laissez-faire* philosophy in America. There had always been government involvement in economic affairs, especially at the state level, but there had been no reasoned national policy of subsidy and control before the Civil War.

[2]The platform of the American Economic Association, founded in 1885, declared that "the doctrine of *laissez-faire* is unsafe in politics and unsound in morals." Among those who subscribed to this view were such rising young economists as John R. Commons, Richard T. Ely, and Simon N. Patten, who wielded considerable influence in the following century. See "Report of the Organization of the American Economic Association," Merle Curti *et al.*, eds., *American Issues: The Social Record* (4th ed. rev.; Philadelphia: J. B. Lippincott Company, 1971), II, 158–162. See also Joseph Dorfman, *The Economic Mind in American Civilization: 1865–1918* (New York: Viking Press, 1949), I, 206–208.

and should involve itself in economic affairs in an effort to move the
economy toward a greater degree of social and economic welfare. An
important issue in the controversy over *laissez-faire* was the appropriate degree of business competition in the market place.

It was argued that the rationale for *laissez-faire* economics depended on intense business competition. If competition were intense, a free market economic system was relatively efficient and
tended to maximize output and minimize costs. If competition were
weak or nonexistent, however, the free market was likely to be inefficient and not capable, therefore, of maximizing output or minimiz-
ing costs in the public interest. It was argued that, in essence, a
monopolistic capitalism had no utilitarian justification and should be
regulated in the best interests of the society as a whole. Antitrust
laws, apparently, were an outgrowth of the belief that competitive
capitalism was not necessarily self-preserving and had to be actively
maintained by governmental policy.

The idea that competition was declining in the post-Civil War
period is familiar enough. Almost every economic historian who has
written about the period has so stated. For example, Joseph W.
McGuire's *Business and Society* provides a typical expression of the
conventional wisdom regarding competition in that period:

> There have always existed many forces which tend to reduce
> competition. In the thirty years following the Civil War, these
> forces began to predominate in the United States . . . Competi-
> tion, so effective as a regulating force on business operations in
> the decades prior to the war, was steadily decreasing as a few
> firms began to dominate our important industries and as these
> and other concerns turned more and more to collusion.[3]

The impression from McGuire (and almost all works) is that the
Sherman Antitrust Act (1890) was passed in an attempt to preserve
—or restore—a rapidly deteriorating competitive market place.
Capitalism, it is implied, was amended to save it.

But is this impression *correct?* Was competition actually declining?
Was antitrust legislation passed to "save" the economy from
"monopoly"? McGuire himself confuses the issue:

> From 1865 to 1897, declining prices year after year made it
> difficult for businessmen to plan for the future. In many areas

[3](New York: McGraw-Hill Book Company, 1963), pp. 39–40.

of business there was a tendency toward overproduction, for the new railroad•links had resulted in a nationalization of the market east of the Mississippi, and even small concerns in small towns were forced to compete with other, often larger, firms located at a distance. At the same time, there were remarkable advances in technology and productivity. In short, it was a wonderful era for the consumer and a frightful age for the producer especially as competition became more and more severe.[4]

But how could competition be "steadily decreasing" while it was becoming "more and more severe"? If competition was declining as a few firms dominated certain industries, how could the post-Civil War period have been a "wonderful era for the consumer"? Was the Sherman Act passed to preserve competition or was it passed to preserve a certain kind of *market structure?* It is the controversy over competition that we shall consider next.

Structure, Conduct, and Performance

What *is* competition and how does it decline? *Webster's Seventh New Collegiate Dictionary* defines competition as "the effort of two or more parties to secure the business of a third party by the offer of the most favorable terms."[5] Inherent in this definition are three important aspects of competition that economists have come to term *structure, conduct,* and *performance.* Structure relates to the number of firms in a given market situation, their respective shares of market output, the relevant entry conditions surrounding the market, and the demand conditions pertinent to that market. Conduct relates to the pricing policies of the firms in a given market structure, their policy of product differentiation, and their general business practices aimed at rival sellers. Performance relates to firm efficiency, cost reduction, and innovation. In the definition quoted above, therefore, "two or more parties" could relate to market structure while the particular "efforts" of the firms involved and "the most favorable terms" could relate to conduct and performance.

Pure Competition and Antitrust

But how do all these aspects of competition come together to make the definition useful? Does competion automatically exist any time

---

[4] *Ibid.,* pp. 38–39.
[5] (Springfield, Mass.: G. & C. Merriam Company, 1971), p. 169. By permission. © From Webster's Seventh New Collegiate Dictionary 1971 by G. & C. Merriam Co., Publishers of the Merriam-Webster Dictionaries.

two or more firms attempt to win business by offering the "most favorable terms"? Does competition increase when the number of firms involved increases, and decrease when the number of firms decreases? Is one pricing, product-differentiation policy more competitive than another? Are all cooperative attempts or efforts anticompetitive? Can "most favorable terms" be offered by a declining number of (larger) firms? Can industry performance improve even though one seller or group of sellers dominates a market structure? Is there an essential link between certain market structures and expected business conduct and performance? In sum, how do we know whether markets are competitive or monopolistic? Or to what *extent* they are competitive or monopolistic?

Between 1880 and 1933 economists defined and constructed mathematical models to encompass a theoretical business competition in terms of a particular *market structure.*[6] "Pure competition" was said to exist when: (1) all producers were small, relative to the total market supply; (2) the commodity produced by all these small firms was homogeneous; and (3) when resources were mobile and no artificial restrictions existed on demand, supply, or price. In addition, "perfect competition" existed when market knowledge was "perfect."[7]

But why *this* definition of competition? This particular definition of competition was popular with economists, and especially with the mathematical economists, because it implied a certain conduct-performance from economic markets that economists came to regard as "optimal." In a word, a purely competitive market structure would automatically generate economic forces that tended to maximize society's wants at the least possible cost: it was the most *efficient.* Accordingly, pure competition became the rationale for *laissez-faire;* departures from pure competition became the rationale for antitrust. As a leading microtheorist puts it:

> . . . economic models set up on the basis of pure competition furnish us with a "norm" or "ideal" situation against which we can appraise the actual operation of the economic system. As we shall see later, *if* pure competition could and did exist

[6]Donald Dewey, *The Theory of Imperfect Competition: A Radical Reconstruction* (New York: Columbia University Press, 1969), pp. 5–10.

[7]See any modern microeconomics text or, specifically, Richard H. Leftwich, *The Price System and Resource Allocation* (4th ed.; Hinsdale, Ill.: Dryden Press, 1970), pp. 26–28.

throughout the entire economy, we would secure the fullest measure of economic efficiency, given the distribution of income. The want satisfaction obtained in the economy would be as great as its techniques and limited resources would allow. The purely competitive model frequently is used in this way as the basis for public regulation of imperfectly competitive situations. Presumably it underlies the philosophy and enforcement of the Sherman Antitrust Act of 1890. . . .[8]

How does this kind of competition produce "optimal" results? If all producers' outputs were so small that each had no effect on market price, then all producers take as given the one and only market price determined by general supply and demand forces. Individual prices higher than market price were not possible; individual prices lower than market price were foolish and irrational. Hence, market price became the individual demand curve facing each firm and was a horizontal line at every possible output level.

Given these demand conditions, individual suppliers attempted to maximize their own profits by producing outputs where their marginal costs equaled the market price; they were price-takers and quantity-makers. If they succeeded in making economic profits, however, additional supplies tending to depress market price were encouraged. A falling market price narrowed profits and closed down inefficient firms. The market price would continue to fall until it reached the minimum point of the average cost curve for some representative firm. At that point, price, marginal costs, and minimum average cost were equated and economic profits were zero. All firms were now producing exactly the number of homogeneous commodities consumers desired, at the absolute minimum cost of production. Scarce economic resources were being used as judiciously as possible, and the community's satisfaction, other things equal, was being optimized. Thus, the purely competitive market structure automatically generated proper behavior and performance; from a classical economic viewpoint, there would be no reason to regulate this "industry" or an entire economy that was purely competitive.

THE MONOPOLY MODELS

The opposite of pure competition is pure monopoly. Pure monopoly is a situation where one firm has somehow obtained con-

[8] *Ibid.*, pp. 28–29. (Copyright © 1970 by Dryden Press, Inc. Reprinted by permission of Dryden Press, Inc.)

trol over the market for some unique commodity or service. In classical terms, a business monopoly was a single seller insulated from
competition that inherently performed poorly *vis-à-vis* competitive
sellers.

Importantly, the monopolist's *structural* characteristics were responsible for a conduct and performance that differed substantially
from pure competition. Since the monopolist was the sole supplier
of some unique product, he could "determine" market price by
determining market supply. Unlike the purely competitive price
taker, therefore, the monopolist had the "power" (monopoly power)
to "administer" price and, in some sense, control the market.

While economists admitted that neither pure competition nor
pure monopoly could actually exist, they did infer that market structures that were closer to pure competition were "more competitive"
(and, therefore, good), while market structures that were closer to
pure monopoly were "less competitive" (and, therefore, bad). Thus,
as business firms got larger, as they merged perhaps, and as they
began to innovate, advertise, and differentiate their products, and
engage in interdependent rivalry for the consumers' dollars, *they
wrecked pure competition and any chance at it,* and moved closer
and closer to "monopoly." The market, economists concluded, was
becoming "less competitive." And that, as might be apparent, was
probably the sort of "competition" that was "declining" in the latter
part of the 19th century.

Since 1933, it has been common to refer to any market structure
that is less than purely competitive as "monopolistic," or "imperfectly competitive," or "oligopolistic," or "monopolistically competitive." It has also been quite common to remark that such market
structures inherently misallocate economic resources and are not as
"efficient" as pure competition. The antitrust implications of this
theoretical approach should be quite apparent to the reader. The
two economists that had the most to do with providing the theoretical tools of analysis in this area are Joan Robinson and Edward Chamberlin.

The Argument of Joan Robinson

Joan Robinson focused the issue of resource "misallocation" under
structural conditions of less than pure competition in her classic, *The
Economics of Imperfect Competition*,[9] first published in 1933. In this

[9]All references that follow are to Joan Robinson, *The Economics of Imperfect Competition* (2nd ed.; New York: St. Martin's Press, 1961).

volume, Mrs. Robinson developed the familiar tools of geometric analysis still employed by undergraduates in economic price theory to "prove" that anything less than pure competition is "undesirable" from an economic point of view. In brief, she demonstrated that a firm producing a "monopolized output" (her terms) necessarily faced a "falling demand" curve, and thus a marginal revenue schedule that was less than average revenue at every output level. Since all profit-oriented firms attempted to equate marginal revenue with marginal cost (supply), and since equilibrium could only be achieved when marginal revenue, marginal cost, and average cost were equal, a monopolistic seller always generated less output than a purely competitive seller. Accordingly, the monopoly price was always higher than the competitive price, and the firm was always of less than optimum size:

> If competition is imperfect the demand curve for the output of the individual firm will be falling . . . and the double condition of equilibrium can only be fulfilled for some output at which average cost is falling. The firms will therefore be of less than optimum size when profits are normal.[10]

Hence, imperfectly competitive markets automatically misallocated scarce economic resources and were necessarily *less efficient* than purely competitive markets.

As a warning to her readers, however, Robinson admitted that the alleged "comparison" between competition and imperfect competition depended upon crucial yet unrealistic assumptions. She stated that:

> In order to make a valid theoretical comparison between competitive output and monopoly output in a particular industry it is necessary to make *very severe assumptions.* First, we must have a definite idea of what we mean by the commodity that we are considering. Secondly, if we wish to discuss what will happen to output and prices if a certain commodity, hitherto produced by competiting firms, is monopolised, we must assume that neither the demand curve for the commodity *nor the costs of production* of any given output are altered by the change. *These assumptions are unlikely to be fulfilled in any actual situation* . . .[11]

---

[10] *Ibid.*, p. 97.
[11] *Ibid.*, pp. 143–144 (Emphasis added).

In addition, there were whole classes of industrial activity (she specifically mentioned railways and the distribution of gas and electricity) where any general comparisons were "meaningless."[12]

While Robinson's models have been reworked, modified, and modernized, the fundamental *welfare* conclusions of the alleged comparison between pure competition and monopoly or imperfect competition have (somehow) survived. It is still respectable to suggest that imperfectly competitive markets inherently misallocate resources and are less than optimal for consumers, since price, average cost, and marginal cost can never be equated.[13] At this point in the analysis, it might suffice to note that such inferences are highly suspect for any *real* market situation or market comparisons—as even Robinson warned—since few if any markets generate homogeneous products, and fewer markets still would find their cost functions completely unaffected by a shift from pure competition to imperfect competition. Thus even on its own terms, the comparison for welfare purposes may be "meaningless."

Pure Competition: The Straw Man

Much more importantly, however, the market structure described as being purely competitive and optimal must certainly appear strange to anyone acquainted with flesh-and-blood consumers or business organizations. In the real-world market place, business competition appears to be almost opposite to economic pure competition. Businessmen and consumers would hardly describe selling markets with no direct price competition, no product differentiation, no brand names, no selling costs, no location advantages, no advertising, no economies of scale, and no innovation as "purely competitive"! In the same light, few, if any, businessmen or consumers would regard the *existence* of these factors as a "movement toward imperfect competition" or, as is clearly implied, toward monopoly and less consumer satisfaction. Instead, businessmen and consumers would recognize these factors as the essence of a competitive market.

Obviously, the difficulties surrounding pure competition surround the assumptions. A least-cost allocation of existing resources, given

---

[12] *Ibid.*, p. 166.

[13] See almost any economics textbook on this point, or see even the more advanced F.M. Scherer, *Industrial Market Structure and Economic Performance* (Chicago: Rand McNally and Company, 1970), p. 400.

existing technology and given existing consumer demand, might be optimal in a changeless, constant, equilibrium world with make-believe businessmen and mythical consumers, but it surely would not be optimal in a world of changing and nongiven consumer tastes, changing and nongiven economic resources, and changing and non-given technology. In the real world, as apart from economic fantasy, competition is a dynamic process where firms—to sustain their exis-tence—must understand and exploit consumer demand, discover and employ economic resources, and adopt and embody technologi-cal change in order to meet the thrusts of the ever-changing market forces initiated by consumers, factors of production, or by one's eco-nomic rivals. This competition is an endless series of "differentia-tions," and is as far from the docile and calm "homogeneity" assump-tions of pure competition as imaginable. Differentiations of product, of service, of quality, of convenience, of advertising, of technology, of innovation, and of price are the very essence of market competi-tion, rather than "imperfections" or departures from some presup-posed "ideal" equilibrium. What is ideal about homogeneous pro-ducts and small, profitless firms, when consumers consistently reward firms that sell differentiated products, quality products, relia-ble products, well-packaged products, convenient products, new products, and, of course, price-competitive products? Consumers, not economists, define market optimality every time they purchase, and for them it is always and only *total* product performance that counts. Hence, any theory that postulates that consumer optimality depends upon some unlikely market structure with improbable con-sumers and impossible firms, is irrelevant and misleading. *That* par-ticular market structure does not, never did, and never could *exist* in a free market. Therefore, it cannot legitimately be hypothesized as optimal nor used to either "measure" departures from competi-tion or serve as a foundation for antitrust policy. If antitrust is founded on pure competition as a standard, it is founded on an impossibility.

Although economists are fond of noting that large stock exchanges approach the assumptions of pure (and even perfect) competition (and they do), attempt to imagine the actual production and distribu-tion of some consumer or capital good under such assumptions. As-sume, for example, that ball point pens are to be manufactured and sold under such conditions. According to the theory of pure competi-tion, we must postulate so many independent sellers such that no one seller has any control over market price. We must also postulate that all the pens are homogeneous "products" as far as consumers are concerned. Further, we must neglect any location differentials, selling costs, and any economies of scale in manufacturing, advertising, or purchasing. And lastly, we must assume that all producers attempt to generate an output that equates their marginal revenue with their marginal costs.

Yet all this is ridiculous since consumers and producers never engage in voluntary exchange under such circumstances. In the first place, all sellers exert some "price control," and demand curves can never be *perfectly* elastic. This is so, since the real world, unlike the mathematical model, does not contain the "infinitely small steps" of the calculus, and all output adjustments for homogeneous products will have some measurable effect on market price. Furthermore, and more important, consumers do not purchase—and sellers do not produce and sell, therefore—"identical" products. In a *free* market, individualism is to be expected on the part of consumers and firms; the goods produced, therefore, will be differentiated to the extent and degree that consumers reward differentiation. For example, if different *colored* pens are sold profitably at different prices, it is not "irrational" or "less than optimal." If different pen *sizes* will sell profitably, they will be innovated by some firms and imitated by others. If pens sell quickly in drug stores, they will continue to be offered there; and to the extent that consumers reward geographic dispersion in marketing, the selling market will be dispersed. If pen durability under adverse conditions becomes an important selling factor, it will be stressed—and advertised. Old fountain pen users will have to be told that there are better ball point pens, and that they are relatively cheaper. Old ball point pen users will have to be told that the new innovations have been accomplished successfully. Price, price changes, and discounts for bulk purchases (since there *are* economies of scale) will have to be communicated and recommunicated to new consumers. Obviously, the consequent rivalry and competition between the separate ball point pen firms (and the fountain pen firms) must take place in the context of the factors just discussed, and there is nothing automatically irrational, imperfect, or less-than-optimal about it. Nor, accordingly, need this competition tend toward any static "equilibrium." Hence, in summation, there is nothing either real or optimal about a purely competitive market structure, nor the pricing behavior (or lack of it) associated with such a market structure.

The Argument of Edward Chamberlin

The idea that real-world competition might contain "monopolistic" structural elements is not new or original. Edward Chamberlin made the same point in *The Theory of Monopolistic Competition*, published in 1933.[14] He used the term "monopolistic competition" to denote economic markets that contained slightly differentiated products, advertising expenditures, and location differentials. He argued that such factors were not always short-run "imperfections" that tended to disappear as markets evolved toward pure competition; as he stated in a later work, the *Atlantic Monthly* and *Popular Mechanics* did not tend to become a homogeneous commodity in the long-run.[15] Instead, product differences were purposeful and permanent and part of business rivalry; to assume them away—as the theory of pure competition and pure monopoly did—was to ignore real competition altogether, since the business world was always a *blend* of competitive and monopolistic elements.

Chamberlin's geometric analysis of monopolistic competition was strikingly similar to Robinson's geometric analysis of imperfect competition. For example, Chamberlin's monopolistically competitive seller also discovers that in equilibrium, average revenue, marginal cost, and average cost are equated at less than minimum average costs. And Chamberlin, like Robinson, quickly concludes that "where monopoly elements are present, the equilibrium price is . . . inevitably higher than the one indicated by the intersection of the competitive demand and cost curves";[16] hence, "the impossibility of production under the most efficient conditions is settled once and for all by the shape of the demand curve."[17]

Chamberlin warned, however, that the conclusions reached above applied *only* when "product variation and selling outlays" were omitted from the analysis; differentiated products could *not* be forced into the mold of purely competitive analysis without committing "definite errors."[18] All firms produced "variables," not homogenous product or "output"; and time, advertising, quality, location, and price always differentiated "product." And if real consumers

---

[14]All references are to Edward H. Chamberlin, *The Theory of Monopolistic Competition* (Cambridge, Mass.: Harvard University Press, 1948).

[15]Edward H. Chamberlin, *Towards a More General Theory of Value* (New York: Oxford University Press, 1957), p. 15.

[16]Chamberlin, *The Theory of Monopolistic Competition*, p. 114.

[17]*Ibid.*, p. 98.

[18]*Ibid.*, p. 116.

really wanted heterogeneous products sold in convenient locations, then it would be foolish and wrong to define optimality as anything but a kind of monopolistic competition. Pure competition was no longer a welfare ideal. As he has concluded so clearly:

> The explicit recognition that product is differentiated brings into the open the problem of variety and makes it clear that *pure competition may no longer be regarded as in any sense an "ideal" for purposes of welfare economics* . . . Differences in tastes, desires, incomes, and locations of buyers, and differences in the uses which they wish to make of commodities all indicate the need for a variety and the necessity of substituting for the concept of a "competitive ideal" an ideal involving both monopoly and competition. How much and what kinds of monopoly and with what measure of social control become the questions.[19]

WORKABLE COMPETITION

Since the 1930s, very few prominent economists have concurred with Edward Chamberlin's views on pure competition. For example, J. M. Clark's attempt to define a "workable competition" has probably been the most referenced effort, and certainly the touchstone of all critical assaults on the concept of pure competition.[20] In more recent years, the writings of such economists as the late Sumner H. Slichter and John Kenneth Galbraith have sounded a similar theme.[21] In this author's view, however, it was the breadth, depth, and intellectual power of Joseph A. Schumpeter that shook the concept of a purely competitive optimality to its very foundations.

Schumpeter: The Nature of Competition

Schumpeter chided his fellow economists for thinking of competition (and hence, of capitalism) in static, Wicksellian-Marshallian terminology, and for supposing that some "golden age" of pure competition had existed in the distant past. There had been no golden age of perfect competition in the past, and it had not, therefore, "metamorphosed itself into the monopolistic age." On the con-

[19] *Ibid.*, p. 214 (Emphasis in original).

[20] "Toward a Concept of Workable Competition," *American Economic Review*, XXX (June, 1940), 241–256. See also Clark's *Competition as a Dynamic Process* (Washington: Brookings Institution, 1961).

[21] See their respective essays, "In Defense of Bigness in Business," and "The Economics of Technical Development," in Edwin Mansfield, ed., *Monopoly Power and Economic Performance: The Problem of Industrial Concentration* (Rev. ed.; New York: W. W. Norton and Company, 1968), pp. 13–18 and pp. 36–44.

trary, Schumpeter argued that perfect competition was more of a reality now than it ever had been.[22]

Of course, the kind of "perfect competition" that Schumpeter referred to differed greatly from the structured models already examined. To Schumpeter, competition was a continuous process of "creative destruction" that came from the "new commodity, the new technology, the new source of supply, the new type of organization . . . which commands a decisive cost or quality advantage and which strikes not at the margins of the profits and the outputs of the existing firms but at their foundations and their very lives."[23] Hence, competition everywhere and always involved innovation or the threat of innovation, and it was strictly a matter of "comparative indifference whether competition in the ordinary sense functions more or less promptly."[24] Importantly, however, innovational competition would, in many cases, enforce a "*behavior* very similar to the perfectly competitive pattern."[25]

But what type of firms from what types of market structures were responsible for creative destruction or capable of innovational competition? Surely not the small, profitless firms from perfect competition!

> The introductions of new methods of production and new commodities is hardly conceivable with perfect—and perfectly prompt—competition from the start. And this means that the bulk of what we call economic progress is incompatible with it.[26]

Instead, the bulk of economic progress was promoted by the large, capital intensive concern that had some degree of control over outputs and prices. These firms could afford the time and expense of research and development, while they could not afford not to do it. If they "exploited," then they surely exploited what they had created, and what would not be but for their activities; hence, the "usual conclusions about their influence on long-run output would be invalid. . . ."[27] On the contrary, these large concerns were "the most

[22]Joseph A. Schumpeter, *Capitalism, Socialism and Democracy* (3rd printing; New York: Harper and Row, 1962), p. 81.
[23]*Ibid.*, p. 84.
[24]*Ibid.*, p. 85.
[25]*Ibid.*, p. 85 (Emphasis added).
[26]*Ibid.*, p. 105.
[27]*Ibid.*, p. 101.

powerful engine of that progress and in particular of the long-run expansion of total output."[28] Therefore, concluded Schumpeter:

> . . . perfect competition is not only impossible but inferior, and has no title to being set up as a model of ideal efficiency. It is hence a mistake to base the theory of government regulation of industry on the principle that big business should be made to work as the respective industry would work in perfect competition.[29]

It would certainly be incorrect to argue that any serious student of antitrust policy believes that "big business should be made to work as the respective industry would work in perfect competition." It would not be incorrect to note, however, that the fundamental criticism of Chamberlin and Schumpeter has never obtained a general degree of professional acceptability in the field of antitrust, and that economists in this area have shown a remarkable reluctance to abandon the arbitrary assumptions of pure competition and of its corollary, the *market structure* approach to competition. The market structure approach to competition is founded rock bottom on the notion that imperfect or monopolistically competitive markets inherently misallocate scarce economic resources from some consumer optimum. Structure is studied because it "*determines* the behavior of firms in the industry, and that behavior in turn *determines* the quality of the industry's performance."[30] The inference is clear: "bad" structure leads inevitably to "poor" conduct and "poor" performance. *But bad structure and poor conduct in relation to what standard?* Again, the market structure determinist must revert to the theory of pure competition as a standard.

An attack on pure competition is an attack on the market structure approach to competition. If pure competition cannot exist, and would not be relevant even if it could, market structures or market structure changes reveal nothing *a priori* about consumer welfare. And without reference to pure competition as a welfare ideal, discussions of entry, mergers, product differentiation, concentration, and the other elements of market structure become interesting but un-

[28] *Ibid.*, p. 106.
[29] *Ibid.*
[30] Richard Caves, *American Industry: Structure, Conduct, Performance* (2nd ed.; Englewood Cliffs, N.J.: Prentice-Hall, 1967), p. 17 (Emphasis added). For an excellent critique of the structuralist position, see Louis W. Stern and John R. Grabner, *Competition in the Market Place* (Glenview, Ill.: Scott, Foresman and Company, 1970).

founded opinions. Reference to the optimality of the purely competitive model might substantiate them, but the model itself is un-
grounded by anything in reality.

FOUNDATIONS OF MARKET STRUCTURE

Unfortunately, almost all the important tools of analysis in the field
of antitrust or "industrial organization" (and that name belies the
emphasis) are still predicated on the unprovable belief that movements away from a purely competitive market structure misallocates
resources and that conduct not compatible with purely competitive
conduct is inferior, i.e., it produces "inferior" performance. It might
be useful to review briefly the more common tools of analysis in
industrial organization, and highlight their dependence on the notion of pure competition as a welfare ideal.

Measurements of "Monopoly"

The Lerner Index: The Lerner index[31] is perhaps the most famous
(and obvious) market structure device for measuring "monopoly." In
the Lerner system, the *coefficient of monopoly* is equal to price
minus marginal cost divided by price; obviously, the greater the
divergence between price and marginal cost, the greater the degree
of monopoly. Since Lerner accepts perfect competition as a welfare
ideal, his coefficient is clearly designed to measure nonoptimal performance. With little encouragement, some economists have since
proceeded to measure the degree of monopoly and the consequent
welfare losses because of monopoly in the economy, under the
Lerner assumption that the divergence of price from marginal cost
measures monopoly and welfare loss.[32]

But if pure competition is not a welfare ideal, all this "measurement" is nonsense. Once heterogeneous consumers, firms, and products are recognized as desirable facts of economic life, a simple
divergence of selling price from marginal cost does not prove inefficiency or nonoptimal resource allocation.[33]

[31]A. P. Lerner, "The Concept of Monopoly and the Measurement of Monopoly
Power," *Review of Economics and Statistics,* I (June, 1934), 157–175.
    [32]For a typical "measurement," see Dave R. Kamershen, "An Estimation of the
'Welfare Losses' from Monopoly in the American Economy," *Western Economic Jour-
nal,* IV (Summer, 1966), 221–236.
    [33]Similar criticism can be leveled at *all* the other familiar "indicators" of monopoly.
For a review of these other indicators see Eugene M. Singer, *Antitrust Economics:
Selected Legal Cases and Economic Models,* (Englewood Cliffs, N.J.: Prentice Hall,
1968), pp. 66–72.

Profit Studies: Profit studies that attempt to "measure" monopoly or to correlate rates of return with some other economic variable (concentration, for example) implicitly make the same sort of error. Although they are concerned with the divergence of price from average costs—and not marginal costs—they also assume that in the long run, pure competition profits would be zero, and that *positive* profits in the long run imply monopoly power. Like the Lerner and welfare-loss model studies mentioned above, these studies frequently hint that the Department of Justice might do well to correct these misallocations.[34]

But again, all this is nonsense. If zero profits are not a welfare ideal (and in a Chamberlin and Schumpeterian sense, there is no reason to assume that they are), then positive profits in the long run are not necessarily a sign of welfare loss. Secondly, all such studies "measure" business or accounting profits and not economic profits. Thirdly, all such studies conceptually assume away demand shifts and cost-reducing innovations and risks as short-run phenomena whose "windfall" gains or losses somehow disappear in the static and peaceful, equilibrium long run. Again, nonsense. There is nothing peculiarly short run about risk, changes in consumer demand, or innovation; since the real business world is never in equilibrium, these dynamic market forces exist as much in the long run as in the short run. Long-run "profits" might be just as attributable to long-run innovation as to anything else. Thus, postulating a frictionless, profitless equilibrium in some undefined long run, where measurements of the divergence of price from marginal cost or average cost can be used to indicate monopoly or inefficiency, is only an exercise in mathematics.

Cross Elasticity: Cross elasticity measurements have been another popular method of measuring the degree of monopoly or competition in a market. The cross elasticity coefficient attempts to record the responsiveness of consumers of one commodity to a change in the price of some other commodity.[35] Assume homogeneous "pencils" made and sold by a group of small manufacturers. A change in the

[34]See, for example, H. M. Mann, "Seller Concentration, Barriers to Entry, and Rates of Return in Thirty Industries: 1950–1960," *Review of Economics and Statistics*, XLVIII (August, 1966), 296–307, especially 300. The "correlations" that have been discovered in such studies are open to serious question. See Eugene M. Singer, "Industrial Organization: Price Models and Public Policy", paper delivered before the Eighty-Second Annual Meeting of the American Economic Association, December 28, 1969. Reprinted in *American Economic Review*, LX (May, 1970), 90–99.
[35]Leftwich, *op. cit.*, pp. 43–44.

price of pencils made by manufacturer X might, other things being equal, significantly affect the consumption of pencils made by manufacturer Y; higher X prices might mean higher Y sales, and lower X prices might mean lower Y sales. Hence, the coefficient of cross elasticity is positive, and one might infer that the "goods" are in the same "industry"; are relatively good substitutes for each other; and are competitive with each other.

On the other hand, a change in the price of pencils made by manufacturer X would not appear to have any direct effect on the quantity of toothbrushes sold by manufacturer Z, other conditions being the same. The cross elasticity coefficient would be *low*, and one might infer that the "goods" are not in the same "industry"; are *not* good substitutes for each other; and do *not* compete directly with each other.

So far, so good. But now assume that two commodities, or a dozen commodities, are *similar* (fulfill the same basic want) *but not identical.* Like all close choices in the real market, the products differ on the basis of appearance, reliability, quality, service, technical assistance, ease of shipment, price, warranty, and many other factors that consumers consider important. If selling price were the *only* relevant factor, and everything else were (somehow) "equal," then low cross elasticity might indicate poor competition and hence high degrees of monopoly. But when price is *not* the only relevant factor and everything else is *not equal,* low cross elasticity might only indicate the *relative insignificance* of price changes as a competitive factor in the market. Like the Lerner-type indexes, cross elasticity implicitly assumes that an optimal competition is *one-dimensional;* it consistently neglects nonprice competitive factors employed by firms in real market situations.[36] Hence it does not and cannot "measure" competition.

Barriers to Entry

The subject matter of so-called barriers to entry occupies a crucial position in the structuralist approach. For it is these supposed "barriers" that unfairly limit—or keep out entirely—potential competitors and allow existing monopolists or oligopolists to charge higher than competitive prices and reap higher than competitive rates of return. Some of the most oft-mentioned barriers that supposedly limit com-

---

[36]Chamberlin, *Towards a More General Theory of Value*, pp. 78–83.

petition are: *product differentiation, scale economies,* and *patents.* Some brief comments on these concepts are in order.

Product Differentiation: Product differentiation can be regarded as an unfair barrier *only* if a purely competitive business world is accepted as ideal, and purely competitive entry conditions are agreed upon as the norm-ideal. As has been pointed out previously, however, differentiation not homogeneity is the context of real world competition, and the degree of differentiation is a function of consumer acceptance. To compare the demand elasticities of differentiated products with the presumed ideal of "perfect elasticity" is meaningless. To conclude that product differentiation is an unfair barrier to entry is to conclude nothing more than the obvious fact that all producers must sell products that please consumers or go out of business. That this process is extremely difficult in the context of modern markets and may require extensive differentiation is a testament to the intensity of competition, and *not* a reflection of its absence.

Scale Economies: The same sort of argument may be made with respect to absolute economies (economies achieved by lowering the structure of costs) and scale economies (economies associated with greater outputs.) That the production and distribution of particular goods take place under conditions of decreasing cost per unit is indeed fortunate—for consumers. In all such cases, firms have innovated processes that drive the entire structure of costs down, or have earned output levels that allow low-cost production: both factors increase the efficiency of production. To conclude that such "economies" are an unfair barrier to entry because they keep out potential competition is to conclude that it is unfair that high-cost and low-cost producers may not be able to compete with each other. If consumers could somehow be persuaded to support the high-cost producer, then this "barrier" would disappear!

Patents: A patent may be described as the legal recognition by government of a property right. When an individual creates something original, i.e., when he creates "new property," it becomes the function of government in our present system to recognize and protect that property claim, just as it protects all "old" property claims. Since governments presently certify and protect ownership claims to personal goods, including land, they would properly certify and protect ownership claims with respect to newly created property. In this context, certification would denote the process of determining exactly *what* had been created and *who* created it. Protection would imply the legal assurance that no one could use, reproduce, or expropriate the property without the owner's permission. The legal owner, in turn, could use, sell, not use, or give away his newly created property as he saw fit.

In this particular context, a patent is no more "unfair" and no more a "barrier to entry" than any other kind of privately owned property. That one may not expropriate private property and use it for "competition" can only appear unfair to those economists who accept theft as a legitimate competitive business practice. Under an economic system founded on private property rights, competition between individuals or business organizations involves the use of privately owned resources. Thus, to the extent that patents secure legitimate property rights, they are consistent and compatible with competitive capitalism.[37]

Concentration

Concentration is currently the most popular structural tool of analysis in industrial organization. Market concentration (concentration ratio) refers to the percentage control that the largest firms in an industry have of that industry's assets, sales, or profits. Average market concentration measures concentration in all markets by averaging the market concentration data for the particular industries. Aggregate concentration (megacorp concentration) refers to the percentage control that the largest industrial firms in the economy have of all industrial assets, sales, or profits, *without* reference to *specific* industries or markets. All three concentration indicators have been popularly used by the structuralists to imply that certain degrees of "market control," or changes in these degrees of control over time, infer something significant about "economic power" and, hence, about business competition. The implication is that increasing concentration in an industry or in the economy is bad for competition and consumer welfare.[38]

[37]To the extent that patents *deny* legitimate property rights (to an independent second discoverer, for example), they may not be compatible with competitive capitalism. See Murray Rothbard, *Man, Economy and State: A Treatise on Economic Principles* (Princeton, N.J.: D. Van Nostrand Company, 1962), II, 652–660.

[38]The highly influential *Studies by the Cabinet Committee on Price Stability* (Washington, D.C.: U.S. Government Printing Office, 1969) arrogantly declared that "market concentration is directly related to the intensity of competition in an industry" (p. 54). For an excellent critique of this concentration-competition approach, see John S. McGee, *In Defense of Industrial Concentration* (New York: Praeger Publishers, 1971).

Once the arbitrary optimality of the purely competitive market structure is admitted, however, concentration or changes in concentration prove precious little *a priori* concerning business competition. An industry or an industrial sector that is becoming "increasingly concentrated" is quite compatible with either more or less competition defined in Schumpeterian terms. For example, small beer producers might decide to merge so that strong regional brands could be marketed in more areas.[39] Or small coal producers might decide to merge to enjoy economies of selling, shipping, and research and development that would allow more vigorous competition with the petroleum industry.[40] Or small, atomistic garment manufacturers might decide to merge to enjoy the lower costs and better qualities possible from a revolutionary mechanical device—the computerized pattern cutter.[41] In all of these examples, the market concentration ratio might have increased, but it is not at all clear that either business competition would necessarily decline(!) or that consumer welfare would be lowered.

The issue is more obvious when consumers themselves "concentrate" an industry by "concentrating" their particular expenditures on the products of some one group of firms, to the consistent neglect of others. Are we to equate this concentration automatically with "monopoly power," or with an automatic welfare reduction? It should be apparent that concentration ratios or changes in those ratios over time, *in and of themselves*, reveal little about desirable degrees of business competition.

But even on its own structural terms, the concept of concentration is subject to much criticism.[42] For example, a simple concentration ratio for an industry does not relate the structural relationship *between* the largest firms. One can draw different conclusions about potentially competitive behavior from an industry whose four leading firms shared their 70 percent market control *proportionately*, as against the same industry with the firms controlling 50 percent, 10

[39]Ann and Ira Horowitz, "Concentration, Competition and Mergers in Brewing," Fred Weston and Sam Peltzman, eds., *Public Policy Toward Mergers* (Englewood Cliffs, N.J.: Goodyear Publishing Company, 1969), pp. 45–56.

[40]Argument in *Appalachian Coals* v. *United States*, 288, U.S. 344 (1933), cited in Irwin M. Stelzer, *Selected Antitrust Cases: Landmark Decisions* (3rd ed., Homewood, Ill.: Richard D. Irwin, 1966), pp. 165–170.

[41]Similar mechanizations have had similar effects on other labor intensive industries. See Chapter 5 in this text concerning mechanization in the cigarette industry.

[42]Much of the following discussion draws ideas freely from Sanford Rose, "Business is a Numbers Game," *Fortune*, LXXX (November, 1969), 113, 115, 226, 228, 230, 232, 234, 237–238.

percent, 5 percent and 5 percent, respectively. Even a structuralist might admit that an increase in concentration in the latter
situation *might* increase competition as some of the relatively
smaller firms gained ground on the industry leader. But if *different* conclusions about competitive behavior or performance are
possible for the *same* industry with the *same* concentration ratio,
it is reasonable to assume that different conclusions about competition in different industries with the same concentration ratio are
also possible. If this is so, then concentration ratios are really not
comparable statistics for measuring competition; accordingly, it
would really not be legitimate to add them together or average
them for all industries in the economy.

Secondly, concentration ratios do not indicate *where* firms compete. Competition always takes place between *particular* firms in
particular markets. Do the industry leaders, for instance, face each
other frequently in the important selling markets, or are many markets "monopolized" by the industry leader? It is conceivable that a
firm with a high market share might face intense rivalry in all of its
selling markets, while a smaller firm with a much lower percentage
of total market sales might sell relatively free of competition. The
point is that a simple concentration ratio cannot reveal the pertinent
selling conditions. Accurate inferences about degrees of competition
from such statistics would not seem rational.

Thirdly, published concentration statistics may exaggerate the
market control of the large firms if these firms are heavily diversified into other industries. For instance, while the four leading
firms might make 70 percent of a particular industry's profit, it is
quite possible that a good part of that "profit" was actually
derived from industrial operations in *other* industries. While the
Bureau of the Census attempts to differentiate this "diversification
factor" for an industry as a whole with "specialization" and "cov-
erage" ratios, it reportedly makes no specific calculation for particular firms. Since the larger firms in the industry are more likely
to be diversified than the smaller firms, all concentration ratios
are likely to overstate the degree of actual concentration in any
particular industry.[43]

Fourthly, it now appears that some of the more important studies

---

[43] *Ibid.*, p. 115.

of concentration have used unrepresentative—even arbitrary—industrial groupings and *unweighted* averages of concentration ratios. As an example, the influential government report released in 1969, titled *Studies by the Staff of the Cabinet Committee on Price Stability*, employed data for but 213 industries even though the Census of Manufacturers classifies over 400 different industries. Almost one half of all the industries in the economy were excluded from the study because their "product" in 1963 was just too different from their product in 1947. Hence the trends in concentration reported in that study were developed for the older, more conservative industries, whose product lines had not changed markedly.[44]

The reported use of *unweighted* data in some of the most important concentration-related empirical studies is even more disturbing, however. Economist Eugene Singer has argued that the Cabinet Committee study used unweighted averages of concentration ratios throughout.[45] He has also argued that two of the most prestigious empirical studies on concentration and profit rates employed *unweighted* averages of profit rates for a *few* leading firms, rather than *weighted* averages for *all* firms classified in the industry supposedly being "measured."[46] It should be apparent to the reader that "empirical studies" employing unweighted and unrepresentative data are open to the most serious question.

As a fifth point, many critics have observed that most aggregate concentration studies, including the Cabinet Committee study of 1969, have included foreign assets and non-industrial assets held by domestic manufacturing firms. But this is not correct if one is attempting to measure *domestic industrial* concentration. Many large American firms, especially since the late 1950s, have invested heavily in overseas facilities, and have diversified into non-manufacturing sectors of the domestic economy. It is not uncommon today to have large industrial firms (and that designation is becoming increasingly inappropriate) owning hotels, rent-a-car agencies, computer software firms, and insurance companies. To the extent that the asset figures used to measure megacorp industrial concentration are not

[44] *Ibid.*, pp. 230, 232.

[45] Singer, *op. cit.*, p. 91.

[46] Singer has stated that both the H.M. Mann study already referenced and J.S. Bain's classic study, "Relation of Profit Rate to Industry Concentration: American Manufacturing, 1936–1940," *Quarterly Journal of Economics*, LXV (August, 1951), 293–324, employ *unweighted* averages of profit rates. See *Ibid.*, p. 93.

deflated for foreign and non-industrial asset holdings, all such statistics *overstate* megacorp concentration or changes in megacorp concentration over time.[47]

In addition, concentration ratios and megacorp concentration statistics overstate the significance of domestic firms since they ignore the competitive importance of *imports*. A simple concentration ratio for the American automobile industry, for example, cannot encompass the effective range of buying alternatives facing the American automobile consumer. To ignore imports (or even second-hand markets) is to overstate the relative importance of concentration in determining "competition."

And finally, all the more famous concentration studies have only dealt with the manufacturing or industrial sector of the American economy. Yet that sector, important though it might be, represents but 28–30 percent of all measured economic activity.[48] Most economic activity is non-manufacturing and in these areas (examples: retailing, construction, entertainment, real estate, business services) it is extremely doubtful whether concentration impairs the competitive process in any way.[49] In fact, increasing concentration in the service sector of the market might provide substantial economies to producing firms and, eventually, to consumers. The point is that no generalizations concerning the dangers of concentration to competition in the *economy* are warranted when at least 70 percent of measured economic activity is systematically excluded from consideration.

Even if concentration were a completely adequate and reliable measure of competition, there is surprisingly little empirical evidence that there has been any tendency for average market concentration to increase over time and, therefore, for competition to decline. Studies of industrial concentration in the period 1901–1947, and some through 1968, have failed to reveal any significant or pre-

[47]See Dr. Betty Bock, *Antitrust Issues in Conglomerate Acquisitions* (No. 110; New York: National Industrial Conference Board, 1969), pp. 26–30; and *Statistical Games and the "200 largest" Industrials: 1954 and 1968* (No. 115; New York: National Industrial Conference Board, 1970); see also Frederick M. Rowe, "Antitrust and Vanishing Boundaries, *New Technologies, Competition and Antitrust* (New York: National Industrial Conference Board, 1970), pp. 25–28.

[48]Joe S. Bain, *Industrial Organization* (2nd ed.; New York: John Wiley and Sons, 1968), pp. 59–60.

[49]See, for example, Victor Fuchs, "The Growth of the Service Industries," in C. Lowell Harriss, ed., *Selected Readings in Economics* (3rd ed.; Englewood Cliffs, N.J.: Prentice-Hall, 1967), p. 67.

dictable upward trend. The work of Adelman,[50] Nutter,[51] and Nelson[52] all tend to confirm the fact that levels of industrial concentration reached in the last decade of the nineteenth century, and approached again in the depression of the 1930s, have remained relatively stable since. Joe S. Bain, a leading economist in the field of industrial organization, summarized the following conclusion on concentration as late as 1968:

> Thus we arrive at the conclusion that overall business concentration certainly has not increased since the early 1930s. We seem at least temporarily (now for three decades) to have reached some sort of a rough plateau in overall concentration. An ever upward trend is not in evidence.[53]

Thus the popular and essentially Marxian hypothesis concerning an inevitable increase in industrial concentration has not been substantiated. Even the Cabinet Committee study rather reluctantly admitted that "average market concentration of manufacturing industries has shown no marked tendency to increase or decrease between 1947 and 1966. . . ."[54]

The extremely high rate of merger activity in the late 1960s revived the concentration-declining competition "hobgoblin." Many prominent economists and government officials, including Richard W. McLaren, former chief of the Antitrust Division of the Department of Justice, were of the opinion that business mergers were "radically restructuring" the American economy.[55] Concentration was growing "dangerously" and competition, as might be expected, was the likely victim of the tale. Given all that has been said concerning the conceptual link between concentration and competition, the concept of concentration itself, and the questionable techniques and assumptions employed in some of the most important empirical stud-

[50]Morris A. Adelman, "The Measurement of Industrial Concentration," *Review of Economics and Statistics*, XXXIII (November, 1951), 269–296; and "Changes in Industrial Concentration" in Mansfield, *op. cit.*, pp. 78–83.

[51]G. Warren Nutter, *The Extent of Enterprise Monopoly in the United States, 1899–1939* (Chicago: University of Chicago Press, 1951).

[52]R.L. Nelson, *Concentration in the Manufacturing Industries of the United States* (New Haven: Yale University Press, 1963).

[53]Bain, *op. cit.*, p. 110.

[54]*Studies by the Cabinet Committee on Price Stability*, p. 58.

[55]The "hobgoblin" view, and an excellent critique of that view, can be found in Robert H. Bork, "Antitrust in Dubious Battle," *Fortune*, LXXX (September, 1969), 103.

ies, it might suffice to note here that independent studies, done with different industry groups and weighted concentration ratios, have produced markedly different conclusions on concentration trends.[56] Whether corporate mergers tend to "reduce competition" will be explored in some detail in Chapter 10.

MONOPOLY POWER, MARKET STRUCTURE, AND ANTITRUST

The tools of industrial organization examined briefly above have sought to (1) measure monopoly power and (2) relate that "power" to a "misallocation of economic resources." Yet, as has been argued, neither aim has been or can be accomplished. What economists call "monopoly power" may only be economies and efficiencies that business firms have earned (absolute and scale economies, patents, etc.) or simple consumer preference for one brand of product over another. And the "misallocation of economic resources"—as usual—only relates to the silly and impossible purely competitive model. Consequently, the economic theory of "monopoly" that pretends to support antitrust policy is both wrong and irrelevant.

Structural analysis fails to "measure competition" because it makes unprovable assumptions about an optimal market structure, and because it inherently deals with *form* and not substance. One way to avoid making unprovable structure assumptions is to go directly to the *substance* of real-world competition itself. Business competition is a process where firms of various sizes attempt to produce and sell various kinds of products and services, expand markets, lower prices if possible, patent inventions, introduce innovations, improve consumer services, and generally attempt to improve consumer satisfaction in a search for greater profits. Monopolies or near monopolies, on the other hand, should attempt to restrict output, raise prices, collude, offer shoddy products and services, suppress invention and innovation, preempt important productive factors of production, and engage in predatory practices designed to eliminate competitors and, eventually, competition itself. Presumably the antitrust laws of the United States were passed to preserve the former and save the economy from the latter.[57] Let us turn in the chapters

---

[56]See Rose, *op. cit.*, pp. 114–115.

[57]If the general criticism of this chapter is correct, however, the laws were passed to preserve particular market *structures*, rather than competition in any Schum-

that follow to the important provisions of the antitrust laws, and to the classic antitrust cases brought under these laws, and attempt to discover the truth about competition.

peterian sense. And to the extent that business competition requires *changing* market structures, the antitrust statutes may have been meant to restrain competition and not monopoly. A more confident inference may be possible after an examination of the leading antitrust cases.

CHAPTER 3

Antitrust Laws and Two Early Cases

THE MAJOR ANTITRUST LAWS

The three most important antitrust statutes are the Sherman Antitrust Act of 1890, the Clayton Act of 1914, and the Federal Trade Commission Act of 1914. The Robinson-Patman Act of 1936 amends Section 2 of the Clayton Act; the Celler-Kefauver Antimerger Act of 1950 amends Section 7 of the Clayton Act.[1]

The essence of the Sherman Act is contained in its first two sections:

Section 1
  Every contract, combination in the form of trust or otherwise, or conspiracy, in restraint of trade or commerce among the several States, or with foreign nations, is hereby declared to be illegal. Every person who shall make any such contract or engage in any such combination or conspiracy, shall be deemed guilty of a misdemeanor. . . .

Section 2
  Every person who shall monopolize, or attempt to monopolize, or combine or conspire with any other person or persons,

[1]For a review of these laws in detail, see any standard text or, in particular, Earl W. Kintner, *An Antitrust Primer* (New York: Macmillan Company, 1967), pp. 266–299.

to monopolize any part of the trade or commerce among the several States, or with foreign nations, shall be deemed guilty of a misdemeanor. . . .

For purposes of our discussion, the most interesting sections of the Clayton Act are the following:

Section 2 (a)
That it shall be unlawful for any person engaged in commerce . . . to discriminate in price between different purchases of commodities of like grade and quality . . . where the effect of such discrimination may be substantially to lessen competition or tend to create a monopoly in any line of commerce, or to injure, destroy, or prevent competition with any person who either grants or knowingly receives the benefit of such discrimination, or with customers of either of them: *Provided,* That nothing herein contained shall prevent differentials which make only due allowances for differences in the cost of manufacture, sale, or delivery resulting from the differing methods or quantities in which such commodities are to such purchasers sold or delivered. . . . [and] (b) *Provided, however,* That nothing herein contained shall prevent a seller rebutting the prima-facie case thus made by showing that his lower price or the furnishing of services or facilities to any purchaser or purchasers was made in good faith to meet an equally low price of a competitor, or the services or facilities furnished by a competitor.

Section 3
It shall be unlawful for any person engaged in commerce . . . to lease or make a sale or contract for sale of goods, wares, merchandise, machinery, supplies, or other commodities . . . on the condition . . . that the lessee or purchaser thereof shall not use or deal in the goods, wares, merchandise, machinery, supplies, or other commodities of a competitor . . . where the effect of such lease, sale or contract . . . may be to substantially lessen competition or tend to create a monopoly in any line of commerce.

Section 7
That no corporation engaged in commerce shall acquire, directly or indirectly, the whole or any part of the stock or other share of capital and no corporation subject to the jurisdiction of the Federal Trade Commission shall acquire the whole or any part of the assets of another corporation engaged also in commerce, where in any line of commerce in any section of the country, the effect of such acquisition may be substantially to lessen competition, or to tend to create a monopoly.

Federal Trade Commission Act of 1914 created the Federal Trade Commission and charged that body with prosecuting "unfair methods of competition in commerce, and unfair or deceptive acts or practices in commerce" (Section 5, as amended by the Wheeler-Lea Act of 1938). Since the substantive provisions of this law overlap the Sherman and Clayton statutes, it will not be discussed separately in this study.

Legality and Morality of the Laws

While the meaning of these statutes might be obscure, legislation regulating interstate commerce has never really been legally challenged. Article 1, Section 8 of the United States Constitution states that Congress has the power "to regulate Commerce with foreign Nations, and among the several states . . ." In *Gibbons* v. *Ogden* (1824), the Supreme Court affirmed the federal government's right to regulate interstate commerce; this interpretation provided the basis for the sweeping exercise of federal power which began with the Interstate Commerce Act (1887). Moreover, court decisions have made it perfectly clear that governments can legally regulate the use of private property whenever it is devoted "to a use in which the public has an interest." In *Charles River Bridge* v. *Warren Bridge* (1837), the Supreme Court gave recognition to the power of government *to police* property rights and *to limit* them in the "public interest." The court held that the rights of corporations are subordinated to the rights of the community, thereby modifying the contract doctrines of the Marshall Court.[2] In the famous *Munn* v. *Illinois* (1877),[3] Munn and his partner, Scott, argued that their private grain storage business was of no concern to the State of Illinois legislature, and that the legislature had no right to require them to make their rates public, or get a license to operate from the state, or comply with maximum storage rates. The court declared—citing English common law—that all private property that involved the public "must submit to be controlled by the public for the common good." Since almost all private property in an exchange economy "involves the public," this case (and many subsequent ones) helped establish clear legal precedent that governments have the power to regulate, through

[2] *Viz. Fletcher* v. *Peck* (1810) and *Dartmouth College* v. *Woodward* (1819). See Stanley I. Kutler, *Privilege and Creative Destruction: The Charles River Bridge Case* (Philadelphia: J. B. Lippincott Company, 1971), pp. 133–179.
[3] 94 U.S. 113.

due process, practically all business activity. As Supreme Court Justice Roberts succinctly put the matter in *Nebbia* v. *New York* in 1934[4]: "a state is free to adopt whatever economic policy may reasonably be deemed to promote public welfare, and to enforce that policy by legislation adapted to its purpose."

Granted that antitrust laws are legal—are such laws *proper* in a capitalistic business system? From a strict "natural rights" or "libertarian" point of view, at least, they are not.[5] This view holds that men have inalienable rights to life, liberty, and property. Moreover, these rights imply the freedom of any person or persons to enter into any noncoercive trading agreement on any mutually acceptable terms; to produce and trade any nonhuman factor or good that they own; and to keep any property realized by such free exchange. Therefore, government's sole function in a capitalistic business would be to protect such rights to life and property, and to adjudicate violations of such rights.[6] The state could not legitimately regulate the manufacture and price of agricultural commodities, limit the production of petroleum, prohibit the sale of labor services below certain fixed terms of exchange, or restrain the voluntary merger of private properties. Such state activities would limit or restrict property rights and, thus, violate the premise of free and voluntary exchange. Antitrust laws, therefore, to the extent that they restrict the voluntary exchange of private property, would not be proper. Thus, part of the case against antitrust can be couched in moral terms.

The libertarian position indicated above is clearly the minority view. Almost all intellectuals, and certainly almost all economists, would hold that property rights are not inalienable or natural. They argue that such relationships are useful social conventions that governments sanction because they tend, under special conditions, to promote the public welfare. For example, if sufficient degrees of competition exist, free trade is desirable because it tends to maximize society's output. If monopoly arises, however, trade might be

[4]291 U.S. 502.

[5]For the clearest exposition of this view, see Ayn Rand, *Capitalism: The Unknown Ideal* (New York: New American Library, 1966).

[6]Some libertarian "anarchists" have argued that *any* government action is immoral and must inherently violate rights. For an explanation of this position, see Morris and Linda Tannehill, *The Market for Liberty* (privately published at P.O. Box 1383, Lansing, Mich., 1970). For an explanation of how a completely laissez-faire economic system would function, and for a detailed criticism of *all* government intervention in a market economy, see Murray N. Rothbard, *Power and Market: Government and the Economy* (Menlo Park, Calif.: Institute for Humane Studies, 1970).

regulated, through legislation, in society's own interest. Because this view makes voluntary exchange relationships conditional or dependent on their supposed contribution to the public welfare, it might be designated as the pragmatic-utilitarian position.[7]

The Economist's Philosophical Position

Historically, almost all economists have rationalized their belief in a capitalistic market system and justified sporadic government regulation of that system by arguing in essentially pragmatic-utilitarian terms. For example, in the first great economic treatise, *The Wealth of Nations*,[8] Adam Smith indicated all the old regulatory economic systems, especially mercantilism, for their economic inefficiency. He opposed government restrictions of free production and trade because, in his view, they hindered the accumulation of capital and the creation of national wealth. Removal of the restrictions and regulations would allow self-interest, regulated by competition, to produce the greatest economic good for the greatest number.

Smith did not extend his argument to all economic areas, however. In fact, *The Wealth of Nations* contains numerous examples which demonstrate that he did not believe that private wills or interest *always* synthesized into the public good. And where they did not, government involvement and even regulation, were clearly necessary. National defense was an obvious exception. More interesting exceptions to the general rule of noninterference were schools, bridges, canals, roads, and the post office.[9] Smith, it appeared, qualified his *laissez-faire* whenever he felt that private pecuniary interests could not, or would not, operate in the public interest as he conceived it.

Jeremy Bentham and the Philosophic Radicals made the semi-utilitarian economic philosophy of Adam Smith more consistent and applicable to the times.[10] Bentham believed that the interests re-

[7]See Gordon C. Bjork, *Private Enterprise and Public Interest: The Development of American Capitalism* (Englewood Cliffs, N.J.: Prentice-Hall, 1969), especially chapters 1, 3, and 5 for a discussion of this position.

[8]Adam Smith, *The Wealth of Nations*, introduction by Max Lerner (New York: Modern Library, 1937).

[9]Smith, *op. cit.*, pp. 682–690 and 737. Also, see Mark Blaug, *Economic Theory in Retrospect* (Rev. ed.; Homewood, Ill.: Richard D. Irwin, 1968), p. 63.

[10]Elie Halévy, *The Growth of Philosophic Radicalism*, tr. Mary Morris (Boston: Beacon Press, 1955), chapters 3 (part 1) and 4 (part 3).

flected in the private, selfish economic activities of individuals were identical and created a stable economic system. The Philosophic Radicals supported free-market capitalism because it provided the "greatest good to the greatest number." Government intervention —not condemned *a priori*—was rejected for the most part simply because the "hedonistic calculus" and experience had shown that its benefits rarely exceeded its costs. Thus, as with Smith, the Radicals made the question of legitimate state intervention in economic affairs a pragmatic-utilitarian issue. They supported the economic arrangements that appeared to function in the public interest as they conceived it.

In fact, this seems to have been the position of most classical economists; it is certainly the position of almost all neoclassical economists. Smith, Ricardo, Mill, McCulloch, Senior, Sidgwick, Marshall—even Keynes—[11] never admitted to a belief in undiluted *laissez-faire;* nor, for that matter, did they imply it in a clear, consistent theory of public policy.[12] For the most part, their only guide to questions of legitimate governmental regulation was utilitarian: though free market activity might be generally acceptable, the state could (and should) intervene whenever its duly elected, well-intentioned representatives thought such action to be in the public interest.

Antitrust laws, according to the libertarian, are immoral, regardless of their supposed contribution to the public welfare. But if a person is more pragmatic—or more "practical"—he should be willing to subject his pragmatic beliefs concerning antitrust and the "public interest" to the test. Chapter 2 has indicated that the theoretical foundations of the market structure approach to competition, and hence to antitrust, are shaky. *But is the "practical" case for antitrust intervention also shaky? Has antitrust functioned in the "public interest"* (whatever that is)?[13] A review of the leading antitrust cases can help answer these questions.

---

[11]John Maynard Keynes, *Essays in Persuasion* (New York: W. W. Norton, 1963), especially pp. 312–322.

[12]William D. Gramp, *Economic Liberalism: The Classical View* (New York: Random House, 1965), II, 75. Also, see Edmund Whittaker, *Schools and Streams of Economic Thought* (Chicago: Rand McNally Book Company, 1960), pp. 168–175.

[13]See Robert H. Bork, "The Legislative Intent and the Policy of the Sherman Act," and George J. Stigler, "The Economic Effects of the Antitrust Laws," *Journal of Law and Economics,* IX (October, 1966), 7–48 and 225–258.

THE E.C. KNIGHT CASE (1895)

The first case involving a new statute is usually very important, for it is often a test of its applicability, even its constitutionality. Such a case concerned the suit brought against the American Sugar Refining Company in 1893 by the Justice Department under the Sherman Antitrust Act.[14] Although a majority of justices admitted that American Sugar Refining Company's acquisition of E. C. Knight Company (and three other independent sugar refiners) tended to create a monopoly in sugar manufacturing and to increase American's share of the refined sugar market to 98 percent; and even though only one significant independent sugar refiner remained;[15] the Supreme Court ruled that the Sherman Antitrust Act could not apply to manufacturers—in this case American—even if they exercised a total monopoly over the making of the product. The justices reasoned that American's near "monopoly" was not necessarily a monopoly or illegal restraint of interstate commerce, and that such "monopolies" only incidentally and indirectly affected interstate trade and commerce.[16] Speaking for the majority, Justice Fuller contended:

> . . . the monopoly and restraint denounced by the Act are the monopoly and restraint of interstate and international trade or commerce, while the conclusion to be assumed on this record is that the result of the transaction complained of (the acquisitions) was the creation of a monopoly in the manufacture of a necessary of life . . .[17]

> . . . it does not follow that an attempt to monopolize, or the actual monopoly of, the manufacture was an attempt, whether executory or consummated, *to monopolize commerce*, even though, in order to dispose of the product, the instrumentality of commerce was necessarily involved. There was nothing in the proofs to indicate any intention to put a restraint upon trade or commerce, and the fact, as we have seen, that trade or commerce might be indirectly affected, was not enough to entitle complaints to a decree.[18]

---

[14] *United States v. E. C. Knight Company*, 156 U.S. 1 (1895).

[15] Elliot Jones, *The Trust Problem in the United States* (New York: Macmillan Company, 1923), p. 44.

[16] Donald Dewey, *Monopoly in Economics and Law* (Chicago: Rand McNally and Company, 1966), p. 214.

[17] *United States* v. *E. C. Knight Company*, 156 U.S. 1 (1895), pp. 328–329.

[18] *Ibid.*, p. 331 (Emphasis added).

As long as there had been no attempt to "put a restraint upon trade or commerce," it appeared that the federal courts lacked jurisdiction over manufacturing "monopolies."

Surprisingly, the post-1895 market structure of the sugar refining industry made the economic significance of the decision not to dissolve almost purely academic. With or without the courts, the competitive market forces in the sugar industry dissolved the "monopoly" position of the "Sugar Trust." American Sugar's relative share of the domestic sugar refining market slipped quickly and continuously from almost 98 percent in 1893 to 25.06 percent in 1927;[19] the reason is not difficult to discover. The high domestic tariff, the more than available raw materials at historically low prices, the relatively easy manufacturing process, the increasing significance of domestic beet sugar, and the absence of any real significant scale economies made entry into the industry easy and profitable. Firms such as United States Sugar Refining, California & Hawaiian Sugar Refining, New York Sugar Refining, Arbuckle Brothers, Federal Sugar Refining, Warner, Revere, Cunningham Sugar Refining, Pennsylvania Sugar, Western Sugar Refining, Godchaux Sugars, W. J. McCahan Sugar Refining and Molasses, Savannah Sugar Refining, Imperial Sugar, and National Sugar Refining (25 percent owned by American) were all—at one time or another—active competitors of American Sugar; many managed to survive and prosper. In 1920, for example, there were at least 105 plants producing sugar from beets alone, and beet sugar had come from nowhere to represent almost 15 percent of the total refined market by that date.[20] Thus, although the "Sugar Trust" dominated the industry *momentarily*, and although it secured a stock interest in a few potential competitors, it failed to keep competitors out of the sugar market permanently.

Furthermore, little statistical evidence exists proving that American Sugar exerted its "monopoly power" in the sellers' market.[21]

[19] *Sugar Institute et al. v. United States*, 297 U.S. 533, 565 (1936).

[20] Joshua Bernhardt, *The Sugar Industry and the Federal Government* (Washington: Sugar Statistical Service, 1948), p. 21; see also his *Governmental Control of the Sugar Industry in the United States: An Account of the Work of the United States Food Administration and the United States Equalization Board, Inc.* (New York: Macmillan Company, 1920).

[21] Price information is taken from Elliot Jones, *The Trust Problem in the United States* (New York: Macmillan Company, 1923), p. 117. For a recently published "revisionist history" of the "Sugar Trust," see Richard Zerbe, "The American Sugar Refining Company, 1887–1914: The Story of a Monopoly," *Journal of Law and Economics*, XII (October, 1969), 339–375.

Refined sugar sold at retail for more than 9 cents in 1880; 6.9 cents in 1890; 5.3 cents in 1895; 6.1 cents in 1900; 6.0 cents in 1905; and 6.0 cents in 1910. Wholesale prices per pound were 9.602 cents in 1880; 6.171 cents in 1890; 4.152 cents in 1895; 5.320 cents in 1900; 5.256 cents in 1905; and 4.972 cents in 1910. The theoretical margin between raw and refined sugar, out of which the refiner must make his profits, fluctuated from a high of 1.437 cents in 1882 (well before the "monopoly") to .720 cents in 1890; .882 cents in 1895; .500 cents in 1899; .978 cents in 1905; and .784 cents in 1910. The "margin" was *lower* in 1895 (when American did 98 percent of the sugar refining) than in 1905 (when they did less than 62 percent). Refined sugar prices were .852 cents *lower* in 1894 than in 1910. In conclusion, the failure of antitrust to break up the "Sugar Trust" did not produce the all-embracing, exploitative monopoly envisioned by simple economic theory.

The U.S. Supreme Court was not interested in conduct-performance information concerning the American Sugar Refining Company. An economic analysis of the tariff on sugar, entry conditions, prices and outputs, and predatory practices played no part in the final decision.

THE NORTHERN SECURITIES CASE (1904)

The Northern Securities case[22] was a turning point for antitrust enforcement because it overturned the precedent established in *E. C. Knight* v. *United States.* In this case, a majority of the Supreme Court agreed that a holding company, the Northern Securities Company, that acquired a controlling interest in two formerly "independent and competitive" interstate railroads, the Northern Pacific and the Great Northern, was necessarily a "trust" or a combination in restraint of interstate commerce. As Justice Harlan stated, in rendering the majority opinion:

> No scheme or device could more certainly come within the words of the [Sherman] act . . . or could more effectively and certainly suppress free competition between the constituent companies. This combination is, within the meaning of the Act, a "trust"; but if it is not it is a combination in restraint of interstate and international commerce; and that is enough to bring it under the condemnation of the act. The *mere existence of*

---

[22] *Northern Securities Company et al.* v. *United States,* 193 U.S. 197 (1904).

such a combination and the power acquired by the holding company as its trustee constitute a menace to, and a restraint upon, that freedom of commerce which Congress intended to recognize and protect, and which the public is entitled to have protected.[23]

Since the Sherman Act embraced *all* restraints of trade and not just unreasonable ones, and since the Trans-Missouri Freight Association[24] decision established that agreements to restrain interstate commerce involving railroads fall within the Act's jurisdiction, Harlan concluded, as had the Circuit Court,[25] that the Northern Securities Company violated the Sherman Act. Although Justice Brewer disagreed with part of Harlan's opinion—arguing that the Sherman Act did not outlaw *all* restraints of trade, only just unreasonable ones—he concurred in condemning Northern Securities as an illegal restraint that threatened to mitigate the benefits of unrestricted competition.

The two written dissents in the Northern Securities decision—one by Chief Justice White, the other by Justice Holmes (Justice Peckham joined with both)—both challenged the logic of the majority decision. White argued that the ownership of stock of two competing railways was *not* interstate commerce. Interstate commerce, according to *Gibbons* v. *Ogden,* implied "traffic, but it is something more, it is intercourse"; but the Northern Securities decision, in White's view, did *not* involve traffic or intercourse, but ownership of property; and ownership of stock in a *state* corporation was a state problem.[26] Since there had been no explicit rate agreement or any other "conspiracy" between the Northern Pacific and Great Northern, there was no restraint of interstate commerce.

Justice Holmes was even more penetrating in his dissent. He, too, agreed that the effect of the stock ownership by Northern Securities on interstate commerce was "indirect" and "not shown to be certain and very great," and that if such a "remote result of the exercise of an ordinary incident of property and personal freedom is enough to make that exercise unlawful, there is hardly any transaction concerning commerce between the states that may not be made a crime by the finding of a jury or a court."[27] But the *real* significance of his

[23] *Ibid.,* p. 327 (Emphasis added).
[24] 166 U.S. 290 (1897).
[25] 120 Fed. Reporter 721, 724.
[26] 193 U.S. 369.
[27] *Ibid.,* pp. 402–403.

dissent becomes evident when he explained that in the common law, conspiracies in restraint of trade "were combinations to keep strangers to the agreement out of the business."

> This restriction by contract with a stranger to the contractor's business is the ground of the decision in *United States* v. *Joint Traffic Association,* 171 U.S. 505, following and affirming *United States* v. *Trans-Missouri Freight Association,* 166 U.S. 290. I accept those decisions absolutely, not only as binding upon me, but as decisions which I have no desire to criticize or abridge. But the provision has not been decided, and, it seems to me, could not be decided without perversion of plain language, to apply to an arrangement by which competition is ended through community of interest—an arrangement which leaves the parties without external restraint. That provision, taken alone, does not require that all existing competitions shall be maintained. It does not look primarily, if at all, to competition. It simply requires that a party's freedom in trade between the states shall not be cut down by contract with a stranger. So far as that phrase goes, it is lawful to abolish competition by any form of union.[28]

Thus, for Holmes, illegal restraint or monopoly did not exist until and unless *something was done to exclude strangers to the combination from competing with it,* and this had *not* been attempted in the Northern Securities case.[29] The inherent elimination of "competition" between any two parties (for example, between two competitive railroads), as the result of a merger or "fusion," was thus perfectly legal. If this were not so, "every such combination, as well the small as the great is within the Act"; and this would not be an attempt to regulate commerce but rather, "an attempt to reconstruct society." But this, Holmes concluded, the Congress had neither the legitimate power nor the inclination to do.[30]

Actually, both the majority and minority opinions in this crucial case ignored (and as far as judicial precedent was concerned, it was quite proper to do so) the essential *economic factors* involved. For example, to what extent were the two roads actually competitive in the first place, how had competition performed, and had their consolidation injured or was it likely to injure the public? As B. H. Meyer aptly put it:

[28] *Ibid.,* pp. 405–406.
[29] *Ibid.,* p. 409.
[30] *Ibid.,* p. 411.

It was assumed that competition had been stifled without first asking the question whether competition had actually existed; and whether, if competition could be perpetuated, the public would profit by it.[31]

In fact, the Northern Securities case arose, *not* from the fusion of two "competitive" roads, but because of the competitive battle between James J. Hill's Great Northern; J. P. Morgan's Northern Pacific; and E. H. Harriman's Union Pacific.[32] While the Great Northern and Northern Pacific appear geographically to be competitive roads between St. Paul and Seattle, rate competition had ended, for various reasons, long before 1904. Meyer indicates that the road had lived in "comparative peace" for at least twenty years.[33] Both had maintained joint rates, and the consequent backloading and even flow of freight realized from such arrangements had increased the efficiency and economy of each line and allowed low rates that would have bankrupted other roads.[34]

Two factors, however, appeared to stand in the way of continued efficiencies: one, a more reliable arrangement was necessary to insure the stability of the joint rates; and two, control of the strategically located Burlington Railroad was crucial. The Burlington stretched east from St. Paul to Chicago and tapped "the principal livestock markets, important cotton, coal and mineral areas of the United States."[35] It was a logical extension of the Hill-Morgan system, and in January, 1901, negotiations began for purchasing the road. Harriman's request to join the negotiations was refused, and a month later the Hill-Morgan interests bought the Burlington.[36]

Harriman then launched his famed Wall Street assault on the Northern Pacific itself. In an effort to get a controlling interest, the price of the Northern Pacific's common stock was bid from $144 to over $1,000 in four days.[37] Although he secured a majority of the common and preferred stock, a technicality[38] kept the Harriman

[31]Balthasar Henry Meyer, "A History of the Northern Securities Case," *Wisconsin University Bulletins*, I (1904–1906), 305. The trial court had raised, but dismissed, these issues. See *Ibid.*, pp. 273–274.

[32]Dewey, *op. cit.*, pp. 214–216.

[33]Meyer, *op. cit.*, p. 227.

[34]*Ibid.*, p. 228.

[35]*Ibid.*, p. 227.

[36]*Ibid.*, p. 231.

[37]Dewey, *op. cit.*, pp. 214–215.

[38]Meyer, *op. cit.*, p. 235.

interests from exercising real control, and, as far as the Hill-Morgan interests were concerned, from wrecking the economic advantages of their close association. Thus, the holding company idea (Northern Securities) was a logical, even necessary, conclusion to the entire episode.

> With the view of presenting the possibility of future "raids" upon the Great Northern and Northern Pacific stock and of fortifying these two roads and their connections in their competitive struggle with "the Suez Canal and the high seas and the entire world," the idea of a permanent holding company was invented. It has been persistently denied that the desire to restrain competition among constituent companies had anything to do with the organization of the Northern Securities Company.[39]

Thus, the Northern Securities Company, incorporated in New Jersey in November, 1901, did not restrain trade between two previously competitive rail systems at all. As far as the people involved were concerned, it finalized an efficient and eminently sensible consolidation of properties. Under the "illegal restraint of trade" rail rates continued to decline between November, 1901, and 1903.[40] But economic facts—as usual—made no difference in the final decision of the court.

Buoyed up by the Northern Securities decision, the Justice Department launched and pressed a number of suits against large industrial corporations. None was more important, however, than the criminal action filed in a St. Louis federal court on November 15, 1906, against the Standard Oil Company of New Jersey. This case is crucial for two reasons: first, it set important precedents in judicial interpretations of the antitrust laws; second, it created or gave rise to "facts that everybody knows" concerning the conduct and performance of big business firms. To set the record straight regarding these two reasons, it will be necessary to examine the entire context of the Standard Oil case, and that context is the petroleum industry itself between 1859 and 1907.

[39] *Ibid.*, p. 236.
[40] 193 U.S. 238.

CHAPTER 4

Standard Oil and the Petroleum Industry: A "Legend" and the Rule of Reason

BEGINNINGS OF THE PETROLEUM INDUSTRY

The petroleum industry, its origins and development, is a fascinating subject for extensive study.[1]

For all practical purposes, the industry began in 1846, when a Canadian geologist, Dr. Abraham Gesner, discovered that oil could be distilled from coal, and that a clear liquid—he called it kerosene —could be drawn off and used as an illuminant. Several years later, a number of firms had entered the business of extracting oil from

[1]For general discussions of the beginnings of the petroleum industry, see J. Stanley Clark, *The Oil Century, from the Drake Well to the Conservation Era* (Norman: University of Oklahoma Press: 1958); Albert H. Carr, *John D. Rockefeller's Secret Weapon* (New York: McGraw-Hill Book Company, 1962); Jules Abels, *The Rockefeller Billions, The Story of the World's Most Stupendous Billions* (New York: Macmillan Company, 1965); Ralph and Muriel Hidy, *Pioneering in Big Business, 1882–1911, History of the Standard Oil Company (New Jersey)* (New York: Harper and Brothers, 1955); Harold F. Williamson and Arnold R. Daum, *The American Petroleum Industry, The Age of Illumination, 1859–1899* (Evanston, Ill.: Northwestern University Press, 1959); Ida M. Tarbell, *The History of the Standard Oil Company*, 2 vols. in 1 (Gloucester, Mass.: Peter Smith, 1950); Allan Nevins, *Study in Power: John D. Rockefeller*, 2 vols. (New York: Charles Scribner's Sons, 1953); and John Chamberlain, *The Enterprising Americans: A Business History of the United States* (New York: Harper and Row, 1963), pp. 146–155.

shale. The kerosene produced would not gum or smoke when burned in properly designed oil lamps; most importantly, the kerosene was relatively *cheaper* than existing illuminants. Whale or sperm oil, always in uncertain supplies, frequently sold for over $3 a gallon; gas, though cheaper than sperm oil, was still 30 percent more expensive than kerosene. Thus, when Yale's professor of chemistry, Benjamin Silliman, confirmed for the Pennsylvania Rock Oil Company the potential value of some oil found floating on marshy creeks in Pennsylvania, the only commercial question left was: can oil be found in great supply? "Colonel" E. L. Drake, a harmless, thirty-nine-year old drifter and one-time railroad conductor, answered that question when he struck oil on in 1859, in Titusville, Pennsylvania. With Drake's well pumping 25 barrels a day, and with the price of a barrel of crude oil at $20, the petroleum industry, and age, had already begun.

When the oil word leaked out, northwestern Pennsylvania was overrun with businessmen, speculators, misfits, horse dealers, drillers, bankers, and just plain hell-raisers. Dirt-poor farmers leased land at fantastic prices, and rigs began blackening the landscape. Existing towns jammed full overnight with "strangers," and new towns appeared almost as quickly. "Smellers" and oil "diviners" worked overtime in a frenzied effort to locate the mysterious deposit of black gold. Hopefully, black gold lay at the bottom of the next "hole."

But getting a rig and sinking a hole on someone's leased land were only the beginning of the problem. The petroleum flow had to be successfully controlled, and the threat of waste and fire was always high. Many potential fortunes burned up in the oil fields. Furthermore, the heavy, corrosive crude oil had to be stored and shipped—somehow. Existing barrels were too weak and new barrels had to be devised. Teamsters had to drive animal teams through hip-deep mud, carrying barreled petroleum from well site to Oil Creek, the nearest available "transportation." The barrels were then floated on top of flatboats down the creek—when there was water. Periodically, freshets would be opened by lumber firms upstream (they usually extracted a toll of a few pennies per barrel), and river boat captains would skillfully guide the precious cargo toward the docks at Oil City. As could be expected, much of the oil did not make it, and many of the producers lost their very lives attempting to transport crude. However, there were eager buyers at Oil City, and the price for crude oil was good; thus, the first dribbles of oil soon turned into a steadily increasing stream.

Investments in industries related to the fledgling petroleum industry quickened. Railroad men smelled money in oil transport and quickly put in track to haul oil from northwestern Pennsylvania to Oil City and then to some early refineries. Barrel makers—some right by Oil Creek—tripled production, then tripled it again; but outputs still fell below demand and consumption. Mules and horses were precious, and courageous river-boat captains were at a high premium. Barge companies acting as crude tankers quickly came into existence to move the crude from Oil City to refineries in Cleveland and Pittsburgh. A crude, two-inch wooden pipe line was erected in 1865, only to be destroyed by suddenly unemployed bands of teamster boys; another built in the same year, destroyed in the same fashion, rebuilt, and then protected by Pinkerton's, proved successful. A metal drum called the "tank car," into which petroleum could be pumped, stored, and transported along a railroad track, was also pioneered in the same year. Crude petroleum could now be found in ample supplies and moved efficiently over land and water to its ultimate destination. The stream of crude had now turned into a torrent.

The development of the industry was, predictably, a mixed blessing to the producers, especially to the small marginal operations. The profit-laden, $20-per-barrel prices for early crude had soured quickly to $14; then to $2; and then in early 1862, to 10 cents.[2] Although the prices would recover somewhat in later years, the expected windfall profits vanished forever. The producers were harshly pushed back to reality by the laws of supply and demand. But the steady production, efficient transportation, and relatively low prices paved the way for another even more important group of oil men—the refiners. It would be the refiners, and particularly the Standard Oil Company, who would turn petroleum into America's greatest growth industry.

By 1865, the development of a petroleum refining industry was well underway. The first region to develop refiners was—as expected —the oil region itself, and there were at least thirty independent refiners there.[3] But, unexpectedly, the costs of refining petroleum in northwestern Pennsylvania were high, due to heavy charges for ship-

[2]Tarbell, *op. cit.*, p. 383.
[3]Abels, *op. cit.*, p. 51.

ping machinery and sulfuric acid, and because land was so expensive. Therefore, other areas that were better situated from a cost point of view grew more quickly than the small, always marginal, oil region refiners. Pittsburgh, for example, less than sixty miles from Oil City, quickly developed into the refining capital of the industry. It was close to some good market areas (Philadelphia), had good rail and water transport, and had a cheap supply of coal and labor. By 1865, eighty refineries were manufacturing kerosene and related products from crude petroleum, and the Pittsburgh sky was heavy with oil smoke.[4] There were other refiners in Baltimore, Philadelphia, and New York, and the industry was growing rapidly. Some sources estimate the total number of refiners at this point to be about 250.[5] But the most interesting developments—as it turns out—were taking place in Cleveland.

Though Cleveland had about fifty refineries by 1866, its strategic position in the refining industry was always precarious. Cleveland was over 150 miles from the oil-producing regions and 600 miles from New York and the eastern markets. Though it had an excellent position to any western markets that might develop, its immediate future rested on transportation rates.

If rates for shipping oil could be pushed down through the Erie Canal; and if rates over the two competitive railroads—the Atlantic and Great Western, and the Lake Shore Railroad—could be lowered and kept low; then Cleveland refineries could be competitive in the eastern markets. The key to refining efficiency and competition in the Cleveland area was transportation, and that key would unlock many of the major developments of the industry.

John D. Rockefeller was twenty-three years old and already a success in his own profitable commission business when he decided to risk $4,000 in a speculative oil refinery operation in Cleveland. The young firm quickly prospered under the technical direction of Samuel Andrews, and a second refinery was constructed in 1866. Later, Maurice Clark, one of the original partners in the firm, was bought out (for $72,500). Rockefeller brought in his brother, William, for entrepreneurial know-how, and his shrewd and slightly wealthy friend, Henry Flagler, was brought in for additional capital. By 1868,

---

[4] *Ibid.*
[5] *Ibid.*, p. 65. *The Petroleum Almanac* (New York: National Industrial Conference Board, 1946) lists 170 "establishments" in 1869. See p. 87.

Rockefeller's complete and undivided attention had turned to petroleum and the profits that could be made by "penny-pinching."

The firm of Rockefeller, Andrews, and Flagler prospered quickly in the intensely competitive industry, because of the economic excellence of its entire operations. Instead of buying oil from jobbers, they made the jobbers' profit by sending their own purchasing men into the oil region. In addition, they made their own sulfuric acid, their own barrels, their own lumber, their own wagons, and their own glue. They kept minute and accurate records of every item from rivets to barrel bungs. They built elaborate storage facilities near their refineries. Rockefeller bargained as shrewdly for crude as anyone before or since. And Sam Andrews coaxed more kerosene from a barrel of crude than could the competition. In addition, the Rockefeller firm put out the cleanest-burning kerosene, and managed to dispose of most of the residues like lubricating oil, paraffin, and vaseline at a profit. Thus, it was not surprising that by the late 1860s, the firm was turning out the industry's best spectrum of petroleum products at the lowest possible costs of production, and that it managed to prosper even while the general industry spread between crude and petroleum decreased significantly. Rockefeller, the eternal optimist, expanded outputs while others were more conservative, and by 1870 the firm was the biggest refiner in Cleveland, and quite possibly the largest in the country.

STANDARD OIL AND THE PETROLEUM INDUSTRY, 1870–1882

In 1870 Rockefeller's share of total refined output was no more than 4 percent, and there might have been as many as 250 independent refiners in existence. By 1874 Rockefeller was refining almost 11,000 barrels a day, or about 25 percent of estimated industry output, and had purchased 21 of his 26 Cleveland competitors.[6] By 1880 his market share had climbed to between 80 and 85 percent, and the number of independent refiners stood at between 80 and 100.[7] During this chaotic period, Rockefeller had gone through unsuccessful collusion with other refiners and railroads (the infamous South Improvement Company episode), numerous battles with railroads to secure rebates (more on this below), and a final, expanded business

---

[6]Abels, op. cit., p. 83.
[7]Ibid., pp. 106–108. Also, see Williamson and Daum, op. cit., p. 471.

war with the Empire Transportation Company and the Pennsylvania Railroad. When it was all over, Standard emerged triumphant with significant interests in pipe lines and tank cars, and an overwhelming bargaining position with the railroads. In 1880, John D. Rockefeller was the undisputed king of petroleum, and his reign appeared unshakeable.

But *how* was all this success accomplished in so short a time? How did Standard Oil of Ohio's (the name had been adopted on incorporation in Ohio in 1870) share of the industry grow so rapidly and why, accordingly, did other firms sell out and thus allow the creation of a "monopoly"? To begin to answer these questions, it must be emphasized that the 1870s were treacherous years for *all* speculative businesses, especially the overbuilt oil refinery industry. The United States Treasury's intentional deflationary policies (withdrawing greenbacks and other "paper" from circulation in an attempt to "resume specie payment" in the late 1870s) and the subsequent post-Civil War decline in general demand and prices hurt all overbuilt production, including, of course, the oil refining business. Prices for refined petroleum (kerosene) fell from over 30 cents a gallon in 1869, to around 22 cents in 1872, and to around 11 cents by November 1874.[8] Many firms that had entered the industry to make a speculative profit during and after the war left as prices dipped with no relief in sight. Others, though less opportunistic, were forced to sell, since they were small, marginal, nonintegrated refiners who could not lower costs as quickly as the market lowered prices. For these two reasons, a general reduction in the number of refiners would have been expected in this period—with or without the presence of the Standard Oil Company.

Much has been made of the fact that the price Standard paid for many of these refineries was significantly below their original cost. But surely, almost all such accounts miss the point completely. The value of almost all property—and particularly refinery property—had deflated as overproduction and deflation lowered exchange values. The original cost of a refinery in 1865 was irrelevant in 1875, since the market conditions were radically different. Surely Standard should not be chided for the fact that it paid the *best* 1875 market prices for properties that were almost bankrupt and so inefficient that most were subsequently closed down by Standard.

[8]Tarbell, *op. cit.*, p. 384.

Actually, many firms were quite anxious to be bought out by Standard, and at "outrageous" prices. The story of George Rice does not appear atypical. In 1882 Rice attempted to bribe and blackmail Standard Oil into paying $250,000 for a refinery he had offered to sell in 1876 for $24,000; in 1890, he wanted $500,000![9] Other examples cited by John McGee are even more interesting.[10]

In addition, the technology and capital requirements of the industry were rapidly changing, and firms too small to invent, innovate, or take advantage of these economies were destined to be of marginal importance only. "Destructive distillation" (the cracking of crude) was introduced in 1875, and the minimum size of an efficient refinery was gradually increased to over one thousand barrels a day. Moreover, large, more efficient refineries and related equipment were relatively more expensive than the simple stills of the 1860s. Furthermore, the increased capital requirements for effective competition certainly limited the role of the very small operator. In point, much of the crude handled in the late 1880s was a very poor grade petroleum (high-sulfur, low-yield kerosene), and it was only handled efficiently because of the successful experiments of chemist Herman Frasch and the $200,000 gamble of the Standard Oil Company.

Efficient operations in the 1870s meant tank cars, pipe lines, adequate crude sources, cheap barrels, huge storage facilities, and export capabilities, all of which the Standard Oil Company had invested in heavily, and most of which the smaller competitors had not. Standard has frequently taken the blame for the fact that its competitors could not enjoy the efficiencies of a tank car fleet, access to cheap pipe lines, and large storage facilities; but, surely, the fact that competitors *would* not or *could* not be as efficient as Standard in these areas is *not* Standard's responsibility. Was it unfair to buy or build pipe lines and then use them to get lower rates for railroad freight? Was it unfair to own tank cars and use them? Was it unfair to invest millions in storage facilities to take advantage of slight variances in the demand and supply of crude or refined petroleum? And was it unfair to surround the Standard organization with singular men of "brainpower, astuteness, and foresightedness"? While competitors who

---

[9] Abels, *op. cit.*, p. 201.
[10] John S. McGee, "Predatory Price Cutting: The Standard Oil (N.J.) Case," *Journal of Law and Economics*, I (October, 1958), 144–148.

could not or would not do these things might have regarded these tactics as "unfair," their ultimate justification was proven again and again in the market place: such policies lowered the costs of production and the price of the product and raised the profits of the Standard Oil Company.

Between 1870 and 1885 the price of refined kerosene dropped from 26 cents to 8 cents per gallon.[11] In the same period, the Standard Oil Company reduced the costs per gallon from almost 3 cents in 1870 to .452 cents in 1885.[12] Clearly, the firm was relatively efficient, and its efficiency was being translated to the consumer in the form of lower prices for a much improved product, and to the firm in the form of additional profits.

Rebates: Bad Conduct?

The issue of rebates has been saved till last since it, above all else, has provoked the most controversy. According to many, it was Rockefeller's unfair and discriminatory rebates that allowed him to triumph over his competitors and "monopolize" the petroleum industry.

A rebate is a price concession (usually secret) granted by a railroad to some shipper(s). Its immediate consequence is to lower transportation costs to some shipper(s). But to understand why rebates are granted and whether they are "fair" or not, it is necessary to understand the economics of railroading.[13]

Railroads are industries which typically have high fixed-low variable costs. Most of their expenses are fixed charges (interest, depreciation) that must be paid regardless of the volume of traffic. Thus, roads are always hungry for traffic, and their rate schedules will reflect this fact. Railroad rates, like all prices in a free market, are determined by competition. And since the variable costs associated with providing railroad services are very low, railroad rates can range well up above average costs where they have little price competition, to rates that fall significantly below average costs where there is intense competition. Railroads always charge "what the

[11]Tarbell, op. cit., pp. 384–385.
[12]Abels, op. cit., p. 98. And this might have been as much as 60 percent less than the industry average; see Williamson and Daum, op. cit., pp. 483–484.
[13]An excellent and brief discussion of the issues involved here appears in Alfred D. Chandler, Jr., ed., The Railroads: The Nation's First Big Business: Sources and Readings (New York: Harcourt, Brace and World, 1965), pp. 159–172.

traffic will bear," *like any other business;* and like almost any other business, the "traffic will bear" *different* rates at *different* times and places, depending on the pressures of competition. Like any firm, it will pay a railroad to take additional freight business as long as the rate covers "out of pocket" costs, i.e., variable costs. Since average variable costs are low (especially if shippers cover some of these variable costs), rates on very competitive runs may fall very steeply, and almost to nothing. But something, be it ever so little, is better than nothing, and railroads will charge it if they have to, and the "deficit" will be funded from above-average cost runs.

In the 1870s much of railroading was very competitive, especially east of the Mississippi.[14] Many roads had overbuilt, and the post-Civil War deflationary period was one of intense and persistent rate competition. Though there were hundreds of voluntary pools, the rates were down throughout the period. Railroad pools attempted to fix and maintain prices, but the agreements often lasted no longer than the meetings necessary to draw them up.[15]

Railroads went through the motions of drawing up rate schedules, but everyone knew that the schedules were the point at which bargaining *began;* everyone bargained for "his" price, and the strength of supply and demand determined the exact rate. Almost always the exact rate was kept secret to prevent a destructive price war. And almost always the real rates were "found out," as some shippers paying one rate attempted to compete in the same market with other shippers paying different rates.

For hundreds of years competition had been limited by the extent of the market, and the market had been limited by transportation costs. Goods of considerable weight could not compete in far away markets because the costs of transportation inflated the selling price. Only with the development of cheap transportation (canals, railroads), and then with competitive cheap transportation, could the rates on freight be bid down to allow intergeographic competition. It was perfectly possible, therefore, to see railroad rates lower from, say, Cleveland to New York than from Titusville to New York, even though the former distance was one hundred miles longer than the latter; it all depended on the relative supply and demand forces in

[14]See Louis M. Hacker, *The World of Andrew Carnegie: 1865–1901* (Philadelphia: J. B. Lippincott Company, 1968), pp. 206–210.
[15]Gabriel Kolko, *Railroads and Regulation, 1877–1916* (Princeton: Princeton University Press, 1965), Introduction and Chapter 1.

both regions. "Distance," like "technology," means little *a priori* in economics; the value of services is determined by the relative strength of demand and supply at any given moment.

If Cleveland shippers, for example, were in a better bargaining position than oil region shippers—and they clearly were—the rates were lower. If the rates drifted down toward average variable costs, this only attests to the poor position of the roads. If these rates were lower than oil region shippers, this was normal, to be expected, and as far as overall competition in New York is concerned, to be encouraged. If competition exists in the final market, almost all such rebates or "discriminations" get translated into price declines and, hence, increases in consumer welfare.

So far, nothing has been mentioned as to whether the firms "deserve" their rebate; or in other words, whether a 10 percent rebate actually represents a 10 percent saving to the road from handling some shipper's business. Almost all commentators have taken Standard Oil to task because it "accepted" rebates far beyond any possible "cost" savings.

Two points are relevant here. In the first place, there were cost savings, and they may have been considerable. Standard furnished loading facilities and discharging facilities at great cost; it provided a heavy volume of even traffic at predictable periods, and even one of Standard's severest critics admits that this led to "savings of several hundred thousand dollars a month in handling" for the railroads;[16] it provided terminal facilities and exempted railroads from liability for fire by carrying its own insurance. Thus, it might have received a legitimate discount for realized economies.

Secondly, realized economies need have nothing to do with rebates; *costs do not determine prices.* If Rockefeller was, in fact, "paying for" a share of railroad's variable costs, so much the better; then the price necessary to secure his business could fall even farther than before. In fact, since Rockefeller probably performed the railroad's "variable expenses" more efficiently than they did, the mechanism of rebate was profitable for both. Still, from the railroad's point of view, the major factor dominating the situation is volume. To secure additional volume, they may have to accept *any* rate higher than average variable costs.

[16]Matthew Josephson, *The Robber Barons* (New York: Harcourt, Brace and Company, 1934), p. 113.

Rockefeller's ability to threaten water shipment, pipe line shipment, or another railroad shipment was the pressure that pushed his rates down. Since his shipments were so important to the roads, they could not afford to lose him. As long as the rates covered *their* variable costs, it was good business. Thus, Rockefeller's rate could be and was considerably different from anyone else's, but the differences are not mysterious. They are a consequence of railroad economics and competitive pressures in the market.

In this light, the "unfairness" of these "discriminations" is certainly debatable. What is "unfair" about securing all the advantages that there are in a free and open competitive market? What is unfair about granting concessions to the biggest, most versatile shipper who can threaten a volume shift, and not to the small producer and shipper whose volume is almost insignificant? One is clearly more valuable than the other. Again, almost all such cries are based on emotion and not economics, and are more concerned with the fate of particular *competitors* than with *competition* and the consumer.

Predatory Pricing

The same emotion still prevails over another of Standard's supposed practices: predatory price cutting. Predatory price cutting is the practice of deliberately underselling rivals in certain markets to drive them out of business, and then raising prices to exploit a market void of competition. Ida Tarbell immortalized this charge in Chapter 10 (titled "Cutting to Kill") of her *History of the Standard Oil Company*. If interested parties had taken the trouble to read that chapter, however, they would have discovered that Tarbell speaks more of railroad discrimination, Standard's efficient kerosene marketing system, and its morally questionable (to her) use of an elaborate industrial espionage system, than of any specific predatory practices. Nonetheless, such practices were (and are) part of the Standard legend.

Unfortunately for lovers of legends "for their own sake," this one has been laid theoretically and empirically prostrate, though much of the profession has still not acknowledged the funeral. John S. McGee hypothesized, in a much neglected article,[17] that Standard Oil did not use predatory practices, because it would have been

---

[17]"Predatory Price Cutting: The Standard Oil (N.J.) Case," *Journal of Law and Economics*, I (October, 1958), 137–169.

economically foolish to have done so. In the first place, such practices are *very* costly for the large firm; it always stands relatively more to lose since it—by definition—does the most business. Secondly, the uncertainty of the length of the forthcoming battle—and its indeterminate expense—must surely make firms leery of initiating a price war. Thirdly, competitors could simply close down and wait for prices to return to profitable levels, or new owners could purchase bankrupt facilities and again be ready to compete with the "predator." Fourthly, such wars would inevitably spread to surrounding markets, thus endangering the predator's "profits" in his "safe" areas. And lastly, predatory practices already assume a "war chest" of monopoly profits to see the firm through the costly battles; firms cannot, apparently, initiate predatory practices unless they are already semi-monopolistic. But if this is true, firms cannot gain initial monopoly positions through predatory practices. Hence, in summation, there are serious logical pitfalls to assuming that large firms gain their "monopoly" position in markets through predatory practices.

The empirical evidence with respect to Standard Oil reinforces these theoretical suggestions. McGee concluded, after sifting through almost eleven thousand pages of the Standard Oil trial record, that:

> Judging from the Record, Standard Oil did not use predatory price discrimination to drive out competing refiners, nor did its pricing practice have that effect. Whereas there may be a very few cases in which retail kerosene peddlers or dealers went out of business after or during price cutting, there is no real proof that Standard's pricing policies were responsible. I am convinced that Standard did not systematically, if ever, use local price cutting in retailing, or anywhere else, to reduce competition. To do so would have been foolish; and, whatever else has been said about them, the old Standard organization was seldom criticized for making less money when it could readily have made more.[18]

Thus, Standard's position in oil refining grew rapidly due to the natural decline of small competitors, the increasing capital and innovational requirements of large-scale oil technology, the economic advantages offered by intelligent entrepreneurship, tank cars, pipe lines, vertical integration into barrels, cans, glues, exporting, and the consequent lower transportation costs from the railroads, and not from any general reliance on short-sighted predatory practices.

[18] *Ibid.*, p. 168.

THE STANDARD OIL TRUST

The 1880–1895 period for the Rockefeller organization was one of rapid expansion (particularly in Europe), continued integration both forward and backward, and experimentation with various institutional arrangements for increased managerial efficiency. The legal organization was particularly bothersome to Standard of Ohio. Almost all states, including Ohio, did not allow chartered companies to hold the stock of other firms. Yet Standard, by 1880, effectively owned fourteen other firms completely and had a considerable stock interest in about twenty-five others, including the giant National Transit Company. How were these companies to be legally and efficiently managed? In addition, Pennsylvania had just unearthed (with the help of Standard's competitors and some producers) an old law that allowed that state to place a tax on the entire capital stock of any corporation doing any business within its borders; other states threatened to follow suit.[19] Thus, a new organizational arrangement was mandatory to allow effective control of all owned properties and to escape "confiscatory" taxation without breaking the law.

The new device chosen was the resurrection of an old common law arrangement known as the "trust." In a trust, men pool their properties and agree to have someone or some group manage those properties in the interests of the owners. Just as "corporations" allow individuals to pool their properties and choose their managers, trusts in the 1880s allowed the same with corporate holdings. Thus, an old trust was a modern "holding company," but without the "formalities" of a name or legal incorporation, and without the necessity of public disclosure.

The formal Standard Oil Trust was formed in January 1882, though smaller informal trustee arrangements had existed before. The 42 stockholders of all Standard's properties in all the 39-odd companies associated with Standard of Ohio agreed to hand over their ownership claims to 9 designated "trustees"; in return, the ex-stockholders received 20 trustee certificates per share of stock tendered. The original Standard Trust was capitalized at $70 million, and John D. Rockefeller, his brother William, Henry Flagler, John D. Archbold, and some others, then managed the entire operations of the Standard organization, setting up committees on transportation, export, manufacturing, lubricating, and others to advise the executive committee.

[19]Abels, *op. cit.*, p. 154.

This organizational arrangement functioned until March 1892, when the Ohio Supreme Court ruled that the "trust" was illegal and ordered Standard Oil of Ohio to withdraw from it. Seven years later the same men and the same firms formed Standard Oil of New Jersey as a legal holding company, and multifirm control over common corporate properties became a reality.

The substantive changes within the structure during this period were equally newsworthy and certainly more significant. Standard closed down many smaller inefficient refineries and built huge ones in their place. Various units of the refining empire were forced to compete with one another, and amazing economies were realized. Outputs expanded so rapidly that enormous expenditures had to be made for tanks and pipe lines to hold and move this vast output. Anything that could be manufactured more cheaply by Rockefeller was manufactured, and innovation (for example, Standard developed machines that turned out 24,000 five-gallon tin cans daily by 1890) came to be almost a matter of routine for the firm. Even Ida Tarbell recognized all this, and her glowing chapter, "The Legitimate Greatness of The Standard Oil Company," pays remarkable tribute to Standard Oil's commercial intelligence. Although that chapter is filled with many excellent examples, the best and most complete, because it demonstrates the economics of integration, is the following:

> . . . Not far away from the canning works, on Newton Creek, is an oil refinery. This oil runs to the canning works, and, as the newmade cans come down by a chute from the works above, where they have just been finished, they are filled, twelve at a time, with the oil made a few miles away. The filling apparatus is admirable. As the newmade cans come down the chute they are distributed, twelve in a row, along one side of a turn-table. The turn-table is revolved, and the cans come directly under twelve measures, each holding five gallons of oil—a turn of a valve, and the cans are full. The table is turned a quarter, and while twelve more cans are filled and twelve fresh ones are distributed, four men with soldering cappers put the caps on the first set. Another quarter turn, and men stand ready to take the cans from the filler, and while they do this, twelve more are having caps put on, twelve are filling, and twelve are coming to their place from the chute. The cans are placed at once in wooden boxes standing ready, and, after a twenty-four-hour wait for discovering leaks, are nailed up and carted to a nearby door. This door opens on the river, and there at anchor by the side of the factory is a vessel chartered for South America or China or where not—waiting to receive the cans which a little

more than twenty-four hours before were tin sheets lying flat-boxes. It is a marvellous example of economy, not only in materials, but in time and in footsteps.[20]

By the late 1880s, the economies of integration that were so important to domestic operations were being transferred to foreign production and distribution as well. In 1895, for example, Standard had 17 manufacturing plants in Europe, hundreds of warehouse and depot facilities under lease, over 150 tank cars, and close to 5,000 tank wagons for bulk shipment to retailers. Though it had considerable foreign competition, especially from Russian and British petroleum operations, the Standard Oil Company was a major factor in the development of foreign oil markets everywhere in the world.

Finally, throughout the 1880–1895 period, the product increased in quality, and the price to the consumer declined. Though Standard's share of the refining market had stayed relatively high (approximately 82 percent in 1895 compared to over 88 percent in 1879), the price of refined oil per gallon in barrels declined from 9⅛ cents in 1880 to 8⅛ cents in 1885 to 7⅜ cents in 1890 to 5.91 cents in 1897.[21] In addition, Standard's refining costs per gallon fell to .29 cents in 1896.[22] Thus, at the very pinnacle of Standard's industry "control," *the costs and the prices for refined oil reached their lowest levels in the history of the petroleum industry.*

THE 1896–1907 PERIOD

Between 1896 and 1907, the petroleum industry changed radically, and Standard Oil of New Jersey's position in the changing market became less and less secure. The most revolutionary change that occurred, and the one that fueled the others, was the product demand shift away from kerosene to other petroleum products. Kerosene sales leveled off as the competitiveness of gas and electricity cut deeply into a once solid growth area; correspondingly, lighter fuel oils, lubricating oils, and gasoline became significantly more important. Between 1899 and 1914, kerosene sales as a percentage of all refined petroleum products declined from 58 percent to 25 percent, while fuel oil rose from 15 percent to 48 percent.[23] The kerosene age was over.

[20]Tarbell, *op. cit.*, pp. 240–241.
[21] *Ibid.*, p. 385.
[22]Hidy and Hidy, *op. cit.*, p. 422.
[23]Clark, *op. cit.*, p. 127.

As new crude supplies in Kansas, Oklahoma, Texas, and California flooded the market, new large, vertically-integrated refinery companies came into existence to direct the crude flow toward the new demand. For example, the Pure Oil Company was formed in 1895, and by 1904 owned 14 refineries, mostly in the oil region; had 1,500 miles of crude oil pipe line, plus another 400 to pipe refined products; handled 8,000 barrels of crude a day; owned steamers and barges; and was capitalized at over $10 million.[24] In addition, firms such as Associated Oil of California were formed in 1901; the Texas Company a year later; and Gulf Oil in 1907.[25] By 1908 there were at least 125 independent refineries in the United States, including such companies as Sun Oil, Union Oil of California, and Tide Water-Associated Oil. By 1911 there were at least 147.[26] The petroleum industry mushroomed, and in more directions, than any one man or any one firm could have predicted or controlled. The competitive market was undercutting Standard Oil of New Jersey's position. As the Hidys so neatly put it:

> Thus even before the breakup of the combination, the process of whittling Standard Oil down to reasonable size within the industry was already far advanced.[27]

Also "far advanced," however, was the "intellectual" criticism of big business, especially of Rockefeller and the Standard Oil Company. Although Standard had remained amazingly clean of political scandal and was never the beneficiary of tariff protection, subsidy, or public land grants—such as the sugar and steel "trusts"—most "muckrakers" directed their fire at the "petroleum combination." Henry Demarest Lloyd set the tone of the era with the great "populist polemic," *Wealth Against Commonwealth*, published in 1894. The Hearst newspapers, *Life, Collier's,* and *Harper's*, quickly discovered that anti-wealth and particularly "anti-monopoly" journalism paid handsomely at the cash register. And when Ida Tarbell's articles entitled "The History of the Standard Oil Company," published during 1902–1903 in *McClure's*, became modern classics, anti-business

---

[24]*Ibid.*, p. 123.

[25]Gabriel Kolko, *The Triumph of Conservatism: A Reinterpretation of American History, 1900–1916* (New York: Free Press of Glencoe, 1963), pp. 40–42.

[26]*Ibid.*, p. 40. Also, see McGee, *Ibid.*, p. 156; and *The Petroleum Almanac*, p. 87.

[27]Hidy and Hidy, *op. cit.*, p. 477.

resentment of the times had reached its zenith. The fact that most
of the attacks were personal, emotional, and even illogical was irrelevant; the fact that some of the attacks were ambiguously motivated
(Ida Tarbell's brother, William, was treasurer of Pure Oil Company),
was ignored. Rockefeller's and Standard Oil's silence on all criticisms
just fired the public indignation more. Between 1904 and 1906 at
least twenty-one state antitrust suits were brought against Standard
Oil subsidiaries in ten states.[28] And on November 15, 1906, the federal government filed the Sherman Act case and petitioned for dissolution of Standard Oil of New Jersey.

STANDARD OIL AND THE COURTS

The Lower Court Decision

Standard was convicted on November 20, 1909, and ordered dissolved back into its "independent" component parts.[29] The four Circuit Court judges (Sanborn, VanDevouter, Hook, and Adams) all
agreed that Standard violated the Sherman Act because it had
formed a holding company in 1899, and the holding company had
not allowed any competition between the merged firms. Judge Sanborn said:

> By the trust of 1899, more than 30 corporations were
> combined with the principal company, and that corporation
> was given the power to fix the rates of transportation and
> the purchase and selling prices which all *these* companies
> should pay and receive for petroleum and its products
> throughout the republic and in the traffic with foreign na-
> tions. The principal company and many of the subsidiary
> corporations were many of them *capable of competing with
> each other* in that trade, and would have been actively com-
> petitive if they had been owned by different individuals or
> different groups of individuals . . . The majority of the stock
> of the New York Company and of 18 other corporations en-
> gaged different branches of the production, manufacture,
> and sale of petroleum and its products was conveyed to the
> New Jersey Company in exchange for its stock, and the lat-
> ter has ever since controlled and operated all these corpora-
> tions and those which they controlled, *and has prevented
> them from competing* with it or with each other.[30]

[28] *Ibid.*, p. 683.
[29] *United States* v. *Standard Oil Company*, 173 Fed. Reporter 179.
[30] *Ibid.*, p. 185 (Emphasis added).

Since "any contract or combination of two or more parties, whereby the control of such rates or prices is taken from separate competitors in that trade and rested in a person or an association of persons, *necessarily restricts competition* and restrains that commerce," and since Standard had necessarily formed such an "association," Standard necessarily violated the Sherman Act:

> ... the power to restrict competition in interstate commerce granted to the Standard Oil Company of New Jersey by the transfer to it of the stock of the 19 companies and of the authority to manage and operate them and the other corporations which they controlled was the absolute power to prevent competition *between any of these corporations* ... and the *necessary* effect of the transfer of the stock of the 19 companies to the holding company was, under the decision in the case of the Northern Securities Company, a direct and substantial restriction of that commerce, that transfer and the operation of the companies under it constituted a combination or conspiracy in restraint of interstate and international commerce in violation of the Anti-trust Act of July 2, 1890.[31]

Nowhere in the decision was there a discussion of the reasonableness or unreasonableness of Standard's competitive practices. Nowhere was there an economic analysis of Standard Oil's performance in the market. The singular relevant issue was that the formation of the holding company in 1899 necessarily restrained trade between the parties to the holding company. As Justice Hook so neatly put it:

> A holding company, owning the stocks of other concerns whose commercial activities, if free and independent of common control, would naturally bring them into competition with each other, is a form of trust or combination prohibited by Section I of the Sherman Act. The Standard Oil Company of New Jersey is such a holding company.[32]

Hence in 1909 the Sherman Act was being enforced literally, as was the tradition up to that point. Trusts or holding companies "necessarily" restrained trade, and Standard was a holding company. In 1909, there was no explicit concern with "intent" or with conduct-performance facts.

---

[31] *Ibid.*, pp. 189–190 (Emphasis added).
[32] *Ibid.*, p. 193.

The Supreme Court Decision

On May 15, 1911, the lower court dissolution decision was reaffirmed by the Supreme Court.[33] The general impression of this case is that the Supreme Court decision is a precedent-setting one, since Justice White argued in the majority decision that not all restraints of trade or contracts or conspiracies were illegal and in violation of the Sherman Act, but only "unreasonable" ones:

> Thus not specifying, but indubitably contemplating and requiring a standard, it follows that it was intended that the standard of reason which had been applied at the common law . . . was intended to be the measure used for the purpose of determining whether, in a given case, a particular act had or had not brought about the wrong against which the statute provided.[34]

According to the logic of the justice's position, no firm (including Standard Oil, presumably) was to be judged guilty *per se* of Sherman Act violations because of, let us assume, its dominant position in the market place. What supposedly was to be the crucial factor determining innocence or guilt was the *reasonableness* or *unreasonableness* of a firm's actions, or whether they are

> . . . of such a character as to give rise to the inference or presumption that they had been entered into or done with the *intent to do wrong to the general public and to limit the rights of individuals,* thus restraining the free flow of commerce and tending to bring about the ends, such as enhancement of prices, which were considered to be against public policy.[35]

It is suggested here that this is the beginning of a conduct-performance approach to antitrust. White, like other justices before him, appears to be concerned with acts that relate an unmistakable intention to "wrong the public" or "limit individual rights." If one discovered such acts and analyzed them, one could infer a restraint of trade and a violation of the law.

Actually, a careful reading of the Supreme Court decision does *not* substantiate the widely held view that Standard Oil was convicted by applying "reason" as a "standard" in a careful examination of

[33] *Standard Oil Company of New Jersey v. United States,* 221 U.S. 1.
[34] *Ibid.,* p. 60
[35] *Ibid.,* p. 58 (Emphasis added).

Standard's conduct-performance behavior in the period under discussion. While White maintained that a "rule of reason" *should* apply to such activities, there is nothing to indicate that the court actually applied a "reasonable" standard to Standard Oil's conduct-performance. The application of such a standard would have required a careful and methodical sifting of all the conflicting evidence concerning rebates, railroad discriminations, predatory practices, the setting up of bogus independents, industrial espionage, and other "unfair" competitive practices as alleged in the government's long-winded petition. But no such "sifting" was detailed in the Supreme Court decision and, consequently, no specific finding of guilt was made with regard to these allegations. Regarding these "acts," we are simply told that:

> . . . no disinterested mind can survey the period in question without being irresistibly driven to the conclusion that the very genius for commercial development and organization which it would seem was manifested from the beginning soon begot an intent and purpose to exclude others which was frequently manifested by acts and dealings wholly inconsistent with the theory that they were made with the single conception of advancing the development of business power by *usual* methods, but which, on the contrary, necessarily involved the intent to drive others from the field and to exclude them from their right to trade, and thus accomplish the mastery which was the end in view.[36]

Yet how can "disinterested minds" be driven "irresistibly" to "conclusions" without facts, and economic analysis applied to those facts? What are these "usual methods" of business development that the court refers to, and are Standard's "unusual" methods to be judged automatically unreasonable because they are not "usual"? How did Standard Oil exclude competitors "from their right to trade," and were these "unreasonable" exclusions? Had the "acts" worked an "injury to the public"? Had Standard raised prices, restricted outputs, repressed technological change, produced shoddy products, and driven all its competition from the market through predatory practices? These are the crucial questions that a "rule of reason" would provoke and did provoke in many subsequent cases, but the Standard Oil decision did not answer them.[37]

[36] *Ibid.*, p. 76 (Emphasis added).
[37] Though a great portion of the actual trial was taken up with these charges, Standard Oil offered rebuttal on all points. See Hidy and Hidy, *op. cit.*, pp. 693–697.

Now the conduct-performance record of the industry indicates, as this account has revealed, that prices fell, costs fell, outputs expanded, product quality improved, and hundreds of firms at one time or another produced and sold refined petroleum products in competition with Standard Oil. Many competitors, particularly in the early period, had, of course, left the market for one reason or another. Many sold out to the Standard organization, and many were glad to; but surely, their right—and the subsequent *rights* of any other refiner to compete and trade—were not involved or *infringed.* The markets were legally open, and Standard neither sought nor obtained any artificial or political exclusions. All had the right to trade. Whether they were equipped to trade efficiently in competition with the Standard organization, and *did* trade efficiently, is another question. If they were excluded because they did not have tank cars, pipe lines, barrel factories, can factories, exporting firms, proper locations, crude supplies, storage facilities, and the consequent ability to obtain rebates from the railroads when necessary, surely, their "right to trade" is not at issue. They were excluded because they could not match the economic advantages employed by Standard Oil. The significant point here is that the Supreme Court did not analyze these issues.

Assuming, then, that all of this is correct, how was Standard Oil of New Jersey convicted? On what basis was the firm found guilty of violating sections 1 and 2 of the Sherman Act? After Justice White had detailed his rule of reason, he turned to an examination of "the facts and the application of the statute to them." Beyond dispute were (1) "The creation of the Standard Oil Company of Ohio"; (2) "The organization of the Standard Oil Trust in 1882"; and (3) "the increase of the capital of the Standard Oil Company of New Jersey and the acquisition by that company of the shares of the stock of the other corporations in exchange for its certificates."[38]

Now this latter aggregation of a "vast amount of property and the possibilities of far-reaching control" over the trade and commerce in petroleum and its products *"operated to destroy the 'potentiality of competition' which otherwise would have existed"* and the lower court had concluded that Standard thus violated Sections 1 and 2 of the Sherman Act. White saw "no cause to doubt the correctness of these conclusions."[39]

[38]221 U.S. p. 70
[39]*Ibid.*, p. 74 (Emphasis added). The issue that mergers restrain "potential competi-

But what were the conclusions, and how were they reached? Was Standard guilty because it had formally created a holding company in 1899 comprised of firms allied to it since the early 1880's, and that *per se* destroyed the "potentiality of competition" in the petroleum industry? Even worse, was the court simply concluding that the destruction of *potential* competition between the now merged firms automatically constituted an illegal restraint of trade, as the lower court had done? White attempted to explain why the Supreme Court had affirmed the lower court decision:

> Because the unification of power and control over petroleum and its products which was the *inevitable* result of the *combining in the New Jersey corporation* by the increase of its stock and the transfer to it of the stocks of so many other corporations, aggregating so vast a capital, gives rise, *in and of itself*, in the absence of countervailing circumstances, to say the least, to the *prima-facie* presumption of intent and purpose to maintain the dominancy over the oil industry, not as a result of *normal methods of industrial development, but by new means of combination* . . .[40]

Now this is hardly a "rule of reason" approach! White simply argued that the creation of the holding company in 1899, or the *formal* merger of firms allied with Standard for almost twenty years (the "new means of combination"), was "in and of itself" *prima-facie* proof of intent and purpose to monopolize, and that this "unification of power and control over petroleum" was an inevitable result" of the "combination." Later, he added that "the exercise of power which resulted from that organization fortified the foregoing conclusions," since

> . . . the acquisition here and there which ensued of every efficient means by which competition could have been asserted, the slow but resistless methods which followed by which means of transportation were absorbed and brought under control, the system of marketing which was adopted by which the company was *divided into districts and the trade in each district in oil was turned over to a designated corporation within the combination, and all others were excluded*, all lead the mind up to a conviction of a purpose and intent which we think so certain as

tion" has arisen (again) in the recent Justice Department's 1969 conglomerate indictments. See Chapter 10.
   [40]*Ibid.*, p. 75 (Emphasis added).

practically to cause the subject *not to be within the domain of reasonable contention.*[41]

But surely, the "reasonableness" of Standard's acquisitions *can* be debated, and surely, it is not always unreasonable for a firm to designate the selling markets of its own subsidiaries and "exclude all others." Though these activities might not have been "normal" or "usual" for the day, they presumably were not (and are not) to be considered unreasonable *per se*. And, finally, it must be the strangest feat of judicial logic in memory to argue, on the one hand, that a "rule of reason" applied to Sherman Act allegations, and then to dismiss the entire subject with reference to Standard Oil as practically "not within the domain of reasonable contention."

In conclusion, while the essence of a conduct-performance "rule of reason" may have been suggested in the Standard Oil case of 1911, there is little, if any, concrete evidence that it was *applied* in that case. No economic analysis of Standard Oil's conduct and performance in the period under consideration was conducted by the court in an effort to determine whether these actions were "reasonable." Standard was convicted and dissolved in 1911, but an economic analysis of conduct-performance had little, if anything, to do with that decision.

In the same year, the same Supreme Court ruled to affirm a lower court decision to dissolve the American Tobacco Company. That decision, the nature of competition in the American tobacco industry between 1890 and 1907, and a discussion of the steel industry and the famous U.S. Steel cases, will be discussed in the next chapter.

[41] *Ibid.*, pp. 76–77 (Emphasis added).

CHAPTER 5

The Tobacco and Steel Monopoly Cases: A Study in Contrasts

THE TOBACCO INDUSTRY IN AMERICA

The legend surrounding the activities of the "Tobacco Trust" is as widely known and repeated as that surrounding Standard Oil.[1] Apparently, many authors have concluded that the violations of the Sherman Act and its newly enunciated "rule of reason" were so obvious in this case that they fail to provide important conduct-performance details that might lead to any independent conclusions.[2] The following account is an attempt to "right the balance" in this regard.

Although cigarettes appeared in America in the early 1850s and

[1]For information concerning the cigarette industry prior to 1911, see Meyer Jacobstein, "The Tobacco Industry in the United States," *Columbia University Studies*, XXVI (1907); Richard B. Tennant, *The American Cigarette Industry* (New Haven: Yale University Press, 1950); William H. Nicholls, *Price Policies in the Cigarette Industry* (Nashville: Vanderbilt University Press, 1951); John Wilber Jenkins, *James B. Duke: Master Builder* (New York: George H. Doran Company, 1927). Much of the following discussion is taken from my article "Antitrust History: The American Tobacco Case of 1911," *The Freeman*, XI (March, 1971), 173–186.

[2]For example, see Clair Wilcox, *Public Policies Toward Business* (3rd ed.; Homewood, Ill. Richard D. Irwin, 1966), p. 139; Elmer E. Smead, *Governmental Promotion and Regulation of Business* (New York: Appleton-Century-Crofts, 1969), pp. 70–71; Hugh S. Norton, *Economic Policy: Government and Business* (Columbus, Ohio: Charles E. Merrill Books, 1966, p. 101.

were unpopular enough with the government to rate their own special penalty tax of up to five dollars per thousand by 1868, there was hardly what could be termed a "cigarette manufacturing industry" before the 1880s. Until then the cigarette business had been concentrated in the New York City area where many small firms employed cheap immigrant labor to "hand roll" mostly Turkish blends of tobacco. The raw material was relatively expensive, and the hand-rolling operation was relatively inefficient and costly; also, there appeared to be great popular reluctance to smoke the small cigarettes. Consequently, the outputs and markets were severely limited. Total output of all "manufactured" cigarettes was never more than 500 million in any one year before 1880.

But the rather rapid shift in public taste to Virginia blends of tobacco, the slow adoption of machinery for manufacturing cigarettes, and the extensive use of advertising to popularize particular brands or "blends" of tobacco, changed the industry radically beginning in the 1880s.

The use of rapidly improving machines that manufactured cigarettes quickly drove down the costs of manufacture and placed a profit premium on mechanization. Labor costs alone were reduced from 85 cents per thousand without machines to 2 cents per thousand with machines.[3] While an expert "hand roller" could make approximately 2,000 smokes a day, a properly operating cigarette machine could make 100,000.[4] A few leased cigarette machines— particularly the "Bonsack" machine—could, in a matter of days, generate the entire yearly output of cigarettes. Thus, almost overnight, the optimum size of an efficient cigarette firm increased manyfold, and almost the entire industry's emphasis shifted to creating or expanding demand for particular blends of "manufactured" cigarettes. Advertising and marketing expenditures began in earnest in the late 1880s, and it was not at all surprising to find only five large firms doing most of the trade in manufactured cigarettes by 1889. Though there were hundreds of small cigarette producers (mostly hand-rolled varieties) in that period, the firms of Goodwin and Company, William S. Kimball and Company, Kinney Tobacco, Allen and Binter, and the W. Duke and Sons Company came to dominate the young

---

[3]Tennant, *op. cit.*, pp. 17–18.
[4]Jenkins, *op. cit.*, p. 66.

industry and did an estimated 90 percent of total domestic cigarette sales.[5]

American Tobacco Company

The name of James Buchanan Duke is almost synonymous with cigarettes and the rapid rise of the American tobacco industry. Although a relative newcomer to the cigarette industry (he entered in 1882), Duke quickly pushed his firm into industry leadership by rapid mechanization of all his operations and, accordingly, huge advertising schemes to increase demand for his increased outputs.[6] He took huge newspaper ads and rented billboard display space to push "Duke of Durham" and "Cameo" brands. In addition, he placed redeemable coupons inside his new and improved cigarette boxes to popularize "Cross Out" and "Duke's Best." He also enticed jobbers and retailers with special bonus plans and gimmicks if they would handle and stress his products. This unusual marketing approach was extremely successful, and by 1889, Duke's cigarette firm had over 30 percent of industry output and was netting almost $400,000 a year on gross sales of $4.5 million. Duke's firm was the largest and most profitable firm in the manufactured cigarette industry, and appeared to be growing much more quickly than its rivals could or would.

In January 1890 the five leading cigarette firms joined together to form the American Tobacco Company and installed J. B. Duke as president. Although competition between the leading firms had been severe in the late 1880s, there is little evidence that the combination was the direct consequence of a "destructive trade war," as some accounts relate.[7] Rather, it was an almost inevitable consequence of the economies of the cigarette industry in 1890.

Potentially, the cigarette industry appeared immensely profitable. The price of leaf tobacco, the raw material, was historically very low (about 4 cents per pound); the costs of manufacture—even with less

[5]Tennant, *op. cit.*, pp. 19–25.
[6]Jenkins, *op. cit.*, pp. 73–84.
[7]Nicholls, *op. cit.*, p. 26, states flatly that the American Tobacco Company was formed in 1890 following an expensive business war begun by James B. Duke. But neither the *Report of U. S. Commissioner of Corporations*, I (February, 1909), which Nicholls indicates was his source, nor the lower court decision against American Tobacco in 1909, appear to bear this out. See William Z. Ripley, *Trusts, Pools and Corporations* (Boston: Ginn and Company, 1916), pp. 269–270; and see 164 Fed. Reporter 722.

than optimal utilization of equipment—were extremely low; and the existing market prices for cigarettes were already high enough to allow adequate profits. Two things alone remained to cloud the potential profits picture of the industry: maximum utilization of the largest, most efficient machinery to drive the costs per unit down to an absolute minimum; and an elimination or severe reduction in total advertising expenditures as a percentage of total output or sales.

Merger provided both of the last-mentioned economies. Consolidation would allow concentration on those blends of tobacco that could be produced most efficiently. Consolidation would also allow great economies of scale to be realized in advertising expenditures. Thus, production and selling expenditures could be lowered per unit of output and profits could grow accordingly. A combination or "trust" of small cigarette firms was thus a natural and predictable economic arrangement, since it was clearly more efficient than a decentralized market structure.

Between 1890 and 1907 American Tobacco diversified into a number of related industries. Diversification was to be expected since cigarettes, although extremely profitable, represented only 3 percent to 5 percent of the entire tobacco industry in 1890.[8] In addition, the public's changing tastes rapidly made obsolete particular brand names and even whole products, and thus made any specialization extremely dangerous.[9] Furthermore, there was a distinct prejudice against machine-made cigarettes, and sales simply did not expand as rapidly as anticipated. While American Tobacco had produced slightly more than 3 billion cigarettes in 1893, they produced only 3.4 billion in 1899, and less than 3 billion annually between 1900 and 1905; American's production of cigarettes in 1907 was only 3.9 billion. Even more importantly, American's share of domestic cigarette sales declined from over 90 percent, when the firm was formed in 1890, to 74 percent in 1907.[10]

For the most part, American Tobacco's diversification and growth

[8]Even in the 1900–1904 period, cigarettes, by weight, represented only two per cent of all tobacco products consumed. See Nicholls, *op. cit.*, p. 7. Cigarettes did not achieve any sort of national popularity until after World War I.

[9]Jenkins, *op. cit.*, pp. 91–92.

[10]*U. S. Research and Brief*, 221 U.S. 106, Appendix "F", p. 318. Also see Jones, *The Trust Problem in the United States* (New York: The Macmillan Company, 1923), p. 140. Higher percentage figures in some accounts (83 percent is a common figure for 1907; see Nicholls) measure American's share of *total* output rather than output for domestic consumption.

in the tobacco industry was accomplished through the direct purchase of existing firms with cash or stock. It is estimated that American may have bought as many as 250 firms between 1890 and 1907.[11] A very few of these purchases were competitive cigarette manufacturers—though the bulk of them were not. Most of these cigarette purchases were made, apparently, to acquire a successful brand-name, since brand-name loyalty was the greatest asset of any tobacco firm.[12] The bulk of American Tobacco's purchases, however, were firms producing non-cigarette tobacco products. For example, diversification into firms that made smoking tobacco, snuff, plug chewing tobacco, and cheroots was begun as early as 1891. These tobacco products were noncompetitive with cigarettes and with each other, and had their own particular markets and used their own particular kind of leaf tobacco.[13] In 1898, after many years of competitive low-price rivalry,[14] American purchased the leading plug manufacturers, including, at a later date, the large and important Ligget and Myers Company. They were subsequently organized into the Continental Tobacco Company, partially owned and completely controlled by Duke and American Tobacco interests. Shortly thereafter, in March 1899 the Union Tobacco Company—manufacturer of the famous Bull Durham smoking tobacco—was purchased. The American Snuff Company was then organized in March 1901, with a paid-in capital of $23 million, and the stock was paid out to the three leading, formerly independent snuff manufacturers. The American Cigar Company was also formed in 1901 and became the largest firm in that sector of the tobacco market. In addition, American purchased licorice firms, bag firms, box firms, firms that made cigarette machinery, firms that produced tin foil, and firms that processed scrap tobacco. By 1902 American Tobacco was manufacturing and selling a complete line of tobacco and tobacco-related products—including over 100 brands of cigarettes—and over 60 percent of the nation's smoking and chewing tobacco; about 80 percent of the nation's snuff; and 14 percent of its cigars. And when the newly organized Consolidated Tobacco Company, Continental Tobacco Company, and the American Tobacco Company all merged in October 1904 to form

[11]Tennant, *op. cit.*, p. 27.
[12]Jenkins, *op. cit.*, p. 149.
[13]*Transcript of Record*, 221 U.S. 106, Volume I, p. 254.
[14]It was not established at court that American Tobacco started this price war; see 164 Fed. Reporter 723, and 221 U. S. 160.

the *new* American Tobacco Company, the last phase of the diversification and consolidation of tobacco properties was complete. The American Tobacco Company was now a major factor in all phases of the tobacco industry domestically and internationally (although relatively weak in cigars), until dissolution by the courts in 1911.

The 1890–1910 Period Acquisitions

Though American Tobacco did acquire many firms in all phases of the tobacco business between 1890 and 1911, the total number of their acquisitions must be put in perspective. While over 200 acquisitions appears high—and creates the impression that only a few independent tobacco firms remained—the tobacco industry contained thousands of independent firms in the period under consideration. While American Tobacco did the great bulk of much of the tobacco industry in a few large manufacturing plants, thousands of smaller independent firms sold their products at a profit in the open market in competition with the Trust.

For example, as many as 300 independent cigarette manufacturers may have existed in 1910.[15] Similarly, while the Trust produced a great percentage of the nation's output of smoking tobacco in fewer than 25 plants, there were as many as 3,000 plants manufacturing smoking tobacco in 1910.[16] In addition, the Trust accounted for only about seven of the nation's estimated seventy snuff manufacturing plants.[17] And finally, the American Cigar Company operated just 29 manufacturing plants in 1906, while the cigar industry contained upwards of 20,000 independent firms.[18] Thus, the tobacco industry contained thousands of firms *in spite of* the acquisition activities of the Trust.

The major reason for the numerous amount of rival sellers is not difficult to discover. With or without the Trust, entry into tobacco manufacturing was relatively easy. The raw material was available to all at the going market rates, and the Trust itself owned no tobacco land whatsoever. Anyone who wanted to compete could purchase the available raw materials and attempt to sell his product in the open market. In addition, the Trust possessed neither discriminatory

[15]See Nicholls, *op. cit.*, p. 17. Jones mentions 528 independent plants in 1906; see Jones, *op. cit.*, p. 146.
[16]Nicholls, *op. cit.*, p. 15.
[17]*Ibid.*
[18]*Ibid.*, p. 13. Also, see Ripley, *op. cit.*, p. 295.

transportation rates or rebates[19] nor any superior production method protected by patent.[20] Thus, it was not surprising to find many independent firms in an industry where neither the raw material nor the efficient means of production were, or could have been, "monopolized."

The major reason for the American Tobacco's policy of acquisitions is not difficult to discover either: it made economic sense. For example, much emotional nonsense has been made out of the fact that American acquired firms and, subsequently, shut them down.[21] The crucial point, of course, is that American concentrated tobacco production—and particularly cigarette production, with only two large plants in New York and Richmond—to achieve quite obvious and substantial scale economies.[22] Most of the obtained facilities were mechanically inefficient, and had been acquired only to secure the immensely more valuable competitive brand name. Once procured, the product itself could be produced more efficiently in American's own modern and efficient facilities. Thus, it made good sense and good economics to close down marginal manufacturing operations, and no tears need be shed for the "dismantled factories." There is no evidence that any of the former owners shed such tears, since American Tobacco's terms (stock in the trust or cash) were admitted to be generous to all concerned. Thus, the plants were not gained *just* to shut them down.

Other economies of the procuration policy were achieved in important, though not so obvious, ways. For example, American's huge production made the ownership of its own foil, box, and bag firms almost mandatory; and the advantages and savings to be realized by accurate and continuous deliveries of these products made economic sense. Its acquisition of MacAndrews and Forbes, and Mell and Rittenhouse, the two leading manufacturers of licorice paste, was predicated on possible economies and on the very real fact that the Japanese-Russian war threatened Near East licorice supplies and, consequently, American Tobacco's expansion of plug tobacco.[23]

[19]221 U.S. 129.
[20]Jacobstein, *op. cit.*, p. 101.
[21]Wilcox, *op. cit.*, p. 139, says that one of American's "unfair" methods of competition was buying plants *to shut them down.*
[22]*Transcript of Record*, 221 U.S. 106, Volume I, pp. 208–211.
[23]*Ibid.*, pp. 227–231.

Independent foil, box, and bag firms still remained in the market place, and at least four other manufacturers sold licorice paste independently of the American Tobacco firms. There is also no evidence that American's paste firms would not sell to anyone who wanted licorice at the going market prices. Thus, this aspect of the vertical integration of American Tobacco was economically logical and certainly cannot be condemned as *necessarily* restraining trade.

American's integration into distribution also realized economies. With the virtual elimination of the middleman, the jobbers' not unhealthy margin could be realized by the tobacco manufacturer.[24] Wholly-owned retail establishments could also push particular brands more effectively and become an important advertising and marketing innovation. American Tobacco's United Cigar Stores, the most famous and effective tobacco products' retail chain—with over a thousand stores by 1910 and at least 300 in New York City alone —was certainly important in this respect.

There were still other more subtle economies. A certain amount of inefficient cross-hauling or cross-freighting was automatically eliminated, since American Tobacco could fill orders for finished tobacco products from a number of different manufacturing locations.[25] In those modernly equipped factories labored nonunion help, and this saved American from 10 percent to 20 percent on its wage expenses *vis-à-vis* most of its competitors, who employed Tobacco Workers' Union labor.[26] The Tobacco Trust could demand prompt settlement of all outstanding accounts (thirty days), while it was quite common for smaller manufacturers to wait two to four months for payment.[27] It could employ fewer salesmen per product, since many of its brands were long established; orders could even be filled by mail without agents of any sort.[28] And lastly, it could employ, and did employ, some of the keenest managerial talent in the industry.[29] They in turn proceeded to implement and extend the potential economies already discussed above.

[24]Tennant, *op. cit.*, pp. 51–52.
[25]Jacobstein, *op. cit.*, p. 126.
[26]*Ibid.*, pp. 125–126.
[27]*Ibid.*, p. 127.
[28]*Ibid.*, p. 128.
[29]*Ibid.*, p. 123.

Policies Toward Consumers and Competitors

But while the Tobacco Trust enjoyed "economies," what became of the tobacco consumer and of the Trust's competitors? Did American Tobacco simply act like a "classical" monopolist by restricting output and raising prices? Or did American act like a "predatory" monopolist and use its market power to lower prices and, consequently, drive its competition from the market? Actually, there is little evidence that American Tobacco followed either monopolistic-like conduct: they neither restricted outputs nor raised prices. Neither did they engage, as a general rule, in predatory pricing practices designed to eliminate their competition.[30] For example, American Tobacco's cigarettes (per thousand, less tax) sold for $2.77 in 1895, $2.29 in 1902, and $2.20 in 1907; fine cut (per pound, less tax) sold for 27 cents in 1895, 33 cents in 1902, and 30 cents in 1907; smoking tobacco sold for 25 cents (per pound, less tax) in 1895, 26.7 cents in 1902, and 30.1 cents in 1907; plug sold for 15.5 cents (per pound, less tax) in 1895, 27.7 cents in 1902, and 30.4 cents in 1907; and little cigars sold for $4.60 (per thousand, less tax) in 1895, $4.37 in 1902, and $3.60 in 1907.[31] In the same period (1895–1907), the price of leaf tobacco per pound rose from 6 to 10.5 cents.[32] Thus, the pricing record indicated above was accomplished during a period when the price of the essential raw material had increased about 40 percent.

Predatory practices are expensive (see Chapter 4), and it is not usually profitable to attempt to eliminate competition through this technique. This would be especially true in an industry where entry was relatively easy, where nonprice competitive factors were crucial, and where there already were hundreds—even thousands—of competitive sellers already in existence. Such a *general* policy on the part of American Tobacco would have been foolish and foolhardy, and no such general policy was attempted. Although there may have been some isolated instances where price-cutting played an important part in merger or consolidation,[33] such practices were not the rule.

---

[30]Tennant, *op. cit.*, pp. 49–57.
[31]*U. S. Research and Brief,* 221 U.S. 106, Appendix "P," p. 329.
[32]Tennant, *op. cit.*, p. 53.
[33]The "plug war" (1894–1898) is probably the most famous example. During this "war," American sold plug at a loss until the large independent plug manufacturers defaulted. The "independents" came together to form the Continental Tobacco Company, whose president was James B. Duke. But some additional facts complicate an easy interpretation of this "war." In the first place, it was not established that Ameri-

AMERICAN TOBACCO AND THE COURTS

The Lower Court Decision

The comments concerning American Tobacco's efficiency and price policy related above are certainly not original. Amazingly, the same sort of comments can be discovered in a reading of the Circuit Court decision (*United States* v. *American Tobacco Company*), 164 Federal Reporter 700 [1908] that first determined that American Tobacco had violated the Sherman Act. Although Circuit Judge Lacombe found American guilty of violating the Sherman Act, he stated, with respect to the economic issues involved, that:

> The record in this case does *not* indicate that there has been any increase in the price of tobacco products to the consumer. There is an *absence* of persuasive evidence that by unfair competition or improper practices independent dealers have been dragooned into giving up their individual enterprises and selling out to the principal defendant . . . During the existence of the American Tobacco Company new enterprises have been started, some with small capital, in competition with it, *and have thriven.* The price of leaf tobacco—the raw material—except for one brief period of abnormal conditions, has steadily *increased,* until it has nearly doubled, while at the same time 150,000 additional acres have been devoted to tobacco crops and the consumption of leaf has greatly increased. Through the enterprise of defendant and at a large expense new markets for American tobacco have been opened or developed in India, China, and elsewhere.[34]

Circuit Court Judge Noyes, while concurring with Judge Lacombe in American Tobacco's guilt, also appeared to concur in the economic issues involved.

> Insofar as combinations result from the operation of economic principles, it may be doubtful whether they should be stayed at all by legislation . . . It may be that the present antitrust statute should be amended and made applicable only to those combinations which unreasonably restrain trade—that it should draw a line between those combinations which work for good and those which work for evil. But these are all legislative, and not judicial, questions.[35]

can *started* the "plug war." Secondly, the price reductions were limited to only a few "fighting" brands; while American Tobacco lost money on plug, all the large independent plug manufacturers *continued to earn a profit.* Lastly, plug sales increased from 9 million pounds in 1894 to 38 million pounds in 1897. See Tennant, *op. cit.*, p. 29.

[34] 164 Fed. Reporter, pp. 702–703 (Emphasis added).

[35] *Ibid.*, p. 712.

It was Judge Ward (dissenting), however, who crystallized the economic issues in the case.

> So far as the volume of trade in tobacco is concerned, the proofs show that it has *enormously increased* from the raw material to the manufactured product since the combinations, and, so far as the price of the product is concerned, that it has *not been increased* to the consumer and has varied *only* as the price of the raw material of leaf tobacco has varied.

> The purpose of the combination was not to restrain trade or prevent competition . . . but, by intelligent economies, to increase the volume and the profits of the business in which the parties engaged.[36]

> A perusal of the record satisfied me that their [American Tobacco] purpose and conduct were not illegal or oppressive, but that they strove, as every businessman strives, to increase their business, and that their great success is a natural growth resulting from industry, intelligence, and economy, doubtless largely helped by the volume of business done and the great capital at command.[37]

Yet, although three of the four Circuit Court judges admitted that there was evidence to indicate that American Tobacco was efficient, had not raised prices, had expanded outputs, had not depressed leaf prices, and had not "dragooned" competitors, Judge Coxe joined Judges Lacombe and Noyes in concurring that American Tobacco violated the Sherman Act! Clearly, the conduct and economic performance of the defendant had nothing to do with the decision. American Tobacco was convicted *in spite of* its economic record because its mergers and acquisitions inherently restrained trade between the now merged or acquired firms, and *that* violated the Sherman Act as interpreted in 1908. Judge Lacombe made the majority's position explicit:

> . . . every aggregation of individuals or corporations, formerly independent, *immediately upon its formation terminated an existing competition*, whether or not some other competition may subsequently arise. The act as above construed [Sherman Act] prohibits *every* contract or combination in restraint of competition. Size is not made the test: two individuals who have

---

[36] *Ibid.*, p. 726 (Emphasis added).
[37] *Ibid.*, p. 728.

been driving rival express wagons between villages in two con-
tiguous states, who enter into a combination to join forces and
operate a single line, restrain an existing competition . . .

Accepting *this* construction of the statute, as it would seem this
Court must accept it, there can be little doubt that it has been
violated in this case. . . . The present American Tobacco Company was formed by subsequent merger of the original company with the Continental Tobacco Company and the Consolidated Tobacco Company, and when *that merger* became
complete two of its existing competitors in the tobacco business
were eliminated.[38]

It was irrelevant to inquire into the benefits of the combination,
argued Judge Lacombe. It was "not material" to consider subsequent
business methods or to judge the effect of the combination on production or prices. The fact that American Tobacco had not abused
competitors, tobacco growers, or consumers was "immaterial." The
only issue that was material was that:

Each one of these purchases of existing concerns complained of
in the petition was a contract and combination in restraint of
competition existing *when it was entered into* and *that* is sufficient to bring it within the ban of this drastic statute.[39]

And thus the three judges (with Judge Ward dissenting) ruled that
the American Tobacco Company must be dissolved.

The Supreme Court Decision

The Supreme Court decision handed down in the American Tobacco case by Justice White in 1911, is a virtual replay of the Standard Oil decision of the same year.[40] Again, White suggests that a
"rule of reason" be applied to the undisputed facts concerning the
activities of the American Tobacco Company.[41] But again, that "rule
of reason" does *not* include a careful economic analysis of the Tobacco Trust's conduct-performance in the period under consideration. All the Supreme Court did (again) was to detail the history of
the tobacco industry between 1890 and 1907,[42] and infer from these
undisputed facts that the intent and "wrongful purpose" of Ameri-

---

[38] *Ibid.*, p. 702 (Emphasis added).
[39] *Ibid.*, p. 703 (Emphasis added).
[40] *United States* v. *American Tobacco Company*, 221 U.S. 105.
[41] *Ibid.*, pp. 155, 178–179.
[42] *Ibid.*, pp. 155–175.

can Tobacco must have been to achieve a monopolistic position in the tobacco industry.[43] This conclusion was "inevitable," said White,[44] and could be "overwhelmingly established" by reference to the following facts: 1) the original combination of cigarette firms in 1890 was "impelled" by a trade war; 2) an "intention existed to use the power of the combination as a vantage ground to further monopolize the trade in tobacco," and tne power *was* used, i.e., the "plug and snuff wars"; 3) the Trust attempted to conceal the extent of its "control" with secret agreements and bogus independents; 4) American Tobacco's policy of vertical integration served as a "barrier to the entry of others into the tobacco trade"; 5) American Tobacco expended millions of dollars to purchase plants, "not for the purpose of utilizing them, but in order to close them up and render them useless for the purposes of trade"; 6) there were some agreements not to compete between American and some formerly independent tobacco manufacturers.[45] With these "facts" in mind, the conclusion was inevitable:

> Indeed, when the results of the undisputed proof which we have stated are fully apprehended, and the wrongful acts which they exhibit are considered, there comes *inevitably to the mind the conviction that it was the danger which it was deemed would arise to individual liberty and the public well-being from acts like those which this record exhibits,* which led the legislative mind to conceive and enact the anti-trust act. . . .[46]

But, as has been demonstrated in our review of the American Tobacco Company, whether such "acts" are a danger to "individual liberty" and the "public well-being" *is* a matter of dispute. To deduce *inevitably*, for example, that purchasing plants and closing them down endangers liberty or the public well-being, *without an economic analysis of the costs and benefits of such an action*, is an unwarranted and faulty inference. If the agreements to secure these "plants" were voluntarily arrived at, then "individual liberty" was *not* endangered; if the plants closed down by American Tobacco were inefficient, and if the products continued to be produced at

---

[43] *Ibid.*, pp. 181–184.
[44] *Ibid.*, p. 182.
[45] *Ibid.*, pp. 182–183.
[46] *Ibid.*, p. 183 (Emphasis added).

larger, more efficient factories, then the danger to the public well-being is *not* obvious. The same kind of questioning can be raised about the rest of the "undisputed facts" and "inevitable inferences" in this case.

Unfortunately, the Supreme Court in the American Tobacco case did not choose to analyze the economic issues involved, nor did it choose to use the rule of reason as an *economic standard* to see whether the public well-being had been harmed. Such an analysis, if performed, would have involved a discussion of prices, outputs, economies associated with merger, growth of competitors (especially in cigarette manufacture), and a host of related issues; no such discussion is discovered in this decision. American Tobacco was convicted of violating the Sherman Act because its acts, contracts, agreements, and combinations were of such "an *unusual* and *wrongful* character as to bring them within the prohibitions of the law."[47] The Circuit Court was directed to devise a plan of dissolving the illegal combination and "recreating" a new market structure that would not violate the antitrust law.

Sparked by impressive victories in the Standard Oil and American Tobacco cases, the Justice Department filed a major antitrust suit against the United States Steel Corporation in late 1911. It is to this suit, and the background details concerning the steel industry in the period prior to the suit, that we turn our attention next.

THE STEEL INDUSTRY IN AMERICA

United States Steel Corporation was formed in 1901, when ten formerly independent steel companies (three steel producers and seven steel finishers) and one other company (which owned the Mesabic ore mines, some railroads, and some ore-carrying ships) came together to form America's first billion dollar holding company. The "firm" had impressive dimensions (66 percent of the nation's ingot capacity; 44 percent of the nation's total output of steel products), and although its principal architects (Morgan, Carnegie, and Moore) talked of economies of scale and lower prices, everyone else talked of *monopoly.*

Surprisingly, there had been little talk of monopoly in the competitive and decentralized steel industry before the late 1890s. On the

[47] *Ibid.*, p. 181 (Emphasis added).

contrary, the industry and its growth had been the personification of the American industrial dream come true.[48] From the small forges and pig iron furnaces of the 1850s, it had developed into one of the country's most capital intensive and progressive industries. Outputs climbed rapidly from a piddling 69,000 tons in 1870, to 1.3 million tons in 1880, and 10 million tons in 1900, and twice the British output in that year. Steel rails—the industry's most important product— went from 84,000 tons in 1872 (when 809,000 tons of iron rail had also been made), to 291,000 tons in 1875. By 1895, iron rails were no longer being made. Eighty-eight percent of the total U.S. railway trackage was made of steel.[49] Consequent with the huge output increases, the price of steel rail tumbled from $106 in 1870 to but $17 a ton in 1898.[50] The price and output record on other steel products was similarly impressive.

This remarkable increase in production and equally remarkable decrease in selling price were a direct function of great entrepreneurial genius, competition, innovation, and the consequent economic efficiencies. The most effective way to illustrate the veracity of these points is to review the history, progress, and success of one of the young industry's most efficient steel producers, originally called the Edgar Thompson Company, but later known as the Carnegie Company.

The Edgar Thompson Company

In 1873, Andrew Kloman, Henry Phillips, David McCandless, John Scott, David Stewart, William Shinn, and Tom Carnegie each subscribed $50,000, while William Coleman subscribed $100,000, and young Andrew Carnegie put up $250,000 toward the construction of a major steel works on a 107-acre plot of land called Braddocks Field, about twelve miles from Pittsburgh. The men involved in the speculative undertaking were an odd mixture of iron and steel experience, railroad knowledge, and financial interests. Kloman, Phillips, and Coleman were iron and steel men, with over one hundred years

---

[48]There are many excellent works on the early history of the iron and steel industry. For an old classic account, see James Howard Bridge, *The Inside History of the Carnegie Steel Company* (New York: Aldine Book Company, 1903). For excellent recent accounts, see Louis M. Hacker, *The World of Andrew Carnegie: 1865–1901* (Philadelphia: J. B. Lippincott Company, 1968), especially pp. 337–439; and Joseph Frazier Wall, *Andrew Carnegie* (New York: Oxford University Press, 1970).

[49]Hacker, *op. cit.*, p. 342.

[50]Bridge, *op. cit.*, p. 83.

of metal-making experience among them in their respective areas; McCandless was a prominent Pittsburgh merchant and vice president of the Exchange National Bank; Stewart was president of the Pittsburgh Locomotive Works; and Scott was a director of the Allegheny Valley Railroad. All became convinced that the success of the "Bessemer process" for making steel in England, could be duplicated with even more profitability in Pittsburgh. Mr. A. L. Holley —who had already negotiated the original Bessemer patents in 1864, and erected the first American hearths in Troy, New York—was commissioned to lay out the most efficient mill possible, and one capable of producing up to 75,000 ingot tons a year. On September 1, 1875, the first steel rail made at the newly completed steel works was forged; and the Carnegie-dominated firm, with strong ties to the Pennsylvania Railroad, was on its way.

Two years after the Edgar Thompson Company was completed, ingot production exceeded rail mill operations, and new uses for fabricated steel were pioneered. For example, billets of high-carbon steel were shaped into buggy springs; axle steel replaced crucible steel for railroad cars; and thin steels were developed for plow shares, stovepipes and cartridge cases. The increasing demand for ingot and steel products prompted the building of a number of pig iron furnaces, and these furnaces turned out to be extremely efficient. In April 1880, for example, a Thompson furnace produced 2,723 tons of pig iron, while consuming 2,536 pounds of coke per ton of iron produced. A decade later 10,075 tons of pig could be produced with only 1,847 pounds of coke per ton. And in December, 1902, over 17,000 tons of pig could be made with but 1,875 pounds of coke per ton.[51]

The record in ingot and steel rail production was similarly impressive. By 1880 the Thompson Company could pour over 10,000 tons of steel ingot a month, and an equal tonnage of steel rails could also be accomplished. By November 1881 the figures for ingot and rail were 16,000 and 13,000 tons per month, respectively, and the Thompson Company had surpassed the monthly outputs of the Troy, Harrisburg, North Chicago, and Cambria steel-producing areas.[52]

In the years that followed, the company expanded operations in-

[51] *Ibid.*, p. 90.
[52] *Ibid.*, p. 93.

ternally, purchased other steel properties (the Homestead mills in 1883; the Duquesne mills in 1890), and engaged in extensive vertical integration. Great ore mines on Lake Superior were leased; railroad and steamship interests were obtained; and harbors were built and operated by the company itself. By 1900 the Carnegie Company (the name had been changed in 1881) controlled every movement of its own materials, from the initial mining and transporting of the iron ore to the finishing and shipping out of the iron rail or whatever, and the firm was easily one of the most impressive industrial complexes in the world.

Hence, in summary, the competitive vigor and economic progressiveness of the steel industry—as represented by its leading firm—before 1901 were unquestioned. The industry, though geographically concentrated in a few major market areas, contained hundreds of producing firms that actively engaged in price and nonprice competition. Gentlemen's agreements and pools to "ease" price competition had been attempted but they had all been short-lived and had all collapsed.[53]

U. S. Steel Formed

The formation of Federal Steel, National Steel, National Tube, American Bridge, American Sheet Steel, and others in the 1898–1900 period, however, began to raise competitive eyebrows. These new incorporations were relatively large corporations formed by the combination of smaller, regional steel makers or fabricators, and although the combinations appeared economically logical, the charge that competition in the industry might be lessened was a distinct possibility; and when *these* firms, the giant Carnegie Company steel works, and eight other major steel firms all combined to become the giant holding company, United States Steel Corporation (in 1901), the insinuation that competition would be lessened considerably, or eliminated altogether, was stronger than ever. It was no surprise to anyone when, on the heels of success in the Standard Oil and American Tobacco cases, the Justice Department brought civil suit against U. S. Steel, claiming repeated violations of the Sherman Act and asking divesture as a remedy.

[53]Walter Adams, *The Structure of American Industry* (New York: Macmillan Company, 1950), p. 147. Also, see Hacker, *op. cit.*, pp. 361–362.

UNITED STATES STEEL AND THE COURTS

Had United States Steel unreasonably restrained trade or commerce in the steel industry, or had it monopolized or attempted to monopolize the market in steel and steel products between 1901 and 1911? The U. S. District Court of New Jersey on June 3, 1915,[54] answered *no* on both counts, and the Supreme Court agreed in a close four to three decision some years later.[55] Although Supreme Court Justice McKenna found U. S. Steel of "impressive size" and "equal or nearly equal to them [competitors] all . . . its power over prices was not and is not commensurate with its power to produce . . . we must adhere to the law, and the law does not make mere size an offense. It, we repeat, requires overt acts. . . ."[56] Since the majority on the Supreme Court in 1920 had apparently found no "overt acts" that violated the statute, the firm was freed.

Unlike any of the antitrust cases previously discussed, the U. S. Steel case was clearly heard and decided on the relevant conduct-performance facts surrounding competition in the steel industry between 1901 and 1911. For example, in the lower court decision of 1915, Circuit Judge Buffington[57] (with Judges Wooley, Hunt, and McPherson concurring)[58] explained that U. S. Steel's position in the steel market between 1901 and 1911 had declined in relative percentage terms in *every* important iron-steel product category except pig iron; there its percentage had increased slightly from 43 percent in 1901 to 45 percent in 1911.[59] But in the crucial area of "finished rolled product," for instance, U. S. Steel's share of the market had gone from 50.1 percent in 1901, to 46 percent in 1911; in steel ingot production, it had dropped from 66 percent to 54 percent; and in wire nails, it had fallen from 67 percent to 55 percent. In addition, continued Buffington, U. S. Steel's competitors managed to produce 78 percent of all domestic wire netting, fencing, and other wire products, and almost 70 percent of the nation's structural steel that was used in bridges, buildings, and auto frames. In sum, a full 60 percent of all the iron and steel products sold domestically in 1911 were produced by at least eighty firms competitive with the United

---

[54] *United States* v. *United States Steel Corporation*, 223 Fed. Reporter, 55.
[55] *United States* v. *United States Steel Corporation et al.*, 251 U.S. 417 (1920).
[56] *Ibid.*, p. 431.
[57] Judge Buffington's decision is reprinted in Ripley, *Trusts, Pools and Corporations*, pp. 97–184. All following references to Ripley are to that decision reprint.
[58] 223 Fed. Reporter, 57.
[59] Ripley, *op. cit.*, p. 106. See also 223 Fed. Reporter, pp. 65–67.

States Steel Corporation.[60] Firms like Bethlehem, Pennsylvania, Inland, LaBelle, Jones and Laughlin, Cambria, Colorado, Republic, and Lackawanna grew very rapidly between 1901 and 1911. Bethlehem, Inland, LaBelle, and Jones and Laughlin had increased their production 3,779.7 percent, 1,495.9 percent, 463.4 percent, and 206.7 percent, respectively, in the period 1901 to 1911.[61] The U.S. Steel Corporation, on the other hand, had increased its total output nowhere as quickly (about 40 percent), and its relative position in the domestic market had accordingly declined.[62] As far as Judge Buffington was concerned, the giant steel firm had not monopolized the steel industry's output, and the trends in the industry were all the *other* way.

The court's position on a possible iron ore monopoly by U. S. Steel was also distinctly clear. U. S. Steel Corporation had no ore monopoly, and "there is no basis on which to attempt ore monopoly."[63] The court was careful to note that all of U. S. Steel's major competitors (notably Pennsylvania, Maryland, and Bethlehem) had adequate ore supplies completely independent of the U. S. Steel-dominated Lake Superior fields. For example, the court pointed out that rich iron ores were readily available from the great Cornwall beds of eastern Pennsylvania, or from the Adirondack regions of New York, or from Sweden, Chile, and Cuba. In addition, steel-producing plants on the Pacific Coast had access to pig iron produced and shipped from China and India at prices that were more than competitive with eastern mill quotes, including rail freight.[64] In no sense, therefore, was U. S. Steel's position in iron ore or pig iron a detrimental factor to steel industry expansion anywhere in the country.[65]

The court also dismissed the notion that any firm (including U. S. Steel) had the market power to initiate a "ruinous trade war" in the steel industry during the period under consideration. An attempt at selective predatory price cutting would have, according to Judge Buffington, "owing to the the sensitiveness and interrelated character of the steel markets, result(ed) in forcing the company that was thus ruinously selling in any particular market or locality to in the

[60]Ripley, *op. cit.* pp. 102–103.
[61]*Ibid.*, p. 103. Also, see 223 Fed. Reporter, 68.
[62]*Ibid.*
[63]Ripley, *op. cit.*, p. 106.
[64]*Ibid.*, p. 111.
[65]223 Fed. Reporter, 68–70.

same way ruinously lower its prices in *every* other community."[66] But this sort of business conduct—as explained in the Standard Oil and American Tobaccco discussions—would threaten to ruin the big firm that initiated the cut. As an empirical clincher, *no* competitor testified that any such business action had occurred in the period 1901 to 1911.[67]

One of the most interesting discoveries in the District Court decision is that there was no evidence that U. S. Steel—or the steel industry itself—was able to charge arbitrary monopoly prices, or increase prices by arbitrarily restraining demanded outputs.[68] On the contrary, Judge Buffington noted that there were significant *decreases* in many important steel product prices between 1901 and 1911. For example, wire nail prices fell from $51 to $36; steel bar prices declined from $33 to $25; steel beams went down from $36 to $27; and billets dropped from $27 in 1901 to $24 in 1911. In fact, U. S. Steel's prices on all fabricated products sold domestically declined 19 percent between 1904 and 1912; its prices on *all* other goods sold fell an average of 11 percent in the same period. And these price decreases occurred at a time when freight rates on coke and limestone had increased more than 10 percent, and wages had risen more than 25 percent.[69] Thus, pricing in the steel industry certainly appeared competitive, and there was little evidence of any general monopoly power over prices or over competitors. As Judge Buffington put it:

The testimony of these men [the competitors of U. S. Steel]— and there is no testimony to the contrary—is that the iron and steel trade in the various products of the steel corporation is and has been open, competitive, and uncontrolled, and that *all* engaged therein have free will and control in selling at their own prices.[70]

And finally, the United States Steel Corporation's net return on investment in the period 1901 to 1911 averaged 12 percent.[71]

But what of the famous and much publicized "Gary Dinners"?[72] Though the District Court agreed that the meetings between U. S.

[66]Ripley, *op. cit.*, p. 113.
[67]*Ibid.*, p. 114.
[68]223 Fed. Reporter, 80–89.
[69]*Ibid.*, p. 81.
[70]*Ibid.*, p. 82.
[71]Jones, *The Trust Problem in the United States*, p. 211.
[72]223 Fed. Reporter, 154–161.

Steel and some of its competitors to discuss price and other common interests amounted "to a combination or common action forbidden by the law," they also noted that 1) the meetings had been started late in the period under consideration (November 1907) and had been continued for only fifteen months; 2) their meetings had been the "only instance" of such cooperation and the "whole movement was exceptional"; and 3) the participants in the movement had not meant to act illegally, and the whole system had been abandoned before the initiation of the Sherman Act case. Most importantly, however, "a large section of the trade paid *little attention, if any,* to this effort at cooperation," and "consumers who testified had *no difficulty* buying at rates sensibly below the prices thus referred to."[73] Thus, the practical economic significance of the "cooperative dinners" was certainly questionable. While the price philosophy of the U. S. Steel Corporation may have reinforced price stability, or at least tempered the usual violent swings in prices in the short run (and almost all customers testified that this was a *desirable* policy), there is little reason to conclude that any steel prices were "fixed," or that independent pricing decisions by individual competitors based on *their* own estimation of supply, demand, and competition had been abandoned. Certainly the economic performance of the steel industry in this period would not lead one inevitably to that conclusion.

Because of the conduct-performance information discussed above, and because U. S. Steel was a major factor in the *world* steel trade, the District Court and the Supreme Court refused to convict the Steel Company of violating the Sherman Act. In 1920, at least—and at last—"size" was no offense.

The "rule of reason," conduct-performance approach taken by the courts in the U. S. Steel cases was subsequently applied in many other important "antimonopoly" cases, and most of the firms involved escaped essentially untouched.[74] In 1937, however, a case was begun that would change the conduct-performance guidelines radically. It is to the famous Alcoa case (and the subsequent United Shoe Machinery case) that we turn in Chapter 6.

[73] *Ibid.*, p. 161 (Emphasis added).
[74] See, for example, *United States* v. *International Harvester Company,* 274 U.S. 693 (1927).

CHAPTER 6

The Aluminum and Shoe Machinery Monopoly Cases: The Rule of Reason and the "Good Trusts"

ON April 23, 1937, in the Federal District Court for the Southern District of New York, the government brought a lengthy antitrust complaint against the Aluminum Company of America, seeking the dissolution of that company as a relief to the petition. Four years, 155 witnesses, 1,803 exhibits, and 58,000 pages later, District Court Judge Francis G. Caffey, in an unusual nine-day oral presentation, exonerated the firm of all wrongdoing, although he reserved judgment on two counts.[1] The government had made around 140 charges involving antitrust violations, supposedly ranging from Alcoa's monopolization of bauxite deposits, water power sites, aluminum castings, alumina and virgin ingot aluminum, to the conscious "squeezing" of fabricators and repeated conspiracy with other aluminum firms. Judge Caffey found the firm innocent of *all* the monopoly and conspiracy charges and dismissed them. On appeal by the government, however, to a special appeals court acting in lieu of the Supreme Court, Judge Hand, speaking for the majority, reversed *one* of Caffey's dismissed charges and found Alcoa guilty of illegally

[1] *United States* v. *Aluminum Company of America et al.*, 44 F. Supp., 97–311.

monopolizing virgin ingot aluminum.[2] Understanding this case and
the two (different) judgments requires placing them in the context
of the aluminum industry before 1937.

THE ALUMINUM INDUSTRY IN AMERICA

Although the element aluminum was discovered and named by Sir
Humphrey Davy in 1807, and although Frederic Wohler improved
a chemical process whereby pinheads of the metal could be obtained,
it was twenty-one-year-old Charles Hall who discovered (1886) and
patented (1889) the first and still only commercially successful
method for making aluminum: the electrolysis of a molten alumina
solution dissolved in cryolite. Hall, after an intensive search, interested a Captain Alfred E. Hunt in the commercial possibilities of the
process, and a $20,000 pilot plant called The Pittsburgh Reduction
Company was constructed in Pittsburgh in 1888. Hall and Arthur V.
Davis, a recent Amherst College graduate (and later Chairman of the
Board of Alcoa), were among those who manned the plant day and
night, and both helped store the initial tiny outputs in the office safe
every night for safekeeping. As must be evident, the entire operation
was a pure speculation.[3]

In 1888 there were no known end uses for the shiny, light metal
and hence no customers. Although the metal had easily recognized
possibilities, it was at that time highly expensive and scarce. The first
prices for aluminum ingot in the open market ranged between $5
and $8 per pound in 1887. In early 1888, Hall and his co-workers
could squeeze no more than ten pounds of metal a day from the
entire operation. The crucial raw material alumina was relatively
expensive, and cheap continuous electrical supplies (ten kilowatts of
electric power per pound of aluminum produced) were simply not
available; the original Pittsburgh plant made its own. Aluminum
would only become commercially successful when and if the raw
materials could be obtained cheaply and, consequently, the price of
aluminum could be made competitive with substitutes.

Through brain power, diligence, money, and productive effort,
outputs of aluminum increased to 50 pounds a day by 1889; over

[2] *United States* v. *Aluminum Company of America*, 148 F. 2d 416 (1945).
[3] For a general discussion of the origins and development of the aluminum industry,
see Charles C. Carr, *Alcoa: An American Enterprise* (New York: Rinehart and Company, 1952); D. H. Wallace, *Market Control in the Aluminum Industry* (Cambridge:
Harvard University Press, 1937).

1,000 pounds a day in 1892; and 8,000 pounds a day by 1897. In a like fashion and coincident with the same business philosophy, prices of ingot per pound fell from $5 in 1887, to $3 in 1889, to 50 cents in 1899, to 38 cents in 1910. The price of aluminum ingot per pound (New York) in 1937 was 22 cents, and it fell to 15 cents in 1941. The output increases and price decreases were sustained by extensive explorations and developments of bauxite deposits in Arkansas. Cheap water power sites were secured, and dams and power stations were constructed to generate billions of kilowatts of cheap power; long-term supply contracts with the Pennsylvania Salt Manufacturing Company for steady supplies of alumina were initiated; and end uses for the metal in the wire industry, for power and paint as a reducing agent for surgical instruments and other medical apparatus, and for fabrication into cooking utensils were all developed and promoted by Alcoa. During 1937 Alcoa produced 500 million pounds of metal and consumed almost 22 billion kilowatts of electricity in the process.

The Pittsburgh Reduction Company's original patent on the Hall electrolysis process ran from 1889 to 1906. Through a complex set of patent infringement suits, claims, and counterclaims, Alcoa managed to extend the legal monopoly on the method for making aluminum until 1910. This three-year extension was accomplished in 1903 when Alcoa purchased the exclusive rights to the "Bradley patents" (that concerned the *heating* of the alumina solution with electricity) from a firm called Cowles Brothers. The patent squabbles between Alcoa and Cowles had begun in 1891, when Cowles Brothers (for whom Charles Hall had been employed for two months in 1886) began producing aluminum with the electrolysis method that Hall had patented. The Pittsburgh Reduction Company quickly sued Cowles and won a patent infringement decision in 1893; on appeal, however, the judgment was reversed in 1903. The difficulties involved were that while Hall apparently had a valid patent on the electrolysis process, the Bradley patents owned by Cowles Brothers dealt with the *heating* of the alumina solution with electricity and was also judged valid. Both patented processes were necessary to reduce aluminum commercially—yet the respective patents were the legitimate property of two different firms. Not surprisingly, Cowles Brothers sold the Bradley patents to Pittsburgh Reduction for $1½ million, some stock, and options to purchase ingot at below-market prices. Thus, in 1910, Alcoa was the sole producer—by law and legitimate patent—of primary aluminum, and had been in that business without direct domestic competition for over twenty years.

The 1910–1937 Period

From 1910 to 1937, various groups tried, though unsuccessfully, to enter the business of producing primary aluminum. In 1912 the Southern Aluminum Company started, with French financial interests, a reduction works complex in North Carolina. The firm had acquired bauxite deposits, but construction of the works ceased in October 1914, because of the impossibility of further financing during wartime conditions in France. When attempts at domestic financing failed, the firm was sold to the only interested buyer—the Aluminum Company of America. This story is described in more detail later in this chapter.

In addition to the Southern Aluminum Company, exploratory investigations concerning the economic feasibility of competitive reduction facilities were begun by a Mr. Lloyd Emory for the wealthy Milwaukee brewing family, the Uihleins, by J. B. Duke, the multimillionaire tobacco and utility entrepreneur, and possibly even by the Ford Motor Company. Certainly, all these groups possessed the financial capital to compete with Alcoa, if they had decided to compete; yet all these explorations were terminated in the planning stage. While thousands of firms flowed easily into the various fabrication areas for aluminum and aluminum-alloyed products, no new domestic virgin ingot competitor dared challenge the preeminent position of the Alcoa Company.

Why no competitors in primary ingot? It will be stated in a *preliminary* form at this point—and later documented with court evidence —that Alcoa had no direct competition for one reason only—the Aluminum Company of America was one of the most inventive, innovative, productive, and eminently efficient organizations in the business world, and no competitor could expect to match, much less excel, Alcoa's economic performance. In 1937, Alcoa produced slightly under one-half billion tons of metal and disposed of it for 22 cents a pound; its average rate of return on capital investment was 10 percent in the period 1912–1936. It had pioneered an extensive and expensive research and development facility that had provided crucial breakthroughs in aluminum and related products. For example, Alcoa research was responsible for major innovations in the processes for the recovery of alumina from fairly low-grade ores and

THE MYTHS OF ANTITRUST

for the obtaining of 99.99 percent pure aluminum in the electrolysis process. In addition, Alcoa developed dozens of methods to increase the strength and anti-corrosiveness of the metal and many alloys used for rolling, forging, or making castings. In a word, users of ingot or sheet, and ultimate consumers of fabricated products made from aluminum by Alcoa, were being served at degrees of excellence, prices, and profit rates that no one chose to match. The risks of direct competition *vis-à-vis* the possible gains were simply too great and, rather wisely, potential investors and entrepreneurs took their funds and talents elsewhere. To have attempted to compete with a firm like Alcoa in the 1912–1936 period would have been unprofitable and, consequently, an economic mistake. It is not surprising—nor regrettable, therefore—that Alcoa retained its singular position in aluminum ingot production.

But if all this supposition is true, what of the government's many charges in the 1937 Sherman Act case? Did Alcoa exclude competitors by preempting or monopolizing bauxite deposits, water power sites and alumina? Had Alcoa conspired to fix prices with a foreign cartel of producers? Had Alcoa acted monopolistically and thus illegally restrained trade? Was its position in the aluminum industry a function of monopolization and restraint? For an analysis of these conduct-performance issues, one should properly turn to the District Court decision where these charges (and many additional ones) were thoroughly investigated.

ALCOA AND THE COURTS

The District Court Decision

District Court Judge Caffey began his examination of the charges against Alcoa by noting that Alcoa had been in court before on similar charges. In 1912, for example, Alcoa had accepted a consent decree and agreed not to enter into "restrictive" covenants with suppliers or with foreign aluminum producers; as a point of fact, Caffey noted that Alcoa had already abandoned such "agreements" before the beginning of that legal proceeding. In another, more complex legal action brought by the Federal Trade Commission in 1925, the FTC examiner had found heavily in favor of Alcoa. Since the issues examined and decided in that lengthy hearing (10,000 pages of testimony) were similar to those listed in the government's latest petition, Judge Caffey thought it relevant to present a review of eight of the examiner's major findings. The examiner's report was dated December 16, 1929, and stated that:

1. The record also shows that respondent [Alcoa] never attempted to monopolize the scrap market; that it is impossible to do so, the scrap market being so scattered and diversified and in such great available quantities that one concern, no matter how large its purchases, could never corner the said market.
2. Respondent has no monopoly on bauxite [the ore of aluminum]; there being sufficient supplies of bauxite in the world, exclusive of respondent's holdings, available for many generations to come.
3. Respondent has no monopoly on water power; its holdings now being only a small per cent of the available water power in the world.
4. The respondent does not now nor has it ever attempted to control or dominate the policy of the Aluminum Goods Manufacturing Company.
5. Respondent has never attempted to control and does not now control the market for foreign aluminum in the United States.
6. That foreign aluminum is imported into the United States and competes with respondent in the sale of virgin aluminum ingots.
7. There is no arbitrary or direct differential between the purchase price of scrap aluminum and the selling price of virgin aluminum. The purchase price of scrap depends upon the law of supply and demand.
8. That respondent has never had a monopoly of the sand castings industry of the United States.[4]

While Caffey admitted that the examiner's report of 1929 could not legally bear *directly* on the present proceeding, he thought it considerably important that "on some of the exact issues now facing me the Commission found squarely in favor of Alcoa."[5]

Judge Caffey then turned to a consideration of the first government allegation. The initial charge of illegal monopolization rested on a paragraph in the 1903 patent agreement between Alcoa and Cowles Brothers which referred to the fact that Cowles had agreed not to engage in the manufacture of aluminum by "electrolysis from a fused bath" in the period 1903–1910. This "restrictive agreement," however, only restated the legal fact that Alcoa had then acquired legitimate *exclusive* right to all the Bradley patents (see the previous

[4] *United States* v. *Aluminum Company of America et al.*, 44 F. Supp. 107.
[5] *Ibid.*, p. 107.

discussion) and could legally prevent anyone—including Cowles Brothers—from engaging in alumina electrolysis in that period. In fact, Caffey noted that the government itself had already *admitted* that, prior to 1909, Alcoa had obtained a legal and lawful monopoly through patent holdings.[6] He therefore dismissed the charge that the contract referred to was evidence of illegal monopolization.[7]

Caffey next turned to the charge that Alcoa had gained and maintained a monopoly over bauxite and had excluded others from a "fair opportunity" to engage in interstate trade and commerce in that article. Unfortunately, the only two witnesses the government could produce to affirm the bauxite monopoly charge admitted, under oath, that they were neither qualified to furnish such information nor had their respective "searches" into available bauxite deposits been more than what the Court labeled "superficial."[8] Curiously enough, as it turns out, both witnesses (Mr. Uihlein and Mr. Haskell) had been the respective parties who had made inquiries into bauxite deposits for the Uihlein family and J. B. Duke.

In contrast to the assertions of these men, Dr. Branner, the state geologist of Arkansas, testified that Alcoa owned approximately 48 percent of the probable deposits of bauxite of aluminum ore quality in Arkansas, and that parties other than Alcoa owned 52 percent. The testimony of Dr. Branner was confirmed by Alcoa's geologist, Mr. Litchfield. Both admitted that bauxite was available in six other states and, according to the court, "outside the United States, the supply of bauxite is practically inexhaustible." Judge Caffey concluded:

> The testimony given by these two experts was quite extensive and quite thorough. It occupied approximately 1,900 pages of the record. These are pages 36,464 to 38,447, except for 53 pages covering the testimony of an out-of-town witness, which was quite brief. And, so far as I can see, the testimony of the government in regard to the amount of aluminum grade bauxite in Arkansas completely fails to sustain its contention. I think the testimony of the two experts is the best we can get and is the kind of testimony which we must rely on if we are to have any information at all on a subject like this.
>
> My conclusion, therefore, as to bauxite, is that the government has not proved its allegation in support of its charge of monopolization with respect to bauxite.[9]

[6] *Ibid.*, p. 115.
[7] *Ibid.*, p. 116.
[8] *Ibid.*, p. 117.
[9] *Ibid.*, pp. 120–121.

Judge Caffey next examined Alcoa's alleged water power or water power sites monopoly. Citing statistics published by the Federal Power Commission, he showed that Alcoa not only produced an insignificant amount of the entire nation's electrical energy, but that it owned only five undeveloped water power sites out of an FPC-compiled list of 1,883.[10] Therefore, the judge held that "the charge against Alcoa of monopolization of water power in the United States is entirely without foundation."[11] Moreover, Caffey continued, if Alcoa had not monopolized bauxite and had not monopolized water power (sites)—the only essential raw materials, by the government's own admission, necessary to produce aluminum—"*it may well be argued that the issue of monopolization is at an end in this case.*"[12]

The issue of monopolization was not at an end, however. Caffey next went on to consider the government charge that Alcoa had monopolized alumina (AL_2O_3). He remarked that the patented Bayer process for making alumina from bauxite had expired in 1903 and that anyone could produce and sell alumina in the United States after that "without any obstruction by patent or otherwise."[13] Alcoa, before 1903, had purchased all of its alumina requirement, and mostly from the Pennsylvania Salt Company; after then, Alcoa manufactured some of the substance itself, although it still relied on Pennsylvania Salt for many years afterward. By 1937, however, Alcoa was making all the alumina used to make primary aluminum—which was obvious, since it was the only domestic producer of primary aluminum. In fact, by then it was making *more* alumina than it required for its own reduction activities. Figures presented at the trial indicated that in the 1928–1938 period Alcoa consumed 78 percent of its alumina production and sold the rest. Additional figures demonstrated that the Pennsylvania Salt Manufacturing Company supplied approximately 33 percent of the alumina available to nonproducers of aluminum; the total of alumina available to non-Alcoa interests for that ten-year period had been slightly less than 251 million pounds. In that period, Caffey pointed out, any other chemical company in the country could have produced alumina from bauxite, and proba-

[10] *Ibid.*, p. 123.
[11] *Ibid.*, p. 124.
[12] *Ibid.*, p. 144 (Emphasis added).
[13] *Ibid.*, p. 145.

bly would have, "if the price which they could get for it were suffi-
ciently inviting."[14] In conclusion, Caffey ruled the government had
"entirely failed to prove any of its charges regarding alumina."[15]

The next charge examined by Caffey concerned Alcoa's (admitted) position in virgin ingot aluminum. In a sense, this was the
easiest and yet most confusing issue of all. For example, it was
beyond dispute that the Aluminum Company of America was the
sole domestic manufacturer of *primary* aluminum. This fact had
been readily admitted by the defendant, and there was no controversy about that. What was at issue, however, was: 1) did such a
monopoly position violate Section 2 of the Sherman Act, and 2)
did Alcoa illegally *exclude* others from primary aluminum production?[16]

With regard to the first question, Judge Caffey's analysis is extremely interesting and important—as subsequent judicial analysis at
the Appeals Court would prove. It would be wise to quote him
exactly:

> On principle it seems to me that it would be little short of
> absurd to construe Section 2 without qualification to mean that
> production of the entire output in the United States of a particu-
> lar article, or of any article, or that the possession or sale of it
> by the producer, *without other complaint or criticism of his
> conduct*, would constitute monopolization of the article. I think
> that such an interpretation would be wrong. I think it would be
> wrong, among other things, because if adopted the statute so
> interpreted thereby would provide punishment for what others
> than the producer (even though wholly unrelated to and dis-
> connected from him) might do or had done.[17]

Caffey then created a hypothetical example to illustrate his point. He
assumed that two producers, *A* and *B*, manufactured the same article
and sold it in the same areas. Over time, producer *A*, because he
could produce and sell the item cheaper than producer *B*, came to
acquire all of *B*'s customers. As a consequence, producer *A* did 100
percent of the business in that article. Was producer *A* now
"monopolizing" in violation of the Sherman Act? Caffey answered
his own question:

[14] *Ibid.*, p. 146.
[15] *Ibid.*, p. 150.
[16] *Ibid.*, p. 151.
[17] *Ibid.*, p. 154 (Emphasis added).

116   THE MYTHS OF ANTITRUST

... if the theory of the government, stated by its counsel, as to what Section 2 of the Sherman Act means be accepted, then obviously A would be punished for what B, or what B's customers, or what B and his customers had done.

So far as I can discover the Supreme Court has never given the slightest support to such an interpretation as the government advocates."[18]

What previous Court precedents *had* implied, Caffey stated, was that the "unexerted power to control is not an offense"; thus, Section 2 could not be construed so as to condemn a sole producer who had gained and held his monopoly position fairly in the open market.[19] To defend this interpretation, Caffey noted that Congress, in drafting Section 2, had been careful to use *verbs* (not nouns) to describe the *conduct* that it meant to make illegal: "every person who shall monopolize, or attempt to monopolize. . . ." Also, during the Sherman Act hearings, Senators Kenna and Edmunds had debated the issue of obtaining a "legitimate" monopoly position in a market. That particular debate, Caffey continued, showed clearly that the "offense of monopolization cannot be established unless there be proved, as one of the constituents, *the element of exclusion.*"[20]

But what of exclusion? Had Alcoa unlawfully excluded competitors or potential competitors from primary aluminum manufacture? The only example of "exclusion" put forth by the government at the trial concerned the case of the Southern Aluminum Company.[21] The French Aluminum Company of France had begun construction of an aluminum facility in North Carolina in 1912, but had been forced to suspend further construction with the outbreak of World War I in August 1914.[22] Thereafter repeated attempts were made, through American attorneys, to negotiate the sale of the uncompleted properties to the Alcoa company. The court record made it clear, Caffey states, that it was Southern's lawyers that pressed and pursued the matter for almost a year until the sale was actually made at a price equal to Southern's costs to that date. The entire matter was reviewed favorably by the Justice Department on September 3, 1915, and the transaction was finalized on November 23,

[18] *Ibid.*, pp. 154–155.
[19] *Ibid.*, p. 155.
[20] *Ibid.*, p. 161 (Emphasis added).
[21] *Ibid.*, p. 161.
[22] The French government actually forbade the transfer of funds from France to continue the American operation. See *Ibid.*, pp. 161–162.

1915.[23] Thus, the charge that Alcoa "excluded" competition by purchasing the Southern Aluminum Company—and supposedly at a price that greatly exceeded its value!—turns out to be groundless. In fact, Alcoa purchased (with much insistence from Southern) at cost, a substantially uncompleted complex (the dam was only one-eighth finished) which it proceeded to redesign radically and complete at its own considerable expense.[24] In summary, Alcoa neither illegally monopolized nor illegally excluded others from the right to trade; or as Caffey put it: "In no respect, related to the production or selling of virgin aluminum, has it been shown that Alcoa violated Section 2 of the Sherman Act."[25]

At this point in the summary, Judge Caffey pointed out that virgin ingot aluminum produced by Alcoa was *not* without competition from a variety of sources. For example, he noted that imported primary ingot competed with Alcoa's ingot; "scrap" and "secondary" aluminum—which, for the most part, was chemically the same as primary ingot—actively competed; and steel, nickel, tin, zinc, copper, and lead were all the "chief industrial competitors of aluminum."[26] The scrap and secondary markets were of particular interest, for there it could be "established without contradiction that, through use of well known processes . . . aluminum of every grade can be produced of the same chemical composition as if it had been produced from virgin aluminum and some factories claim that they can produce from secondary aluminum all the commodities that can be produced from primary aluminum . . . which includes aluminum of 99.75 percent purity."[27] And it was *there* that 125 million pounds of scrap and secondary aluminum had been produced and sold in 1937 at prices competitive with primary ingot. In fact, on a few occasions, and "under appropriate market conditions, secondary aluminum is sold at prices higher than the price of primary aluminum."[28] Thus, if the issue was a relevant one, primary ingot faced competition from a variety of substitutes, although Alcoa was admittedly the only domestic primary aluminum manufacturer at the time of the trial.

[23] *Ibid.*, pp. 162–163.
[24] *Ibid.*, p. 163.
[25] *Ibid.*, p. 165.
[26] *Ibid.*
[27] *Ibid.*, p. 305.
[28] *Ibid.*

The rest of the government's charges, relating to Alcoa's supposed monopolization of aluminum castings, cooking utensils, pistons, extrusions and structural shapes, foil, and miscellaneous fabricated articles, *were all dismissed* by Judge Caffey, while final consideration of the charges dealing with "sheet" and "cable" were delayed. In summary, the judge concluded the entire area of monopolization by stating that "*none of the monopolization charges has been satisfactorily proved* and that in regard to them the Government has not shown that it is entitled to any relief."[29]

Much had been made of Alcoa's supposed conspiracy with a cartel of European firms, and the second half of Judge Caffey's decision dealt with these Section 1 allegations. The government had charged, among other things, that Alcoa conspired directly, and through Aluminium Ltd., with several European firms and *The Alliance* to limit output, raise price, and restrict the importation of aluminum and aluminum products. Though the government had once admitted that "conspiracy constitutes only 5 percent of this case,"[30] Caffey devoted fifty pages to the charges and countercharges. After thoroughly examining all charges relating to the supposed "sundry conspiracy," he concluded:

> In consequence, I conclude that the government has failed to establish the charge of conspiracy between Alcoa and European producers of aluminum or Aluminium or either or any of them.
> I further conclude that the Government has failed by credible evidence to show that either (1) there was ever a conspiracy between Alcoa and Aluminium or (2) that since January 23, 1915, there has ever been a conspiracy between Alcoa or any of the other foreign producers to fix prices or to restrict importations or to limit the quantities of production or to allocate customers or shipments to customers of aluminum or aluminium products of any kind.[31]

The final part of the court decision dealt with "other misconduct" by Alcoa, specifically the allegation that Alcoa charged "extortionate prices" and thus made "exorbitant" profits.[32] Although Caffey admitted that neither allegation, *even if* sustained by evidence, was itself

[29] *Ibid.*, p. 224 (Emphasis added).
[30] *Ibid.*, p. 225.
[31] *Ibid.*, pp. 285–286.
[32] *Ibid.*, p. 286.

a violation of the Sherman Act, and that he had already ruled against the federal government "on all the issues raised by the bill involving monopolization and, therefore, against all those involving prices or profits," he proceeded to examine the relevant price-profit information. Alcoa had submitted evidence that its average rate of return on investment for the period 1887–1937 was 9.96 percent; the government's figure for the same period was "a small fraction excess of 10 percent."[33] Since the court dismissed the relevancy of examining profit rates on particular items or profit or profit rates in particular years, it concluded that as a general matter Alcoa had not "exacted extortionate prices" nor "been shown to have made exorbitant profits."[34]

To summarize and conclude the entire proceedings, Judge Caffey had examined and dismissed the entire government petition with regard to illegal monopolization, conspiracy, and "other misconduct." He had not found sufficient proof to sustain *any* of the government's 140-odd charges and allegations against the Aluminum Company of America. On October 10, 1941, Caffey ruled Alcoa innocent of violating the Sherman Act.

The Appeal

Judge Caffey had expected an appeal from the losing party in this complex case, and such an appeal was quickly forthcoming by the government. The Supreme Court, however, was unable to hear the appeals case because four of its justices had previously participated in antitrust actions against Alcoa when they had been with the Justice Department. After over two years of delay, the Congress passed a special act on June 9, 1944, allowing a U. S. Circuit Court of Appeals to hear the Government's appeal and act as a "court of last resort." Judges Learned Hand, Augustus N. Hand, and Thomas Swan presided over the appeals case, with Learned Hand delivering the decision.[35]

The government's appeal and the emphasis in the Appeals Court decision clearly centered on one issue—Alcoa's "monopolization" of the virgin ingot aluminum market. Though District Court Judge Caffey had examined and dismissed that charge on at least three

[33] *Ibid.*, p. 298.
[34] *Ibid.*, p. 304.
[35] *United States* v. *Aluminum Company of America*, 148 F. 2d 416 (1945).

grounds,[36] the Circuit Court of Appeals argued that Caffey's analysis of Alcoa's market share was incorrect. Caffey had suggested—as part of his argument—that if one *excluded* the primary ingot that Alcoa fabricated itself, and included scrap or "secondary" aluminum ingot, Alcoa's share of the aluminum ingot market was approximately 33 percent, and not enough for monopolization *per se.* Judge Hand argued instead that it was improper to exclude Alcoa's own fabricated ingot since Alcoa's fabrication "pro tanto reduce(s) the demand for ingot itself," and thus affects the primary ingot market and ingot price.[37] In addition, secondary should not be included (even though he stated that "at any given moment . . . 'secondary' competes with 'virgin' in the ingot market"),[38] since Alcoa's monopoly over virgin ingot in the present allows an influence over all "future supply of ingot" including, necessarily, secondary ingot. Thus, Hand reduced the relevant market under consideration to virgin ingot aluminum, and concluded (not surprisingly) that Alcoa "monopolized" it with 90 percent control (10 percent was imported primary ingot).

To arrive at such a conclusion, the court broke all judicial and economic guidelines as to the meaning of "monopolize" and to the relevant market under consideration. A relevant market for a product "should include all firms whose production has so immediate and substantial an effect on the prices and production of the firms in question that the actions of the one group cannot be explained without direct reference to the other. One should include in a market all firms whose products are, in fact, good and directly available substitutes for one another in sales to some significant group of buyers, and exclude all others."[39] Secondary or "scrap" was chemically and economically competitive with "virgin" and therefore a part of the relevant market for aluminum ingot. Just as clearly, Alcoa's fabricated ingot was not available for "marketing" and therefore not part of the aluminum ingot "market." To exclude scrap and include "own-use" ingot was an arbitrary, nondefensible construction, which proves only that *markets defined narrowly enough can make "monopolies" out of any firm.*

[36]See 44 F. Supp. 150–165.
[37]148 F. 2d p. 424.
[38]*Ibid.*
[39]Henry Adler Einhorn and William Paul Smith, eds., *Economic Aspects of Antitrust* (New York: Random House, 1968), p. 9.

Alcoa was not monopolizing, even in Hand's terms, any reasonably defined market.

Hand also rebuked Caffey for placing any relevance on the fact that Alcoa had not "monopolized" since its net return was calculated at only 10 percent. Hand stated that:

> ... the whole issue is irrelevant anyway, for it is no excuse for "monopolizing" a market that the monopoly has not been used to extract from the consumer more than a 'fair' profit. The Act has wider purposes.[40]

Since Congress "did not condone 'good trusts' and condemn 'bad' ones, it forbade all," and since the court had already proven that Alcoa's share of the market was enough for it to qualify as a "trust" or monopoly, the *exercise of monopoly power* was irrelevant to the issue. Alcoa was a competent, ingenious firm—no one disputed that; in fact, the court's praise was almost embarrassing at points.[41] But Alcoa monopolized, and that was the only relevant issue here.

But was Alcoa's monopoly "thrust upon" the firm?[42] Was it the "passive beneficiary" of a monopolistic position earned legitimately in the market? Supposedly, according to Hand, the court would not indiscriminately condemn a single producer that had gained his position "merely by virtue of his superior skill, foresight, and industry."[43] Yet, in the next breath, Alcoa's superior skill, foresight, and industry were condemned as "exclusionary" and illegal.[44] Hand stated that Alcoa "forestalled" competition by stimulating demand and then efficiently supplying a demand "it had evolved"; it anticipated increases in demand for ingot and "doubled and redoubled" its capacity to fill that demand; it embraced every new opportunity with a "great" organization manned with elite personnel. That Alcoa meant to keep its monopoly position through such efforts and thus violate the Sherman Act was an obvious conclusion for Judge Hand and the Circuit Court of Appeals.[45]

That Alcoa's industrial efficiency per se was being condemned was just as obvious. Neither Judge Hand nor anyone else overturned *any*

[40] *United States* v. *Aluminum Company of America*, 148 F. 2d 416 (1945), p. 427.
[41] *Ibid.*, pp. 430–431.
[42] *Ibid.*, p. 429.
[43] *Ibid.*, p. 430.
[44] *Ibid.*, p. 430–431.
[45] *Ibid.*, p. 432.

of Caffey's other conclusions concerning bauxite, water power sites, alumina, castings, excluded competitors, conspiracy with foreign firms, and so on. Thus, Alcoa was convicted of being the (efficient) single supplier in an artificially defined market.

Not unreasonably, however, the court refused to dissolve "an aggregation which has for so long demonstrated its efficiency . . .";[46] instead, it hoped that the government-owned aluminum properties that had been constructed for the war effort would be disposed of in a fashion that would create competition in the aluminum industry. Subsequently, of course, many of the government reduction plants were sold to Reynolds Metal and Kaiser Aluminum. In 1948 both the government and Alcoa petitioned for a reopening of the case: the government was not satisfied with the competition market structure and wanted divesture of much of Alcoa's properties, while Alcoa wanted Hand's "guilty of monopolization" decision overturned because of the existence of Reynolds and Kaiser. Again, as in the Caffey trial, Judge Knox (Caffey had retired in 1947) of the New York District Court ruled against the government petition on almost all counts.[47] Knox praised Alcoa for its war efforts, for its royalty-free licensing of patents, for a record free of unfair competition of any kind, and concluded that competition was quite vigorous in the aluminum industry. He thus rejected the divesture petition. Although no specific findings of illegal activity, collusion, or conspiracy were proved, he did order ingot stockholders in both Alcoa and Aluminium, Ltd. to divest themselves of one or the other. On January 16, 1951, Judge Knox accepted a stock disposal plan, and the thirteen-year court battles of Alcoa came to an end.

THE UNITED SHOE MACHINERY CORPORATION
The United Shoe Machinery Company was formed in 1899 when four formerly independent shoe machine makers merged. In March 1899 two additional shoe machine firms joined the company. On May 2, 1905, the United Company, containing the once-independent shoe machine manufacturers, formally incorporated in the state of New Jersey as United Shoe Machinery Corporation, with corporate headquarters and essential manufacturing facilities at Beverly, Massachusetts. After still another reorganization in 1917, United Shoe

[46] Ibid., p. 446.
[47] United States v. Aluminum Company of America, 91 F. Supp. 333.

Machinery had attained a position in the shoe machine manufacturing industry such that it leased or sold approximately 85 percent of the nation's shoe machinery.[48] Although at least ten other shoe machinery firms sold or leased equipment throughout the period, United maintained its 1917 market share for the next thirty years.

Prior to 1947, United Shoe had been in the courts twice before. In a 1918 Sherman Act case,[49] the government had sought to dissolve the reorganized shoe machinery corporation, since it (clearly) dominated that industry and was allegedly extending its "control" through various tying arrangements. The Supreme Court, however, released the firm under the theory that efficient firms using legitimate patents do not necessarily violate the Sherman Act, even though they may "dominate" their industry. In a second case, however, decided in 1922,[50] Section 3 of the Clayton Act was used successfully to purge some of the "restrictive" and "tying" features from United's leasing controls; the leasing system and the dominant position of United in that industry, however, were accepted and left intact. In December 1947, a third antitrust action was launched under Section 2 of the Sherman Act,[51] in still another attempt to end United's "monopoly" and "exclusionary" practices.

UNITED SHOE MACHINERY AND THE COURTS

The District Court decision, written and handed down by Judge Wyzanski in 1953, began with a brief discussion of the shoe machinery industry and United's position within it. Through a set of tables[52] indicating the number of machines leased or sold by United—compared to the rest of the sales made by other shoe machinery manufacturers—Wyzanski estimated United's share of the market to be between 75 and 90 percent.[53] This position was attributable, Wyzanski said, to the firm's original constitution creating the United Shoe

[48]For background information about the shoe machinery industry see *United States* v. *United Shoe Machinery Corporation* 110 F. Supp. 295 (1953), and Carl Kaysen, *United States* v. *United Shoe Machinery Corporation* (Cambridge, Mass: Harvard University Press, 1956), pp. 1–24.

[49]274 U. S. 32.

[50]258 U. S. 451.

[51]110 F. Supp. 295.

[52]*Ibid.*, pp. 304–306.

[53]*Ibid.*, p. 307. Dry thread sewing machines, though admittedly substitutable for United's machines, were excluded from the definition of the "market" since United did not make any! See Lucile Keyes, "The Shoe Machinery Case and the Problem of the Good Trust," *Quarterly Journal of Economics*, LXVIII (1954), 294–295.

Machinery Corporation in 1905 and reorganized in 1917, to the company's "superior products and services," and to the company's business practices, notably the *leasing system*. Now, since the first factor had been thoroughly investigated and reviewed (and dismissed) in 1918, the only relevant issues at this trial were to be United's supposed efficiency and United's supposed restraining and exclusionary leasing system.

The court's first action was to dismiss the government's contention that the purchase of a few firms by United Shoe Machinery since 1917 had violated the antitrust laws. Although there had been thirty-odd acquisitions valued at $3½ million between 1916 and 1938, Wyzanski concluded that "they have not been one of the principal factors in enabling defendant to achieve and hold its share of the market."[54] In like manner, he summarily dismissed the government-alleged, anticompetitive effects of certain "restrictive agreements" between United and other firms.[55]

The District Court then considered United Shoe's leasing policies and agreements. United manufactured 342 different types of shoe machines in 1947: 178 of these machines were available on a lease basis only, 42 were available on an outright sale basis only, and the other 122 shoe machines could be sold or leased, depending on the preferences of the customer.[56] Although almost 50 percent of all United's machines could be sold, it was the other 50 percent that could be leased—and especially the 178 machines that could only be leased—that concerned the court.

Leasing shoe machinery was the accepted practice in the shoe industry, had been since the Civil War, and was used by all of United's important competitors. The court noted emphatically that the practice of leasing shoe machinery had made entry into shoe manufacturing easy (there were 1,462 shoe firms in 1947, an increase of almost 500 over 1937),[57] and that small shoe manufacturers could grow quickly under the leasing system, with small capital expenditures.[58] The court also noted that the leased machines from United Shoe performed excellently and were serviced by United's 1,500 roadmen "promptly, efficiently and courteously."[59] Furthermore,

[54] 110 F. Supp. 312.
[55] *Ibid.*, pp. 313–314.
[56] *Ibid.*, p. 314.
[57] *Ibid.*, p. 301.
[58] *Ibid.*, p. 323.
[59] *Ibid.*, p. 322.

the rates for leasing machines had been uniform and fair, and the 1,220 factories that employed United equipment had shown *no expressed dissatisfaction with the system.*[60]

The leasing system also worked successfully for United Shoe Machinery, since it greatly stabilized revenues (unusual for a capital goods firm), allowed constant contact with shoemakers and their particular machinery needs, and consequently spurred expenditures for research and development to produce and market more efficient machines for shoe manufacturers. On the whole, United Shoe and its customers were quite happy with the leasing arrangement.[61]

There was also no unhappiness from customers—or the industry as a whole—concerning United's pricing policy. The nine examples of pricing conduct presented by the court demonstrated that United *reduced* its rates in the face of competitive challenges, and that its rates throughout the period under discussion had hardly been excessive. In addition, the firm had not sold "below cost"—as the government had alleged—nor engaged in "predatory price cutting," or coercive practices of *any* kind.[62] As a result, its pricing policies had not generated any "monopoly return." Judge Wyzanski concluded that "United's book earnings on its total operations 1925–1949 were about 10 percent net, after taxes, on invested capital."[63]

Furthermore, the court praised United's research facility ("United has a research organization of efficiency, intelligence and vision"),[64] and the fact that it explored "every branch of science and every modern scientific device which could be brought to bear upon the problems of shoe making."[65] Moreover, United's fundamental research had been turned quickly into technological developments and "has *not* been slowed down or withheld . . . until competition appeared, or until the demand for its own models abated. It has not shelved developments."[66] The court concluded that there was no reliable evidence that United repressed invention or innovation (United held almost 4,000 patents) nor had it "refused any reasonable offers for licenses made by others."[67]

[60] *Ibid.*, p. 322–323.
[61] *Ibid.*, p. 323.
[62] *Ibid.*, pp. 325–329.
[63] *Ibid.*, p. 325.
[64] *Ibid.*, p. 330.
[65] *Ibid.*
[66] *Ibid.*, p. 332.
[67] *Ibid.*, p. 333.

But if all the above information is to be accepted, what was wrong with the United Shoe Machinery Corporation? If its prices were competitive, nondiscriminatory, and nonpredatory; if its services were excellent; if its research complex was famous throughout the world; if it had not repressed innovation; and if its net profits had averaged 10 percent on capital, then where did the monopoly or restraints of trade exist? To discover the "illegal restraints" one must return, with the court, to the leasing agreements.

The government had alleged—and the court accepted—that the standard, ten-year leasing contract was just too long.[68] Too long *for whom?* Shoe manufacturers who leased machines from United had *not* requested a reduction in the leasing period. In fact, it had been their combined pressure that had *raised* the lease period from seven to ten years in the 1922 antitrust proceeding against United Shoe![69] Long-term leasing was economically advantageous to United Shoe and its customers, and provided few difficulties for the parties involved. But the court was not particularly concerned with the parties involved. It was the *competitors* and *potential competitors* of United Shoe Machinery that were of particular concern. With ten-year leases, Wyzanski stated, "a *competitor* may not get a chance to have his machine adequately tried out by a shoe manufacturer."[70] The fact that all leases ran out, or could be terminated, or that "competitive" machinery could be tried out by firms employing United Machinery during "experimental periods,"[71] did not sway the court from its position that the leasing period must be shortened so as to "increase competition."

The next issues in the leasing contracts were much more serious and concerned United's policy of requiring that the lessee "shall use the leased machinery to its *full capacity* upon all footwear . . . ,"[72] and that machines returned before the expiration of the contract leasing period were subject to a *"return charge."*[73] The "full capacity" clause implied that United could penalize lessees who employed non-United shoe machinery in their shoe manufacture. The return charge implied that firms that returned leased machinery before the

[68] *Ibid.*, p. 324.
[69] *Ibid.*
[70] *Ibid.*, p. 324 (Emphasis added).
[71] *Ibid.*
[72] *Ibid.*, p. 320.
[73] *Ibid.*

expiration dates paid a pro-rata return charge; firms that replaced the returned machine with another United shoe machine paid a smaller "return charge" than those shoe manufacturers who intended to replace United's machines with shoe machinery of "outside manufacture." This "variation" was accomplished by applying the *credits* from an amortization plan, or "deduction fund" that the lessee contributed to, toward the "deferred payment" or return charge when United machines were replaced with other United machines. The court regarded this as a "discriminatory" practice and not merely one defendable on revenue grounds.

> The discrimination is designed to operate as, and does operate as, a method of excluding from the shoe factories shoe machinery competitive with United's.[74]

Supposedly, there were ninety such instances of full capacity or return charge tactics to deter competition (the court lists eight), and even the president of United Shoe Machinery admitted that the practice deterred factories from employing competitive machines.[75]

And so it did, somewhat. But are we to infer that a significant proportion—or even the dominant position—of United Shoe Machinery was attributable to *this* particular practice? Hardly. At best, this discrimination would have been a marginal deterrent to the adoption of competitive machines.[76] If the competitive shoe machines were that much better, cheaper, and more reliable, they certainly would have been adopted despite the return charge, and in increasing numbers, at the termination of the United leasing period. That such was not the case implies that it was not necessarily "unfair exclusion" or discrimination that limited sales by competitors, but the fact that United offered superior experience, terms, services, and "a long line of machine types while no competitor offers more than a short line."[77]

The District Court's examination of United's repair system

---

[74] *Ibid.*, p. 321.

[75] *Ibid.*

[76] Carl Kaysen, *op. cit.*, devotes pp. 64–69 to this issue. Although he cautiously concludes that the long lease period and the return charge were "substantial" deterrents to competition (p. 68), his examples, though admittedly fragmentary, are far from convincing. Of 299 machines *returned* and *replaced with competitive* machines, 229 were returned to United *without* charge! The other 70 machines returned involved an average cash outlay of $300 per machine (p. 67).

[77] 110 F. Supp. 343.

confirms the view expressed immediately above. Judge Wyzanski
regarded United's free repair maintenance system (or, more exactly,
including repair in the original leasing contract without separate
charge) as "exclusionary" because it made it difficult for both large
independent repair companies to come into existence and for foreign machine makers to compete without offering similar "repair
services."[78] Again, the court displayed a notable degree of concern
and sympathy for firms as yet "unborn" and for other firms that had
difficulty competing with United Shoe because they could not, admittedly, offer comparable terms. In Judge Caffey's terms, firm A was
again being chastised for what firm B or B's customers had done or
had failed to do. The interests of the existing shoe machinery leases
and, ultimately, of the *consumers* of shoes themselves, were ignored
throughout.

As a final example of "exclusion," the court pointed out that
"United's lease system makes impossible a second-hand market in
its own machines," and thus excludes potential competition.[79]
Though not even an accurate statement—since at least 148 shoe
machines could be purchased and ultimately appear in a second-
hand market[80]—Wyzanski in effect condemned United for not
making it easier for competitors or potential competitors to compete with it! Since it is extremely doubtful that the court would
have considered a second-hand market in shoe machinery "competitive" anyway—since shoe machinery becomes technologically
dated and obsolete quickly—the entire issue is economically
trivial. In this trial, however, it served to demonstrate that concern for the difficulties of *competitors* far outdistanced concern
for competition or the consumer.

The rest of the District Court decision concerned United's supposed attempt to monopolize the trade and commerce in "shoe factory supplies." Fourteen such supplies—ranging from shoe boxes to
clicking dies—were examined by the court and, in most of these
cases, "it is too plain for argument that United has *not* achieved a
share of the market which prima facie indicates a monopoly."[81] What
was indicated was that United did a substantial share of the business

78 *Ibid.*, p. 325.
79 *Ibid.*
80 *Ibid.*, p. 314.
81 *Ibid.*, p. 335.

in some of these supplies because United had regular contact with 85 percent of the shoe manufacturing industry. As the court put it:

> Customers already know United, have current relations with it, trust it generally, believe it able to specify, select, or manufacture suitable supplies, and are aware that because of the lease provisions United is, as it were, a partner interested in the effective functioning of the machines.[82]

But was United's success in the "supplies" area due in any way—as the federal government had alleged in their petition—to predatory practices or to "coercion"? The court thought not and dismissed the charges in this area.

> . . . there's *nothing whatsoever* to the Government's allegations that customers are coerced, or are subservient, or a captive, or are deliberately mislead by United's representatives.[83]

Yet, after the court admitted that United functioned efficiently and in a nonpredatory manner in these supply areas, it ordered divesture of United's nail, tack, and eyelet subsidiaries![84]

In conclusion, the court determined that specific provisions of United's standard leasing contract were restraints of trade in violation of Section 2 of the Sherman Act. The full capacity clause and return charge were not "practices which could be properly described as the inevitable consequence of ability, natural forces, or law." Instead, they were business practices that "unnecessarily exclude actual and potential competition [and] restrict a free market."[85] Hence, the court ordered United Shoe to purge the restrictive features:[86] the maximum standard leasing contract was reduced to five years; the full capacity and return charge system was modified to make it nondiscriminatory; service charges were ordered separated from leased machine charges; and any shoe machine that United leased, it also had to offer for direct sale on substantially comparable terms. In addition, the court ordered United to license out *all* patents at uniformly reasonable rates and not to purchase any

[82] *Ibid.*, p. 336.
[83] *Ibid.* (Emphasis added).
[84] *Ibid.*, pp. 352–354.
[85] *Ibid.*, pp. 344–345.
[86] *Ibid.*, pp. 351–354.

shoe or shoe machinery manufacturer if the transaction exceeded
$10,000; nor were they to purchase *any* second-hand shoe machin-
ery "except for experimental or like purposes."[87] Saddling United
with special rules not faced by other shoe machinery manufacturers,
the court argued that this action was necessary to "root out monopolization." It was further argued that these rules were not "discriminatory" since United was *already* in a class by itself; indeed, these
provisions would help put United back in the same class with its
"competition."[88]

In a way, the decisions reviewed in this chapter are an appropriate climax (and dead end) to the market structure approach of
"measuring competition." Both decisions manipulated relevant
markets, ignored existing substitutes, placed importance on the
degree of concentration, disregarded objective conduct-performance information, and showed a distressing degree of concern
(even sympathy) for competitors or potential competitors. If the
rule of reason had ever implied a dispassionate examination of
conduct-performance, it was abandoned with a vengeance. Efficient firms were a "threat," it appeared, *because* they were efficient. Investing in productive facilities to supply future demands
"preempted" potential rivals. Offering a full line of machinery
was "unfair," since no competitor offered more than a short line.
Purchasing power plant sites was "exclusionary." Offering "free"
service made competitive entry more difficult. And retaining a
high market share—a most extraordinary business accomplish-
ment in a free market—was inevitably "to monopolize" and to violate the antitrust law. Clearly, to this author, Alcoa and United
Shoe Machinery were indicted and convicted in spite of (indeed,
because of) their unique industrial virtues, the protestations of the
courts to the contrary. It was their self-made positions within a
particular market structure, arbitrarily regarded as nonoptimal,
that condemned them.[89]

[87] *Ibid.*, p. 354.
[88] *Ibid.*, p. 350. The District Court decision was upheld by the Supreme Court in
1954. Still, however, the Justice Department was not satisfied. After much legal ma-
neuvering, the Supreme Court in 1968 ruled that United Shoe must further reduce
its share of the shoe machinery market to approximately 33 percent. See, *United States
v. United Shoe Machinery Corporation.*, 391 U.S. 244.
[89] Even where firms have successfully defended themselves under Section 2, their
conduct-performance has been irrelevant or, at worst, positively damaging. See, for
example, *United States v. E.I. DuPont de Nemours and Company*, 351 U.S. 377 (1956).

The last four chapters have dealt with the most classic "monopoly" cases in antitrust history. Reviewing the conduct-performance history of these firms *in context* has certainly *not* verified the assumptions that "bad" structure leads inevitably to improper conduct and poor performance. If the primary concern of political economy is really scarcity/efficiency, then these "monopolies" should have been commended, not condemned.

CHAPTER 7

Price Fixing in Theory and Practice

WHILE some landmark monopoly cases have at least enjoyed the pretense of a "rule of reason" approach, price fixing conspiracies have, for the most part, been judged illegal *per se* since as early as 1898. For the last seventy years, the courts have consistently argued that collusion to fix prices and restrict outputs is an inherent violation of Section 1 of the Sherman Act, and that there can be no question of "reasonableness" with respect to such agreements.

The traditional rationale for a *per se* approach to price fixing agreements depends on two crucial assumptions. *If* price and output agreements are actually effective, and *if* the performance of the firms under conspiracy is inferior to what it might have been under competition, then the power to fix prices might well be condemned in and of itself. According to this line of reasoning, the power to effectuate a price conspiracy would become the power to destroy consumer optimality and distort the efficient allocation of economic resources. Since buyer welfare is automatically lowered, a minute inquiry into the sundry details of any particular conspiracy would be superfluous.

If these agreements are not effective, however, or if there are nonprice competitive factors that outweigh the welfare losses of conspiracy, a *per se* approach can be misleading. The *a priori* economic misallocations associated with a conspiracy *that does not work* are not obvious to this author. In addition, one could argue the relative costs and benefits of a price conspiracy when nonprice competitive factors are important, or where the alternatives to temporary "conspiracy" are multiple bankruptcies or mergers. To avoid a knee-jerk approach to price fixing, therefore, this account will examine the landmark price fixing cases from a conduct-performance point of view.

THE THEORY OF PRICE FIXING

The simple theory of price fixing suggests that an agreement by firms to restrict their output and raise the market prices of their product could be profitable, *under appropriate conditions.* Theoretically the firms would sell less, charge more, and reap the "monopoly" bonuses associated with collusion. Or, alternatively, the collusive agreement might bind the parties to submit noncompetitive bids at a public letting; somehow one of the firms would be selected to "get the job," and it would split the monopoly profits with the rest of the group. In some fashion, the firms involved would be taken out of direct price competition with each other—to their mutual benefit.

But what are these "appropriate conditions," and are they likely to occur? The widely-held presumption among economists for some time has been that price conspiracies would be common in the American business system without antitrust legislation. The intent of the following discussion is to challenge such a presumption and suggest, instead, that there are diverse economic factors which would tend at all times to limit the success, and hence the significance, of price-fixing agreements in a free market. It is to be assumed that the hypothetical firms under discussion here *want* to fix prices at more than competitive rates. What is being challenged is their collective ability to effectuate such a situation.[1]

Substitutes: The responsiveness of buyers to price changes (elasticity) is of crucial importance when considering the potential effectiveness of price-fixing agreements. If, for example, the commodity to be price fixed has few good substitutes in the short run, an increase in its price may increase total revenues of the conspiracy and make price collusion financially rewarding. But if, as more often is the case,

[1]The following discussion is taken from my article, "The Inherent Weakness of Price Collusion," *The Freeman,* XX (January, 1970), 40–43.

there is a plentiful array of goods that might be substituted for the commodity that is being price fixed, the higher fixed price may push marginal buyers to the cheaper substitutes, and thus lower total conspiracy revenues.

This consequence encourages firms to break the agreement to maintain a uniform price since the agreement does not, apparently, work in their interests. Certainly some firms will be *relatively* worse off with regard to substitute competition than others, and would be the first to feel the pinch of a revenue squeeze, and the first to consider a policy of selective price reductions. Thus, the threat of substitute competition may make price conspiracy difficult to form in the first place, or lead to competitive price reductions that break up the conspiracy.

Changes in Demand: A slight, even temporary reduction in demand for the price fixed commodity may break apart the price agreement; recession is the natural enemy of successful price collusion. A decrease in demand at fixed prices will curb sales, and the temptation to ease the decline with a price reduction will be strong, especially for the low-profit firms involved. Since all firms differ in financial strength, and in their willingness to "ride out" a demand decline, there must be such temptations and such pressures. When the relatively weaker firms cut prices in an attempt to increase or maintain sales, the formal price-fixing agreements tumble.

Output Agreements: Firms that agree to fix prices also agree to some marketing arrangement. Somehow, particular firms must be selected to "get" particular "jobs," or a particular percentage of industry output. This part of the conspiracy is crucial since it must produce proper revenues to all firms involved, else one or more of the conspirators will "chisel" prices to steal orders. However, these marketing arrangements are all but impossible to sustain for any extended period of time. Will the present market shares be maintained? And if they are maintained, how long will they last? What arrangements will exist for altering the status quo? Will a smaller firm attempt to cut the fixed price when it feels that its allotted share or territory is too restrictive, and no operational procedures for change exist? And what about *new* firms attracted to the market by the higher-than-competitive prices? By definition, they have no allotted outputs or selling instructions. Will they be content to just take a slice of the existing action? But which of the existing sellers in the conspiracy will give up sales to make room for the newcomer? The tendency of output restrictions is to frustrate all aggressive sellers and attract new producers, and thus to weaken and eventually break apart price-fixing agreements.

Costs: Assume a manufacturing firm A whose average production and selling costs per unit decline as output increases. As almost every businessman realizes, there are certain economies associated with larger outputs; spreading the overhead and purchasing supplies in larger quantities tend to lower average costs per unit of output, and make larger outputs cheaper to produce and sell than smaller outputs. The significant point for this discussion is that firms that *restrict* outputs as a part of a price conspiracy invariably raise their average costs per unit. Hence, profits will decline unless the extra revenue associated with the conspiracy exceeds the extra costs associated with the output restriction.

This important consideration must surely make firms hesitant to join such restrictive agreements. Smaller firms especially will be anxious to increase—not decrease—output, in order to enjoy the economies associated with larger scale output. To compete with the larger, more efficient firms in the future may make this output expansion mandatory. In conclusion, price-fixing and output agreements are difficult to conclude when firms find it advantageous to increase, not decrease, their sales.

Imports: As long as international markets are free (and it is within our power to lower our quotas and tariffs to zero on all goods), a domestic price-fixing conspiracy appears limited by foreign competition. When foreign goods are price competitive, domestic price-fixing agreements are inherently unstable. A world-wide conspiracy is possible, but almost all such arrangements have existed and functioned successfully in the past with active *governmental* support.

Honesty and Trust: Honesty and trust between the firms involved in conspiracy is absolutely crucial to its successful operation. If one of the conspirators thinks, or is led to think, that anyone else is not living up to the price-output agreements (and they will have to police their own agreements), then price cutting is likely. And since it is hard to turn down old customers and their price requests, and difficult not to discount from book price when demand is flat, and since all firms know this, the *suspicion* of secret price concessions will always be strong. Furthermore, since firms don't trust each other in open competition, it is difficult to understand why they should suddenly trust each other in price conspiracy.

Buyer Power: It appears that some assumptions concerning the market "power" of the buyers is necessary before price collusion can be understood. The buyers must, obviously, have a relatively weak bargaining position *vis-à-vis* the selling conspiracy. If buyers are large firms that can threaten to make the price-fixed item or import it, or can use reciprocal agreements to the detriment of the price conspirators, then successful price conspiracy certainly becomes more difficult. It is hard to imagine firms such as Sears, DuPont, American Can, or any of America's industrial giants being the victim of price conspiracy in *their* purchasing markets.

Differentiated Products: Other things equal, one would expect price fixing to be more difficult in industries where the "products" being sold are highly differentiated. By definition, firms selling homogeneous products (e.g., cement) concentrate most of the competitiveness of their output in one bit of significant data: price/unit weight. A price fix on homogeneous products would, therefore, be relatively simple since the range of competitive variables is "managable." The greater the number of competitive variables or, correspondingly, the less important unit price becomes, the greater the difficulty that a simple *price* conspiracy could be arranged or could function in the interests of the parties involved. Consumer goods industries, with their usual emphasis on diversity and differentiation, would appear to be poor candidates for successful price collusion.

Transportation Costs: Local or regional price conspiracies would appear to be limited by transportation charges from areas where competition is still open. For example, to fix the price of septic tanks in area A, the area A septic tank sellers would have to take into account the fact that sellers in area B could begin to compete (and thus destroy the price conspiracy) when production costs plus transportation approached the price fix. Thus if the manufacturing costs of all the area sellers were roughly similar, the price fix in area A would be limited by the freight rates between themselves and the nearest competitive market. Put slightly differently, if transportation costs between markets were low relative to final price, a local price conspiracy would find it extremely difficult to increase and "fix" prices for any extended period of time.

Summary of Theoretical Factors

In summation, a price-fixing agreement would be unstable or unworkable when substitute competition is important, demand is falling, large producers are not party to the conspiracy, production quotas are to be agreed upon, larger outputs are cheaper per unit than smaller outputs, imports are an important part of market competition, mutal distrust and suspicion abound, buyers are in a position to bargain, products are widely differentiated, and where transportation costs are negligible between markets. Any of these factors might be enough to prevent successful price conspiracy. Since a great many markets, at one time or another, display these various conditions, it appears reasonable to assume that successful price collusion would be of minor proportions even without antitrust legislation. To test this conclusion, let us turn to an examination of some of the landmark price-fixing cases prosecuted under the Sherman Act, and attempt to discover what the "conspirators" were actually doing.

THE ADDYSTON PIPE CASE (1899)

The Addyston Pipe Case[2] is an antitrust "landmark" for at least three different reasons. In the first place, it represents one of the few early victories for the Justice Department under the Sherman Act. Secondly, its successful prosecution may have been a factor in the significant structural changes that took place in American manufacturing during the 1895–1902 period.[3] Finally, the case is classic because it details vividly the difficulties of price collusion in a free and unstable market situation.

In 1896 the Justice Department brought suit in the Circuit Court for the Eastern District of Tennessee against six cast-iron pipe manufacturers: Addyston Pipe and Steel Company; Dennis Long and Company; Howard-Harrison Iron Company; Anniston Pipe and Foundry Company; South Pittsburgh Pipe Works, and the Chattanooga Foundry and Pipe Works. The firms were charged with rigging bid prices for cast-iron pipe to certain municipalities. Although the Circuit Court decision of 1898 argued that the "combination" only affected "manufacturing" and not interstate trade and commerce,[4] Circuit Court Judge Taft, on appeal, reversed the lower court decision on the grounds that such "associations" were *always* void at common law, and that there was "no question of reasonable-

[2] *Addyston Pipe and Steel Company* v. *United States*, 175 U. S. 211.
[3] Donald Dewey, *Monopoly in Economics and Law* (Chicago: Rand McNally and Company, 1959), pp. 53–55.
[4] *United States* v. *Addyston Pipe and Steel Company*, 78 F. 712 (1897).

ness open to the courts with reference to such a contract."[5] Besides, Taft indicated, even if the reasonableness of the conspiracy were at issue, the facts in the case clearly demonstrated that the Addyston "group" was indeed charging unreasonable prices.[6]

On December 4, 1899, the Supreme Court agreed with Judge Taft's decision and reaffirmed the reversal of the appeals court. Justice Peckham, writing the majority opinion, simply quoted Taft's "analysis" of the unreasonableness of the Addyston group's prices and concluded that . . .

> The facts thus set forth [Taft's quoted decision] show conclusively that the effect of the combination was to enhance prices beyond a sum which was reasonable, and therefore the first objection above set forth need not be further noticed.[7]

In his history of the Addyston Pipe conspiracy, Almarin Phillips indicates that the object of the conspiracy was rather simple and logical.[8] The six firms involved were the major suppliers of cast-iron pipe in the Southern market area. Although there were many other cast-iron pipe producers in the rest of the country (particularly in the New Jersey area), transportation costs from the Eastern plants limited competition for jobs in the "safe" areas immediately surrounding the Southern manufacturers. The general idea of the conspiracy was to end competition between the six firms for the local (reserved cities) jobs altogether, and to prearrange collusively a bid and a bidder for the public lettings in the "pay territory." Hopefully the internal reduction in price competition between the Southern firms —and the consequently higher prices—would increase group revenues and profits.

But there were difficulties with the scheme from the beginning. The major operational difficulty concerned the allocation of "pay territory" jobs. Which firms were to get them, and how were the final bid prices to be arrived at? The prearranged bid price in the pay territory certainly had to be below the delivered price of any (Northern) producer not a party to the conspiracy else the Southern group would get no business at all. Yet, at the same time, the price actually

[5] 85 F. 293.
[6] *Ibid.*, pp. 293–295.
[7] 175 U.S. 238.
[8] Almarin Phillips, *Market Structure, Organization and Performance* (Cambridge, Mass.: Harvard University Press, 1962).

bid had to be close to the nonmember bid in order to realize a profit for the conspiracy.

In addition, the bid price had to be at least competitive with firms *in* the pay territory and not a party to the conspiracy. Judge Taft admitted that there were 170,500 tons of cast-iron pipe capacity in the pay territory associated with nonconspiracy firms.[9] Some of these nonconspiracy pay territory manufacturers were in Texas, Colorado, and Oregon; more important mills were in St. Louis, Columbus, in northern Ohio, and in Michigan.[10] Thus the prices worked out by the Addyston group would have to be tempered by potential competition from within and without the pay territory.

How, exactly, were the bid prices (and the bidder) determined? The solution to this problem was to allow secret bidding for pay territory jobs by conspiracy members. When a bid price was selected, the members were allowed to "bid a bonus" price per ton for the privilege of submitting that bid at the public letting and actually doing the production. Other things equal, the firm with the lowest marginal production costs plus transportation could "bid" the largest bonuses and could get the jobs. Bidding bonuses introduced the necessary element of "competition," and allowed the conspiracy to allocate the appropriate jobs to the most efficient firms. Consequently, as should be obvious, the firm that bid the largest bonus and secured the job, derived little if any *additional* profit from the arrangement since the bonuses were paid to the group.

Was the attempt at price collusion successful? If the test of success is made to be a significant and sustained advance in the final price of cast-iron pipe sold by the Addyston group companies between 1893 and 1896, then clearly the collusion was far from successful. For example, the first preliminary attempts to advance prices and profits in 1893 and 1894 were admitted failures.[11] During this period, prices charged by the conspiracy members were actually lower (in some cases as much as 20 percent lower) than they had been in the preconspiracy period. Amazingly, prices bid in some of the *reserved city* areas were significantly lower than prior to the conspiracy.

Although the Addyston group did agree on a "new plan" in late 1895, and although some bid prices did advance briefly, most bid

[9]The defendants capacity was estimated at 220,000 tons. See, 85 F. 291.
[10]*Ibid.*, p. 292.
[11]Phillips, *op. cit.*, p. 108.

prices by the middle of 1896 were as low *or lower* than in the previous periods. For example, in a statement by M.L. Holman, Water Commissioner of St. Louis, dated January 15, 1897, it is indicated that the contract price for cast-iron pipe per ton was $24.95 on April 12, 1892, $25.48 on July 26, 1892, $19.94 on August 7, 1894, $19.85 on March 26, 1895, $22.47 on September 17, 1895, $19.64 on July 28, 1896, and $19.94 on October 6, 1896.[12] These price movements are fairly typical of the patterns in other pay territory cities.

Were the prices charged by the conspiracy "fair and reasonable"? Almarin Phillips suggests that Judge Taft likely erred when he concluded that the prices charged by the conspiracy were unreasonable.[13] The rather incomplete cost-price information available suggests to Phillips that conspiracy prices in the period under consideration were frequently below average costs, and possibly even below average variable costs.[14] He speculates that a price of $20 per ton would have covered full costs including transportation if the mills had been operating close to capacity. Since they were operating well below capacity in 1896, Phillips concludes that the "charge that the general level of prices was exorbitant seems unjustified."[15]

The Record and Briefs in the Addyston Pipe case supply additional information concerning the "fairness" of the prices charged by the conspiracy during the period. Although Judge Taft summarily *dismissed* the fifty-odd affidavits from private contractors, gas and water companies, and public officials testifying to the reasonableness of the prices charged, nothing (for our purposes) could be more *relevant.* Affidavit after affidavit swore to the fact that the buyer was acquainted with all the firms that manufactured cast-iron pipe, with the past and present prices of pipe, and with the price of the basic raw material, pig iron. On that basis, all testified that the prices actually charged for pipe were fair and reasonable. The last paragraph from the affidavit of A.W. Walton dated December 30, 1896, is not atypical:

The prices at which said pipe, and all other pipe, which aggregated large amounts have been purchased by me and furnished by the Addyston Pipe and Foundry Company and others are

---

[12]*Addyston Pipe et al.* v. *United States*, 175 U.S. 211, *Transcript of Record*, Supreme Court of the United States, October Term, 1899, No. 51, pp. 196–197.
[13]Phillips, *op. cit.*, p. 111.
[14]*Ibid.*, p. 112.
[15]*Ibid.*

the lowest that could be obtained from any of the pipe works in the United States. From my knowledge and long experience, extending over a number of years past, respecting the cost of manufacturing cast-iron pipe, the loss entailed, and the capital required, I consider the prices at which said pipe was purchased as fair, reasonable and just. From my knowledge of such things I do not believe that the prices could reasonably have been less. The prices at which cast-iron pipe has sold since December, 1894, have been uniformly moderate, even low in a number of instances, much lower at all times that pipe could be purchased prior to that time.[16]

Now surely the sworn testimony of the supposed *victims* of the dastardly conspiracy (the buyers of cast-iron pipe) to the effect that they believed that they were *not being victimized* is important and relevant information. Yet almost all accounts of the Addyston case conveniently ignore this information.[17]

The probable reason for the inability of the conspiracy to increase and sustain high and unreasonable prices is not difficult to discover. Although many of the theoretical factors discussed earlier in this chapter would appear to favor successful price collusion, the one crucial nonfavorable factor was the level of demand. The period of the middle 1890s was one of extremely poor and unstable economic performance, even depression. In that context, it is doubtful that the number of bids for cast-iron pipe sought by contractors and municipalities would have been sufficient to sustain then-existing plant capacity without a severe reduction in market price. Further, idle capacity on the part of the nonconspiracy firms would have made them hungry for additional business at *any* price that covered out-of-pocket expenses. With the decrease in demand for pipe on the part of private contractors, and the uncertainty associated with the demand for pipe on the part of the municipalities, it is not surprising that prices could not even be maintained at 1892 preconspiracy levels, let alone pushed higher. *The general level of demand and the level of operating capacity of all pipe works (there were twenty-one firms operating in the United States) were, it appears, much more important influences on price than conspiracy.* Thus, in one of the

---

[16]*Addyston Pipe et al.* v. *United States*, 175 U.S. 211, *Record and Briefs*, p. 195.
[17]The mention of the affidavits is omitted from Justice Peckham's opinion in the Addyston Pipe case as excerpted in Irwin M. Stelzer, *Selected Antitrust Cases: Landmark Decisions* (3rd ed.; Homewood, Ill.: Richard D. Irwin, 1966), p. 163.

landmark price fixing cases of all antitrust history, prices were not really fixed and monopoly profits were not obtained.

THE TRENTON POTTERIES CASE (1927)

A.D. Neale, in his widely respected volume, *The Antitrust Laws of the U.S.A.*, declares that the Trenton Potteries case is the leading Supreme Court decision on price fixing.[18] And so it may well be. But few antitrust volumes—including Neale's own excellent survey—supply any substantial conduct-performance information that would allow the reader to determine what actually transpired during the alleged conspiracy, and during the very interesting proceedings at the trial court. The most general and repeated summaries of the Trenton Potteries case are legalistic. In this case, almost all accounts relate, Chief Justice Stone reaffirmed the Addyston Pipe precedent on price-fixing agreements, and stated that:

> Agreements which create such potential power may well be held to be in themselves unreasonable or unlawful restraints, without the necessity of minute inquiry whether a particular price is reasonable or unreasonable. . . . [19]

Thus price-fixing agreements were always *per se* illegal, and there was to be no "rule of reason" with regard to such conspiracies.

Such a legalistic approach, of course, leaves the most interesting *economic* questions unanswered—or even unasked. Did, for example, these so-called "price agreements" in the Trenton Potteries case actually accomplish "agreement," i.e., were the actual market prices for vitreous pottery bathroom and lavatory fixtures "uniform, arbitrary, and noncompetitive" as the federal grand jury indictment had charged?[20] It would be both informative and ironical, indeed, if in the "leading case on price fixing" it could be discovered that prices were *not* actually fixed and *not* uniform. Before we explore this and similar questions concerning the conduct-performance of the firms involved, a brief sketch of the industry and the supposed conspiracy is required.

At the time of the alleged illegal agreements, the pottery industry was regionally concentrated in New Jersey along the Delaware River.[21] Although there were pottery firms in Chicago, Kalamazoo,

[18](London: Cambridge University Press, 1970), p. 33.
[19]*United States* v. *Trenton Potteries Company et al.*, 273 U.S. 397.
[20]Phillips, *op. cit.*, p. 164.
[21]*Ibid.*, pp. 162–173.

Evansville, and Wheeling, West Virginia, at least eight important firms (including Trenton Potteries and Thomas Maddock and Sons, the two largest firms) were located in Trenton, New Jersey. Also headquartered in Trenton was the Sanitary Potters Association, the trade organization to which at least 23 firms representing 82 percent of the industry's 1922 output belonged.

The activities of the Sanitary Potters Association were varied—and eventually controversial. There is evidence to suggest that the association encouraged its members to adopt a more standardized approach to the design of certain bathroom fixtures, and that it strongly encouraged the use of a uniform system of cost accounting. It also kept records of the particular wholesalers (jobbers) to whom association members sold so-called "first line" class "A" material, and occasionally admonished its members for selling imperfect (class "B") fixtures in the home market. Its most controversial activity, however, involved the preparation and publication of an official industry "price list."

The price lists (there were six different lists for six different geographical areas of the country) were prepared from statistics of actual sale prices submitted monthly by the association members,[22] and from the recommendations of the Sanitary Potters "price list committee." The lists were then sent out to the member firms and, supposedly, served as the basis for *their* own price bulletins. In the individual firm price bulletin one might find the "list" price on a particularly styled wash bowl; in addition, the "discount" off that list price might also be indicated. Further, there were "surcharges" that might be added to actual order invoices on particular bathroom ware. If all firms in the same regional zone followed the *same* list price in their bulletins, and then applied the *same* discounts and the *same* surcharges to the *same* class A items, the final selling prices for these particular firms would have been identical.

In August, 1922, a federal grand jury returned an indictment against twenty-three vitreous pottery manufacturers, claiming that they had conspired through their trade association to "fix and exact non-competitive prices for the sale of said pottery," and that the firms had "refrained from engaging in competition with each other as to the prices of said pottery."[23] In addition, the indictment also

---

[22]This practice was reportedly abandoned in 1920.
[23]300 F. 551.

charged that the defendants had illegally conspired to confine their sales of bathroom and lavatory fixtures to "legitimate jobbers."[24] The case was tried by Judge William C. Van Fleet, and on April 17, 1923 the jury returned a guilty verdict on both counts.

The convicted defendants appealed and on May 9, 1924, a Circuit Court of Appeals reversed the trial court decision on the basis of certain procedural errors in the conduct of the trial. Circuit Court Judge Hough (apparently speaking for Judges Rogers and Mayer, also) maintained that "the learned court erred" when *it had refused to allow defense witnesses to testify as to the existence of competition between the indicted defendants,* and that it had erred when it instructed the jury that "if they found the defendants did conspire to restrain trade, as charged in the indictment, *then it was immaterial whether such agreements were ever actually carried out...* " (emphasis added).[25] Judge Hough argued that it "was essential for the prosecution to prove the absence of competition" and, thus, "incumbent upon the defense to show, if possible, the presence of actual competition in respect of prices."[26] This was especially important, Judge Hough observed, in view of the fact that none of the defendants lived in the district where the trial had been conducted (Southern District of New York), and that the federal indictment had not charged that the conspiracy was formed in that district.

> ... consequently there was no jurisdiction there to bring the indictment or there to try the case, unless it was shown that the jurisdiction was conferred by the commission of an overt act within the Southern District.
>   The pleader understood this, for otherwise all the allegations concerning acts done in the Southern District in pursuance of the object of the conspiracy were mere surplusage. Why the United States was so anxious to institute and prosecute this case in the city of New York we do not know, but the frame of indictment compared with the undisputed facts show that New York was intentionally selected, and trial of these defendants in the Third Circuit, where most of them resided, was sedulously avoided. Such a choice as this carried with it the burden of proving something done in the Southern district, i.e., an overt act—justifying the finding of the indictment. The pecularity of this transplanted litigation was overlooked below, and *it was*

[24]It was the common practice of almost *all* manufacturers to market products exclusively through wholesalers. There was no evidence presented to indicate that any particular wholesaler had been discriminated against. See Phillips, *op. cit.,* p. 168.
[25]300 F. 552.
[26]*Ibid.,* p. 555.

error, and very material error, to instruct a New York jury in so many words that it was immaterial whether any effort had ever been made to carry out the conspiracy complained of.[27]

The essential question, therefore, and the one totally ignored by the lower court, was: had the firms *successfully* conspired to fix arbitrary and uniform prices and, hence, "injure the public"?

Both the trial court record and the *United States Supreme Court Records & Briefs*[28] contain abundant evidence that selling prices during the period of the alleged conspiracy were *not* fixed and *not* uniform, and that there was active competition—active *price* competition—between the defendants. The many *buyers* of vitreous pottery, to the extent that they were *allowed* to testify, indicated that the defendants were in active price competition with each other, and that the bulletin prices were not actual selling prices. As one buyer recounted:

> . . . I received their bulletins . . . I did not make use of the bulletins except to put them in the waste basket, because I went around shopping and bought just as I found the market ripe to buy. My prices were not affected or controlled by these bulletin prices that I know of. . . .[29]

Although the government attorney repeatedly objected—and Judge Van Fleet sustained almost all objections—to the introduction of defense testimony regarding whether actual competition existed in the market for the wares of the defendants, the official record of the case still contains conclusive evidence that such price competition did. The following excerpt is a summary statement from respondents brief pertaining to price determination in the market; the trial record page references are in parentheses:

> During all of the period in question sales of sanitary pottery were made at prices below those announced in the current bulletins (R; p. 344, fols. 1030–1031; p. 375, fol. 1123; p. 397, fols. 1189–1191; p. 422, fol. 1264; p. 442, fols. 1324–1325; p. 445, fol. 1335; p. 459, fol. 1375; p. 459, fol. 1376; p. 460 fol. 1378; p. 498, fol. 1453; p. 512, fol. 1535; p. 516, fol. 1547 and p. 521, fol. 1562). Some buyers never paid bulletin prices. (R., p. 424, fol.

---

[27] *Ibid.*, p. 552 (Emphasis added).
[28] *United States* v. *Trenton Potteries Company et al.*, 273 U.S. 392, *Brief for Respondents, No. 27, United States Supreme Court Records & Briefs*, October Term, 1926.
[29] Phillips, *op. cit.*, p. 167.

1271) Others bought oftener below than at the bulletin prices.
(R. p. 448, fol. 1342; p. 452, fol. 1356; p. 459, fol. 1375; p. 459,
fol. 1376; p. 460, fol. 1378; p. 464, fol. 1391). The prices at which
the various companies sold were usually different. (R., p. 528,
fol. 1582) Sometimes the bulletin prices varied. (R., p. 450, fol.
1348; p. 459, fol. 1376). The prices charged by some of the
companies were always lower than those of any of the others.
(R., p. 381, fol. 1142). Some of the manufacturers regularly gave
certain customers a stated reduction from their published
prices (R., p. 513, fol. 1539) Salesmen of defendant companies
found themselves in competition as to price with those of other
companies (R., p. 398, fols. 1193–1194), and manufacturers, if
they wanted the business, met their competitors prices. (R., p.
471, fol. 1412). Buyers found manufacturers bidding against
each other for their business (R., p. 422, fols. 1265–1266; p. 492,
fol. 1475; p. 514, fol. 1541; p. 525, fols. 1573–1575) and reducing
their prices to get orders (R., p. 439, fol. 1317; p. 446, fol. 1336;
p. 450, fol. 1349). Some buyers obtained prices from several
manufacturers at the same time and found that these prices
differed (R., p. 436, fol. 1306; p. 438, fol. 1314; p. 440, fols.
1318–1319; p. 446, fol. 1336; p. 465, fol. 1393; p. 528, fol. 1582).
Some of the buyers thought so little of price bulletins that they
threw them away (R., p. 439, fol. 1316).[30]

Further, an analysis of the actual sales invoices of 21 of the 23
defendants between June 1, 1918, and July 31, 1922, showed that 26
percent of the tanks sold by the defendants sold at bulletin prices,
while 64 percent sold below bulletin and 10 percent above bulletin.
Of the bathroom bowls invoiced, only 28 percent sold at bulletin
prices, while 68 percent sold below bulletin and 4 percent above
bulletin.[31] And the differences from bulletin prices were not slight.
Almarin Phillips has noted that some actual prices for tanks and
bowls may have varied as much as 40 percent from the "official"
bulletin prices. Clearly, then, the Trendon Potteries conspiracy was
not able to fix "uniform, arbitrary and non-competitive" prices for
vitreous pottery in the period under consideration. And in the "leading case on price fixing," prices were not being "fixed."

One can speculate as to why the "conspiracy" failed. Almarin
Phillips suggests that the industry lacked "the leadership required to
establish an effective market organization";[32] the markets were dis-
organized, the pottery firms had widely different objectives, and
there was no "dominant firm" to whip the smaller firms into price
line. With no assurance that *anybody* was following bulletin prices,

[30]*Records & Briefs, Brief for Respondents, No. 27*, pp. 10–11.
[31]*Ibid.*, p. 11.
[32]Phillips, *op. cit.*, pp. 173–176.

all had to "cheat" to insure their proper share of new orders. And since there were no penalties associated with "shading" bulletin prices (outside of occasional admonishments), the financial benefits of competition apparently exceeded the costs of unsure price agreement. Under such conditions, a successful price collusion was extremely unlikely.

The 1918–1922 period was also high in other economic uncertainties. The disequilibriums of World War I must have been severe, especially in an industry as sensitive to construction spending and housing starts. At the same time, a major technological change had threatened to revolutionize the manufacturing process in the industry.[33] All these factors together must have placed intense competitive pressure on the existing market structure of independent pottery manufacturers, and made them extremely price conscious.

As already noted above, however, the Supreme Court regarded such contextual information as "immaterial," and reversed the Appeals Court decision that such economic evidence or analysis should have been part of the deliberations of the jury. In 1927, and rather consistently since then,[34] any price agreement—or any sort of combination that "tampers with price structures"[35]—has been regarded as unlawful. Whether the prices have *actually* been fixed, or whether they have been fixed at unreasonable levels, has been immaterial to a determination of guilt or innocence. To presume automatically, therefore, that "price-fixing" antitrust cases demonstrate that successful price fixing is easy or common throughout the American business system—or would be without a protective Sherman Act— is not justifiable. In many cases, the information relevant to decide such an issue has been "immaterial" at court.

THE GREAT ELECTRICAL EQUIPMENT CONSPIRACY

Undoubtedly the most celebrated price-fixing antitrust case of modern times is the electrical equipment manufacturers price conspiracy, decided in 1961.[36] Involved were some of the nation's largest

---

[33] *Ibid.*, pp. 175–176.

[34] *Appalachian Coals, Inc.* v. *United States,* 288 U.S. 344 (1933), is a strange exception to the *per se* approach in price fixing cases. See Stelzer, *op. cit.*, pp. 165–170.

[35] *United States* v. *Socony-Vacuum Oil Company,* 310 U.S. 150 (1940), quoted in Stelzer, *Ibid.*, p. 175.

[36] Background information can be obtained from Richard Austin Smith, "The Incredible Electrical Conspiracy," *Fortune,* LXIII (April and May, 1961); John Fuller, *The Gentlemen Conspirators* (New York: Grove Press, 1962); John Herling, *The Great*

and most prestigious firms, such as General Electric, Westinghouse, Allis-Chalmers, Federal Pacific, I-T-E Circuit Breaker, Carrier, and many others. The charges: that various employees of said firms had, between 1956 and 1959, combined and conspired to "raise, fix, and maintain" the prices of insulators, transformers, power switchgear, condensors, circuit breakers, and various other electrical equipment and apparatus involving an estimated $1.7 billion worth of business annually.[37]

A series of Philadelphia grand jury indictments were returned during 1960. After much discussion between the defendants and the Department of Justice, the firms were allowed to plead guilty to some of the more serious charges, and *nolo contendere* to the rest. On February 6, 1961, Judge Ganey sent seven executives off to jail, gave twenty-three others suspended jail sentences, and fined the firms involved nearly $2 million. Subsequent triple damage suits, brought against the equipment manufacturers by the TVA and private firms that had been "overcharged," increased the financial penalty many times. And so ended the most publicized price conspiracy in all business history.

The fact that there were price "meetings" among various electrical equipment producers between 1956 and 1959 was indisputable. The meetings were a "way of life" in the industry.[38] Some of the meetings were little more than hastily called "gripe" sessions where the various firm representatives complained about price discounting and foreign competition. But others were more sophisticated and, apparently, involved the determination and application of secret bidding formulas and the allocation of market business. Certainly the most incredible aspect of the conspiracy was not the price meetings but the absolute disclaimer by top General Electric and Westinghouse executives of any knowledge of any "conspiracy." The executives actually involved in the meetings bore the brunt of the financial and social penalties.

Price Conspiracy: The Story of the Anti-trust Violations in the Electrical Industry (Washington: Robert B. Luce, 1962).

[37]Clarence C. Walton and Frederick W. Cleveland, Jr., *Corporations on Trial: The Electric Cases* (Belmont, Calif.: Wadsworth Publishing Company, 1964), p. 12.

[38]*Ibid*, p. 11. The best source of information about the conspiracy meetings is the Hearings on Administered Prices by the United States Senate Committee on the Judiciary, Subcommittee on Antitrust and Monopoly, *Price-Fixing and Bid-Rigging in the Electrical Manufacturing Industry*, Parts 27 and 28, 87th Congress, 1st session, April, May, and June 1961.

If an "agreement" to fix prices is price fixing, then the electrical manufacturers were certainly guilty of price fixing and the issue is a dead one. Or if "tampering with price structures" constitutes price fixing, then these meetings were illegal and in clear violation of the Sherman Act. But for the purposes of this discussion the important questions are not legal (or moral) but *economic*. Did the conspiracy in fact "raise fix and maintain" unreasonable prices as the twenty-odd indictments had charged? Did it "restrain, suppress and eliminate" price competition with respect to the selling of various kinds of electrical machinery or apparatus? Did the conspiracy work to "cheat" buyers of the benefits of free competition?

To comprehend correctly the issue of price conspiracy, one must understand the usual and normal pricing practices in this multi-product, oligopolistic industry. General Electric, Westinghouse, and to a lesser extent, the smaller manufacturers, sell hundreds of thousands of electrical products that have been "standardized" to a high degree by the industry's trade association. The products are sold out of huge catalogues where potential customers may obtain a detailed description of the product and its suggested list price. Almost all the catalogue products are so-called "shelf" items that the huge manufacturers produce continuously and hold in inventory. When an order is received a computer fills the request and directs that the particular product be shipped from the closest warehouse to the customer.

Since the products produced by the electrical equipment manufacturers are almost identical, and all firms quote delivered prices, the selling prices for standardized shelf items are almost identical to all buyers.[39] Any price decrease by one seller—usually announced with a mimeographed price sheet to customers—is quickly matched by other sellers. On sealed bid business, the price cut is "announced" when the bids are opened. In any case, the pressure of the marketplace, i.e., the desire on the part of each manufacturer to keep or increase his customers, makes the new (lower) price the new catalogue price, which is, again, nearly identical for all firms that want to be "competitive." Although there may be recognized quality differences that eventually "sell" an order, it still appears that the price of the higher-quality product must nearly equal its lower-qual-

---

[39]There was testimony to the effect that the Robinson-Patman Act made quantity discounts difficult. See *Price-Fixing and Bid-Rigging. . .* , p. 17619.

ity competitor. The testimony of John K. Hodnette, executive vice-president of Westinghouse, illustrates the pricing procedures with respect to such a shelf item, electric meters:[40]

> This is a standard item. It is the meter that goes on the outside of the house that measures the use of current, protects the customer, tells the utility how much electricity has been used so that they can render a bill. We have been manufacturing these meters for 75 years. The selling price is approximately $16 . . . About 60 days ago, I think it was, one of our competitors decreased the price of his watt-hour meter that corresponded to the one in question in Cleveland. When we learned of this, which we do very promptly, because they send out published catalogs, and our customers call them to our attention, so with the large number that are printed it is very easy matter to get a copy of a competitors' catalog and determine his prices, they reduced the price of the meter 30 cents per meter, when the new pricelist came out. We had just concluded the development of a meter which we thought was superior, better than any in the industry. We advised our field salespeople that we were not at that time planning to reduce our prices. We felt that we could sell a superior product at a higher price. We very soon learned that customers would not pay us the price, and many of them came to us and asked us to reduce our price to the same as those charged by competitors, so that they could continue to buy meters from us.[41]

Thus, Hodnette argued, competition produced identical prices. And the pricing procedure was no different with reference to "sealed bid" business. As he explained:

> The City of Cleveland and many other people recognize no brand preference or quality preference of one meter manufactured by one company as against another. In order to obtain business in any location, it is necessary that he be competitive with respect to price. This is total cost to the customer, whether he be the city of Cleveland or TVA, delivered to him at the site he wants it. He will not pay more . . . In order for a manufacturer to get an order, he must quote a competitive price. He must quote a price that is equal to that of any of his competitors, delivered to the customer, and without any qualifications.[42]

---

[40]All the quoted testimony to follow in this chapter is taken from *Price-Fixing and Bid-Rigging in the Electrical Manufacturing Industry*, unless otherwise indicated.

[41]*Ibid.*, p. 17430.

[42]*Ibid.*, p. 17431.

From these remarks, it is clear that the normal forces of competition tended to produce identically quoted list prices in the electrical equipment manufacturers industry. To regard such identical quotations as *per se* evidence of collusion or conspiracy would be naïve and wrong. A final note on this extremely important issue from Ralph Cordiner, president of General Electric during this period, will suffice:

> In the course of these hearings, considerable attention has been devoted to the frequent identity of prices charged by competitors. It has been suggested that this identity, where it occurs, indicates a lack of competition, or even continuing conspiracy, among competing manufacturers. In all candor, may I say that identity of prices on standard, mass-produced items normally indicates no such thing. On the contrary, such price identity is the inevitable and necessary result of the force of competition —a force that requires sellers of standardized items to meet the lowest price offered in the market. The manufacturer who makes a product on a mass-produced basis and where minimum performance or quality standards are a part of the customer specifications will not long be in business if he prices that product above the market. The customers will purchase elsewhere unless his product has demonstrable additional values accepted by a reasonably large number of customers. The manufacturer who prices his products below the market will quickly discover there is no advantage to him because his competitors drop their prices to the price level he establishes . . . It is simply not true that uniformity of prices is evidence of collusion. Nor it is true that uniformity of prices on sealed bids amounts to an elimination of price competition. The facts are that vigorous price competition continually takes place with one effect being a uniformity of catalog prices and, therefore, a uniformity of sealed bid quotations. Suppliers come to the conclusion—some possibly reluctantly—that if they want to continue to offer a particular product for sale that they will have to offer it at market prices equal to the lowest available from any supplier of any acceptable product.[43]

Even if the product being sold is *not* a standardized shelf item, firms desiring to be "competitive" tend to meet the already established price. This procedure will hold even if a firm has not as yet manufactured the specialized electrical apparatus; it will quote the price of its competitor to announce to its potential customers that it *can* and *will* be competitive if orders should appear. Thus the "costs" in the short run, or even before the product is actually made,

---

[43] *Ibid.*, pp. 17672–17673.

are *irrelevant* to price determination. Again and again, the business-men that testified before the Senate Subcommittee on Antitrust and Monopoly pointed out that market prices were determined by the firm willing to sell at the lowest price. But again and again, many of the Senators on the committee, particularly Kefauver, refused to accept that explanation. Like many economists, Senator Kefauver implied that competitive prices should have been determined by "costs"—completely ignoring the fact that buyers of electrical apparatus have no idea what producer "costs" are, and care less. Note the following exchange of views with respect to "costs" and competition:

> SENATOR KEFAUVER: How does it happen that each one of these other companies comes up with exactly the same cost figures and decides that should be their price?
> MR. HODNETTE: I have no idea what their costs are. The prices are determined by competition in the market place, not by cost.[44]

Or note the discussion below between Senator Kefauver and Mark W. Cresap, Jr., president of Westinghouse, with respect to the nearly identical prices ($17,402,300) submitted by different companies on a 500,000 kilo-watt turbine:

> SENATOR KEFAUVER: . . . did you arrive at that price independently?
> MR. CRESAP: Yes, sir.
> SENATOR KEFAUVER: You figured it yourself?
> MR. CRESAP: We arrived at that particular one on the basis of the fact that General Electric Co. had lowered its costs for this type of machine, and we met it.
> SENATOR KEFAUVER: You mean you copied it from G.E.?
> MR. CRESAP: No, we met the price.
> SENATOR KEFAUVER: Have you ever made one?
> MR. CRESAP: Have we ever made—
> SENATOR KEFAUVER: A 500,000 kilowatt turbine?
> MR. CRESAP: We had not at that time, no sir.
> SENATOR KEFAUVER: Have you made one yet?
> MR. CRESAP: No.
> SENATOR KEFAUVER: Has G.E. ever made one?
> MR. CRESAP: Yes, they are making one.
> SENATOR KEFAUVER: They have never made one, though?
> MR. CRESAP: Well, this is the price that they established for this machine, and we met it.

[44] *Ibid.*, p. 17438.

SENATOR KEFAUVER: You mean you copied it?

MR. CRESAP: We didn't copy the machine. We met the price because it was the lowest price in the marketplace.

SENATOR KEFAUVER: In other words, you copied the figures exactly, $17,402,300, from General Electric?

MR. CRESAP: Senator, we had a higher price on the machine on our former book, and when they reduced, we reduced to meet them, to meet competition.

SENATOR KEFAUVER: If you never made one, how would you know how much to lower or how much to raise?

MR. CRESAP: You would know by the basis of how much you needed the business, what the conditions of your backlog was, what your plant load was, what your employment was, and what you thought you had to do in order to get the business.

SENATOR KEFAUVER: In any event, you would not know whether you were making money or losing money on this bid, because you had never made one, and Mr. Eckert told us you had no figures on which to base this price. You just followed along with G.E. Is that the policy of your company?

MR. CRESAP: The policy of our company is to meet competitive prices, and this is the manner in which the book price on this particular machine was arrived at . . .

SENATOR KEFAUVER: Even if you lost money?

MR. CRESAP: Even if we lost money, if we needed the business to cover our overheads and to keep our people working . . .

SENATOR KEFAUVER: On something that you had never sold, had never made, and that you have not made yet, and they have not made one yet, their price is $17,402,300, the same as yours.

MR. CRESAP: They would have to be, Mr. Chairman, if we are going to be competitive. We cannot have a higher price than our competition.

SENATOR KEFAUVER: How about a lower price?

MR. CRESAP: If we had a lower price, I am sure they would meet it, if they wanted to get the business very badly.[45]

The Effectiveness of Conspiracy: The Conspirators' View

The essential question to be answered in this section is: did the electrical equipment manufacturers successfully conspire to raise, fix and maintain prices? Did the meetings—which many executives admitted attending—actually fix the level of prices and price changes, or did competition? Was the driving force behind price identity collusion or competition?

The most acceptable generalization concerning the nature of the price conspiracy meetings must be that they were a failure or, as one

[45] *Ibid.*, pp. 17628–17630.

executive rather disgustedly put it, "a waste of time." Without exception, every witness queried before the Senate Subcommittee on Antitrust and Monopoly stated that the meetings were *not* effective at all.
(Why they attended will be discussed below.) Because this particular
aspect of the conspiracy is so important—and so neglected—it must
be documented thoroughly with direct testimony. The following
exchange concerns "collusion" on *medium turbine* sales:

> SENATOR KEFAUVER: How would it work out? Just tell us how
> it worked.
> MR. JENKINS: It didn't work very good.
> SENATOR KEFAUVER: It looks as if it had the possibilities of
> working good.
> MR. JENKINS: The thing that is important, this is a dog-eat-dog
> business and everybody wanted it. There has never been
> enough business.[46]

And again, with Mr. Jenkins with respect to the end of the price
meetings on *turbines:*

> SENATOR KEFAUVER: When did they break up?
> MR. JENKINS: In early 1959.
> SENATOR KEFAUVER: What happened then to cause this ces-
> sation?
> MR. JENKINS: It was a waste of time and effort. There was very
> little business. We were at the bottom of a buying cycle. Every-
> body wanted every job, and it was of no value.[47]

The following exchange concerns price "collusion" on *electrical con-
densers:*

> SENATOR BLAKLEY: If I understand, then, if your competitors
> were of the same mind as you, then it would be a general feeling
> that these meetings for the purpose of fixing prices would be in
> order; is that the way to interpret it?
> MR. BUNCH: An attempt may have been made to fix these
> prices, but, it was entirely unsuccessful.[48]

The following exchange concerns price "collusion" on *small turbine
generators:*

[46] *Ibid.*, p. 16608. Jenkins was sales manager of medium turbine sales for Westinghouse.
[47] *Ibid.*, p. 16614.
[48] *Ibid.*, p. 16639. Bunch was manager of the condensor division of Ingersoll-Rand
Company.

MR. FLURRY: What was decided at that meeting with respect to price level?

MR. SELLERS: This meeting consisted of perhaps—I say "perhaps"—there were six manufacturers in this small turbine generator business represented. This was recognition of the fact that the prior bid price discussions which had been going on among the manufacturers *was so ineffective as to be rather useless,* and to try to determine whether or not people were serious in this endeavor or whether—well, it had become so useless that there was a question as to whether you should continue, and this was a meeting to discuss that. Also, an effort to stabilize the market at some place within a few percent of a published price, rather than 10 or 15 percent, where the market had drifted. Again, the meeting *was so ineffectual as far as I am concerned, because it promptly all fell apart.* This rugged individual type of business that we are in simply ignored—I will put it a different way. The forces that were coming about from lack of volume, and the pressure that was on a manufacturer to get volume, negated any price discussion. It just did not amount to anything.[49] (Emphasis added.)

The following exchange concerns meetings and alleged price collusion with respect to *medium voltage switchgear:*

MR. FLURRY: I understood you to say that this broke off some time before 1959?

MR. HENTSCHEL: That is right, sir.

MR. FLURRY: What was the cause of that break-off?

MR. HENTSHEL: Basically the thing wasn't working. In other words, everybody would come to the meeting, the figures would be settled, and *they were only as good as the distance to the closest telephone before they were broken.* In other words, so the thing just wasn't working.[50] (Emphasis added.)

The following exchange concerns meetings that were designed to set and maintain the prices of *power transformers:*

MR. FERRALL: What do you mean, Mr. Smith, when you say you did not know whether any good would come of it or not?

MR. SMITH: Well, I meant by that, whether there was anything done at the meeting with competitors, which would in any way improve the price situation. Past meetings with competitors had been rather unfruitful in that respect.

[49] *Ibid.,* p. 16669. Sellers was manager of the turbine generator division of the Carrier Corporation.

[50] *Ibid.,* p. 16884. Hentshel was general manager of the medium voltage switchgear department for General Electric.

MR. FERRALL: You mean you did not know whether they would abide by their agreements?
MR. SMITH: I don't know whether you can say that we had real agreement at any time . . . [51]
MR. SMITH: (continuing) My experience in meeting with competitors, as I have said before, indicated to me that it was a rather fruitless endeavor. It might be one day, it might be two days, after a meeting, before jobs would be bid all over the place, and there seemed to be no real continuity that came out of those meetings in the way of stabilizing prices at any level.[52]

And again with Smith of General Electric with respect to "price agreements" on *power transformers:*

SENATOR CARROLL: In other words, you reached agreement that there could be some stabilization?
MR. SMITH: There could be, but we agreed upon no stabilization.
SENATOR CARROLL: I understand that. I am not asking you to commit yourself, but there was this general agreement that you could stabilize?
MR. SMITH: General understandings that it would probably be best if it was possible.
SENATOR CARROLL: Did you remove the threat of price cutting?
MR. SMITH: No, sir.
SENATOR CARROLL: Was there any price cutting after that?
MR. SMITH: Surely, sir.
SENATOR CARROLL: Did it continue?
MR. SMITH: Yes, sir . . .
SENATOR CARROLL: (Continuing) I think I have asked this question, but I will ask it again. Do the records then reflect that you got some price stabilization after that time? I mean, not the records, but the practice, your profits.
MR. SMITH: The price curves which were maintained by the power transformer department all the way through this whole period is one of this kind of picture, up and down all the time.
SENATOR CARROLL: Did it improve after your last conference, the conference in 1958? Did it improve in 1958 after the two presidents got together?
MR. SMITH: No, sir, not to amount to anything.
SENATOR CARROLL: Did it improve any in 1959?
MR. SMITH: It got worse in 1959.[53]

The following exchange again concerns price meetings with respect to fixing prices on *power transformers:*

[51] *Ibid.*, p. 16961. Smith was the general manager of the transformer division for General Electric.
[52] *Ibid.*, p. 16962.
[53] *Ibid.*, pp. 17013, 17029.

SENATOR HRUSKA: By and large, Mr. Ginn, you have had considerable experience in the business of meetings with competitors. How effective were those meetings to get the job done that they purported to have as an objective?

MR. GINN: Senator, this is the way I will put it. *If people did not have the desire to make it work, it never worked. And if people had the desire to make it work, it wasn't necessary to have the meetings and violate the law.*

SENATOR HRUSKA: So that your preliminary discussions and meetings with competitors—

MR. GINN: *Were worthless.*

SENATOR HRUSKA: Were not necessarily controlling?

MR. GINN: *Were worthless . . . I think that the boys could resist everything but temptation.* No sir, I'll tell you frankly, Senator, I think if one thing I would pass on to posterity, that it wasn't worth it. *It didn't accomplish anything,* and all you end up with is by getting in trouble.[54] (Emphasis added.)

And a final exchange with respect to the effectiveness of "fixing" *transformer* prices:

MR. ROSENMAN: And you fixed prices, you participated in the fixing of prices?

MR. MCCOLLOM: That is right.

MR. ROSENMAN: Fixing of the book price–

MR. MCCOLLOM: We discussed those in meetings.

MR. ROSENMAN: But you maintain that there was no agreement as to these?

MR. MCCOLLOM: We discussed these generally, and I say that there was no agreement, because *it didn't result in prices being quoted at those levels that were discussed.* There was just no evidence of any agreements in the actions that were taken by the parties in the meetings. There was no formal definite agreement in writing on this thing.

SENATOR KEFAUVER: None of it was in writing?

MR. MCCOLLOM: There was no verbal agreement, just a discussion.

SENATOR KEFAUVER: Just an understanding?

MR. MCCOLLOM: Just a discussion of it.

SENATOR KEFAUVER: Was there, or was there not, an understanding about what was going to be done?

MR. MCCOLLOM: Well, *I think the results indicate that there was no understanding.*

SENATOR KEFAUVER: *I am not talking about results.* I am asking whether at the meeting there was an understanding about what was going to be done?

MR. MCCOLLOM: Well there was a discussion of price levels 15

---

[54] *Ibid.,* pp. 17069–17070. Ginn was vice president and general manager of the turbine division for General Electric.

percent off book. I might have gone out of the meeting thinking the other people understood it; they might have gone out thinking I did; *but there was no action that supported any understanding of it*, that there was any understanding because it did not occur. It did not happen.[55] (Emphasis added.)

Summary and Conclusions

Through the entire period of the conspiracy, the firms could not suspend price competition. Although there had been repeated *attempts* to fix, raise, and maintain prices, the attempts rather monotonously failed. Price agreement might last a day or two, and "then somebody would break the line and there would be another meeting."[56] In most cases, the prime purpose of the meetings was an attempt to restore "agreements" that were being openly and regularly violated in the marketplace. In other instances, the meetings were an attempt by some firms to "get the line on prices," i.e., to find out what a competitor might do with his price in the near future.[57] Such information would allow a firm to bid just under its competitor and secure the desired business. As Raymond Smith, former general manager of the transformer division at General Electric, put it:

> . . . my prime objective was to find out whether the Westinghouse people had received any instructions from their people, and failing to do so, I thought the meeting was worthless.[58]

The Ineffectiveness of Conspiracy

Hard and fast evidence on *actual* prices and price changes during the period of the conspiracy is extremely spotty. The Bureau of Labor Statistics (BLS) indexes of wholesale prices show substantial increases for various kinds of electrical apparatus. Switchgear prices, for example, increase from an index number of 112.7 in 1950 to 127.4 in 1952, to 135.1 in 1954, to 154.1 in 1956, to 172.8 in 1958, and to 176.6 in 1960.[59] Since there were "meetings" with respect to the prices of switchgear—at least during the latter part of the 1950s—the

[55] *Ibid.*, pp. 17378–17379. McCollom was the manager of the power transformer department for Westinghouse.
[56] *Ibid.*, p. 17883.
[57] *Ibid.*, p. 17523.
[58] *Ibid.*, p. 17013.
[59] *Ibid.*, p. 17767.

impression conveyed is that prices were rather routinely raised and maintained at "unreasonable" levels.

The impression conveyed by the BLS statistics is an altogether incorrect impression. The statistics are based on catalog prices, and they do not necessarily relate to the *actual* prices being charged in the marketplace. The fact remains that all during the "conspiracy" period, switchgear sold at particular percentages off of book or catalog price. This "discounting" was particularly pronounced during the infamous "white sale" of 1954 and 1955, when switchgear was selling for as much as 45 percent to 50 percent off of book.[60] This "sale" was repeated in late 1957 and early 1958 when market prices were as much as 60 percent off of book.[61] Ironically, the entire purpose of the switchgear meetings was to "do something" with respect to the "unreasonably" *low* switchgear prices. The meetings ended in failure and were abandoned before the conspiracy was discovered by the Department of Justice. There was no effective price fixing in switchgear at all.[62]

The fact that there was no effective price fixing in switchgear, or in many other electrical products, might be substantiated by an examination of profit data for some of the firms involved during the period of conspiracy. Although a positive relationship between "periods of conspiracy" and "unreasonable profit" would not prove cause and effect, the complete *lack* of any such relationship might be indicative of ineffectual price collusion. Indeed, if price conspiracy cannot produce "unreasonable" profit levels—and, thus, generate the misallocation of resources that so concerns the economists—why is it important at all? If collusion does not generate substantial profits, economists—for at least a generation—have made mountains out of molehills.

The twenty separate indictments returned by the grand jury in 1960 charged that a price conspiracy had been in effect in the electrical equipment manufacturers industry between 1956 and 1959. A comparison of the rates of return on both capital and sales for that

[60] *Ibid.*, p. 16740.
[61] *Ibid.*, p. 17103.
[62] The same conclusion might be made with respect to the prices of "large circuit breakers." See George J. Stigler and James K. Kindahl, *The Behavior of Industrial Prices* (New York: National Bureau of Economic Research, 1970), p. 31. See also Jules Backman, *The Economics of the Electrical Machinery Industry* (New York: New York University Press, 1962), especially Chapters 5 and 6.

period, with some previous period, is reproduced below for four of the most important firms involved in that conspiracy.[63]

Table 1

General Electric

Years	Profits on Capital (Percentage)	Profits on Sales (Percentage)
1950–1955	20.5	5.9
1956–1959	20.1	5.8

Table 2

Westinghouse

Years	Profits on Capital (Percentage)	Profits on Sales (Percentage)
1950–1955	10.8	5.1
1956–1959	7.0	3.0

Table 3

Allis-Chalmers

Years	Profits on Capital (Percentage)	Profits on Sales (Percentage)
1950–1955	11.3	5.1
1956–1959	6.6	3.7

Table 4

Carrier

Years	Profits on Capital (Percentage)	Profits on Sales (Percentage)
1950–1955	12.9	4.4
1956–1959	7.9	3.5

It can be observed from these tables that in *all* cases, without exception, the rates of return on capital and on sales were actually *lower* during the period of alleged conspiracy than during the previous period.[64] If the conspiracy was successful, the price and prcfit behavior of the firms involved certainly does not reflect that "success." More than likely, the conspiracy was a sad failure from the start to finish.

[63]The tables are based on figures taken from *Moody's Industrial Manual*, and from *Price-fixing and Bid-Rigging in the Electrical Manufacturing Industry*, Exhibits 54A, B, C, pp. 17960–17961.

[64]The profits may have been lower for a good many reasons; the 1957–1958 recession in the economy is the best candidate. The point here, however, is that the collusion did *not* generate monopoly profits.

To understand why the conspiracy failed, it is necessary to examine two crucial elements of the electrical equipment manufacturers industry: the industry's cost structure, and the nature of the demand for electrical apparatus.

Although there are thousands of firms that produce and sell electrical apparatus and machinery—and although entry remains relatively easy[65]—the important parts of the industry are dominated by a relatively few, extremely capital intensive firms. As might be expected, these firms are rather sophisticated innovators, and all maintain substantial research and development facilities at great expense. More important for our purposes, however, is the fact that the extremely high capital intensity, and the resultant scale economies,[66] generate pressures for "selective" price cutting when demand is low to gain volume.

The demand for electrical equipment is derived almost equally from industrial firms and electric utility companies. Since a high proportion of the total demand for electrical equipment is associated with new construction, or new generating capacity on the part of utilities, it becomes extremely sensitive to money market conditions. In addition, since it is a demand for a (postponable) producer's durable good, it can be expected to display the violent instability commonly associated with the "feast or famine" capital goods industry. Both factors foretell an extremely cyclical demand for electrical apparatus.

Given the instability in the economy and in the money markets during the period 1955–1960, and given the cost structure of the equipment manufacturers, it is not at all surprising to discover that price competition was severe and that catalog prices were not being honored. Here were expensively equipped firms with huge overhead costs hungry for a volume of business that did not materialize at existing price levels; this volume simply had to be attracted. In such circumstances price cutting was inevitable. Although there is numerous testimony to support this view,[67] the remarks of George E. Burens, former division general manager of switchgear at General Electric, are indicative of the real situation:

[65]The *Census of Manufacturers* reports that there were 7,066 "establishments" in the electrical machinery industry in 1958, compared with 3,970 in 1947.

[66]Walton and Cleveland, *op. cit.*, p. 13.

[67]See, for example, *Price-Fixing and Bid-Rigging in the Electrical Manufacturing Industry*, p. 16614.

Everybody has their plant in shape. They have the facility. They have the organization. But they have no business. So, they are out grabbing. I think that is the thing.[68]

It was, indeed, the thing.

Price fixing was also difficult because t'ere were always competitors who did not compete on a national basis. When demand was flat or falling, electrical firms closer to potential customers might simply figure the cost of a particular job, and quote a price to cover that cost.[69] Hence, price could be significantly different from national catalog prices, and "could be anywhere over the lot." In addition, there were so-called "tin makers" (firms that made "inferior" electrical equipment) that would make it a practice to underbid national competition, especially on sealed bid jobs.[70] Rarely would the nonnational firms or the "tin makers" abide by any price agreement.

Further, there was the "problem" of price competition from the foreign firms. They could not be controlled directly, and they were not a part of the price conspiracy; accordingly, their pricing practices made it difficult—if not impossible—to raise, fix and maintain prices on electrical equipment. For example, prices on certain turbogenerators were cut 20 percent when foreign competition entered the market, and meetings to "fix" that particular situation were "unsuccessful . . . quite unnecessary and very foolish."[71] The ability of such meetings to contain price competition under such circumstances was nil.

Price collusion was ineffective in the electrical equipment manufacturers industry, therefore, because demand was unstable, economies of scale were substantial, competitors had different price and profit objectives, honesty and trust were nonexistent, and foreign imports were (increasingly) important. Under such circumstances, a successful price conspiracy would have been nearly impossible. The Justice Department, it appears, with all its legal fuss, fines, and headlines, ended a nearly impotent arrangement.

The general meaning of this chapter should not be misunderstood. It is not being argued here that "price conspiracy" is impossible, or

[68] *Ibid.*, p. 16876.
[69] *Ibid.*, pp. 16693–16694.
[70] *Ibid.*, p. 17472.
[71] *Ibid.*, pp. 16945, 17061.

that such a successful conspiracy might not work an "injury" to the buyers. What is being argued is (1) that the inherent market forces in a free market make most price conspiracies completely unworkable, and (2) that a sampling of the most famous price-fixing antitrust cases in history has revealed that they involved just such unworkable conspiracies.

CHAPTER 8

Price Discrimination in Theory and Practice

ALTHOUGH there is a high degree of unwarranted professional unanimity over the theory and practice of the Sherman Act, Section 2 of the Clayton Act with its Robinson-Patman Act amendments and Federal Trade Commission enforcement enjoys no such unanimity of opinion. Indeed, Section 2 of the Clayton Act has come in for an unusual—yet entirely appropriate—amount of "roasting" from economists, business spokesmen, lawyers, and jurists alike.[1] The point of contention is that Section 2 tends to make vigorous price competition *more difficult* and tends to protect particular competitors, rather than competition. It has been argued that this section of the Clayton Act is, in its own way, an anticompetition law rather than an antitrust one.

The criticism stems, understandably, from the origins of the Clayton and Robinson-Patman acts themselves. Unlike the Sherman Act it is readily admitted that Section 2 of the Clayton Act and its more important Robinson-Patman Act amendments were passed to protect small, independent business firms from the buying and selling practices of larger corporations, particularly large

[1]See, for example, M.A. Adelman, *A&P: A Study in Price-Cost Behavior and Public Policy* (Cambridge, Mass.: Harvard University Press, 1959), pp. 160–161.

chain stores.[2] Large chains, for reasons to be discussed below, were able to buy cheaper and sell cheaper than some of their smaller competitors. The inevitable economic pressure, supposedly, was to force the "independents" out of particular product lines and/or out of business altogether. The independents argued that the price concessions enjoyed by the larger firms were unjustified by any real cost savings. According to the independents, it was "economic power" and not any economies or efficiencies that allowed the chains to be more "competitive." And it was to curb this unreasonable economic power—in the public interest!—that the small business pressure groups pushed through the strong price discrimination law.

THE THEORY OF PRICE DISCRIMINATION

The theoretical objections to price discrimination, like almost all classical antitrust theory, are rooted deep in the market structure approach to pure competition. In pure competition, no seller would have any "monopoly power" and, therefore, no seller would be able to discriminate on the basis of price. With "perfectly elastic" demand functions in the factor and product markets, prices for all "goods of like grade and quality" sold by identical producers to identical buyers would necessarily be identical in equilibrium. Thus, the absence of price discrimination fits in nicely with the preassumed welfare ideal that is pure competition. Presumably that is the foundation of the theory that supports the law.

Pure competition does not fit well with real world competition, however (see Chapter 2). And if pure competition is not a welfare ideal, then neither is a state of zero price discrimination. In fact in a non-purely competitive economic world with heterogeneous sellers and buyers, price differences would be perfectly normal and to be expected. They certainly would not be considered anticompetitive *per se*. Such differences in price might typically be based on the number of units purchased, the distance delivered, the incomes of the buyers, the estimated demand elasticity, the price decisions of other sellers, the degree of product familiarity, and many other factors.[3] Some discriminations might, undoubtedly, be based on "real

[2]The Robinson-Patman Act of 1936 was actually drafted by the U.S. Wholesale Grocers' Association. See Richard Caves, *American Industry: Structure, Conduct, Performance* (2nd ed.; Englewood Cliffs, N.J.: Prentice-Hall, 1967), p. 86.
[3]For a good review of these factors, see Ralph Cassady, Jr., "Techniques and Purposes of Price Discrimination," *Journal of Marketing*, XI (October, 1946), 135–150.

cost differences." But in a non-purely competitive disequilibrium—
the typical selling situation—one would not expect that all discriminations would be related to cost, or that cost differences would be
instantly and fully reflected in price differences. Yet the economic
literature seems heavily biased against all such non-cost justifiable
discriminations, and consistently refers to these price differences as
"noncompetitive."

What is Illegal Price Discrimination?

Section 2 of the Clayton Act as amended makes price discrimination on goods of like grade and quality illegal when the effect would
substantially lessen competition or tend to create a monopoly. Price
discrimination at law means a difference in price.[4] Illegal price discrimination is a price difference that cannot be "justified" on the
basis of a cost savings or one made in "good faith" to meet the lower
price of a competitor.

There are many conceptual difficulties with the theory of a law
making price discrimination illegal. The first serious problem concerns the "threshold" phrase, "of like grade and quality." What goods
are to be classified "of like grade and quality"? Will minute differences in fundamentally "similar" commodities be enough to exempt
application of the price discrimination statute? But who will determine what is minute and what is fundamentally similar? Will firms
successfully avoid prosecution by making marginal adjustments in
"similar" products? Or will the courts interpret such artificial differences as evidence of the fact that the goods are *truly* of like grade
and quality?

Are chemically similar products that sell under different brand
names and different labels to be considered "equal" under the law?
Certainly, the market (buyers) may treat the chemically similar products differently and, hence, in the mind of the buyers they would
not be equivalent products. To assume automatically that physically
identical commodities are of "like grade and quality" would be to
neglect the utilities associated with popular brand names. Yet the
Robinson-Patman Act was probably intended to ignore such "artificial" differentials.[5]

The second difficulty is much more fundamental and has been

---

[4] *Federal Trade Commission* v. *Anheuser-Busch, Inc.*, 363 U.S. 536.
[5] *Federal Trade Commission* v. *Borden*, 383 U.S. (1966), pp. 641–644.

well-documented by many scholars. While the law aims at preventing price discrimination—price differences—from occurring, it enhances what the economist defines as *economic* price discrimination. Economic discrimination is a price differential that does not correspond with a true cost differential. And, therefore, price *identity* when costs actually differ would be economic discrimination. To the extent that the law aims at price uniformity, and particularly price uniformity at some higher price, it tends to promote economic discrimination, especially against the low-cost seller.[6]

Yet the entire conception of economic discrimination has its difficulties as explained above. Here, in its clearest form, is the overwhelmingly accepted economic notion that prices based on "costs," particularly long-run marginal costs, are "competitive" and "just" and, therefore, desirable. While it may be admitted here that there might be a *tendency* under competitive conditions for prices to tend toward cost (especially as additional supplies are channelled to the high-profit margin markets putting pressure on prices) there is no reason to expect prices at any given moment in time to reflect costs. *Prices are determined by demand and not by costs.* All real prices in all real markets are discriminatory; nondiscriminatory prices are reserved for the imaginary competitive equilibrium. Hence, both the law *and* the classical economic theory—to the extent that they condemn "discrimination"—are dealing in competitive fantasy and illusion. They are decrying and condemning a kind of pricing behavior that is natural, normal, and to be expected in a free market.

A third difficulty with the law is that the "cost justification" defense assumes a level of sophistication in cost accounting that has not and never will be attained. Costs, as every economist knows, are difficult to define and harder to measure. There are joint costs and overhead costs that make the precise expenses associated with *particular* outputs almost impossible to determine accurately. As a practical matter, no firm could begin to justify a particular price discrimination on the basis of "marginal savings," especially if the cost savings must just match the price difference. Thus, as will be shown more clearly below, the "cost justification" defense is *not* a defense at all, but only a legal *pretense* at one.

There are certain parts of Section 2 of the Clayton Act where all pretense at a "cost justification" is dropped, and the real meaning of

---

[6]Adelman, *op. cit.*, p. 60.

the price discrimination law is clearly revealed. For example, Section 2 (c) makes price allowances for "brokerage" that an integrated buyer performs illegal *per se*.[7] And a proviso on Section 2 (a) states that certain quantity discounts may be declared "unjustly discriminatory" and, hence, illegal, *even if full cost savings support these price discounts!* It might be noted that here, at last, the price discrimination act is honest concerning its intent to limit price competition and restrain efficiency.

A fourth difficulty with the law is the same one encountered in all Sherman Act cases: definitions of terms. What particular actions shall be interpreted as "substantially lessening competition" or tending to create a monopoly? Will price decreases, for example, that attract *new* customers be "an attempt to monopolize"?[8] Will price decreases that *prevent* competitors from taking business away be considered an "injury" to competition? Will the loss of some undetermined amount of customers, or the *potential* loss of customers be enough to violate the antitrust statute? If so, then the law will tend to preserve the economic status quo rather than promote dynamic competition.

A fifth difficulty surrounds the so-called "good faith" provision, i.e., that prices may legally be lowered to *meet* the prices of a competitor in good faith. But how is a seller to know *ex ante* whether the price he is about to meet is itself a legal discount? To meet an illegal discount is also illegal.[9] Yet unless a seller is able to analyze the cost information of another seller, he can never be sure whether the price discount he is meeting is a "just" price. Such practical difficulties may discourage the likelihood that *any* prices will be cut *at all to anyone.*

And finally, it appears that a strict interpretation of Robinson-Patman would rule out delivered pricing with freight absorption, and all basing point pricing. Imagine a market with different sellers located at different distances from some important group of buyers. To be competitive with customers and the closest potential seller, other sellers would find it necessary to "absorb" freight and handling charges, and charge a price that does not fully reflect "costs." Since

---

[7]". . . brokerage payments are *per se* illegal, even though no injurious or destructive effect on competition has resulted and even though the challenged concession reflected actual savings in the sellers distribution costs." *Federal Trade Commission* v. *Simplicity Patterns Company*, 360 U.S. (1959), p. 55.

[8] *Standard Oil of Indiana* v. *Federal Trade Commission*, 340 U.S. 231 (1951).

[9] See the discussion in *Federal Trade Commission* v. *A.E. Staley Manufacturing Company and Staley Sales Corporation*, 324 U.S. 746 (1945) to be detailed below.

the practice is voluntary, one could assume that the firms find it more profitable to lower prices than to lose the business altogether. The net result of the "competition" is that the buyers are presented with additional alternatives, no customers are considered "safe," and the extent of geographic rivalry is broadened considerably. Large sellers with extremely low production costs can "absorb" freight and compete almost everywhere. The ultimate effect is to extend competitive pressures into all "local" markets.

The Robinson-Patman Act—as might be expected—views the matter differently. Freight "absorption" is a price concession that cannot be cost justified; it is discriminatory *vis-à-vis* buyers located nearer the plant of the seller. While some buyers have costs absorbed others do not. The situation is inequitable since the prices that either buyer pays do not reflect true costs. According to this line of reasoning, only f.o.b. pricing would not be discriminatory.

Nowhere is the clash between "prices should be determined by costs" and "prices are determined by demand" more vividly illustrated. And nowhere is the *trade restraining* effect of Robinson-Patman more obvious and odious. Rigidly enforced, such a prohibition would end free market competition between national firms, and return buyers to the mercy of geographic monopolists.[10] There, indeed, prices would reflect costs with a vengence. The only thing more regrettable is the fact that some economists would actually support such pricing systems.[11]

Imagine a seller who knows that buyer A is a poorer bargainer than buyer B; he cannot legally charge A a higher price if competition might thereby be lessened. Imagine a seller who knows that lower prices to buyer A will produce additional orders, but that lower prices to buyer B will not; he cannot charge A lower prices unless he can demonstrate a "cost savings." Imagine a seller who meets the lower price of a competitor and discovers that "meeting competition in good faith" requires a *price differential* between his product and the product of his competitors; he must, therefore, *raise* price back to the accustomed differential! Imagine a buyer who accepts a discount and discovers *ex post* that it was illegal. Imagine salesmen in the field complaining that they are losing business because they

---

[10]Murray N. Rothbard, *Power and Market* (Menlo Park, Calif.: Institute for Humane Studies, 1970), p. 47.

[11]Clair Wilcox, *Public Policies Toward Business* (3rd ed.; Homewood, Ill.: Richard D. Irwin, 1966), pp. 232–233.

cannot "bargain" rates that differ from uniform book rates without either lowering *all* rates, or determining an exact "cost saving" associated with a particular order. And, finally, imagine an efficiently integrated seller that cannot even use his in-house brokerage activity as a cost justification for offering lower prices. And then ask, again, what the price discrimination statute was designed to preserve and what it was designed to prohibit.

Section 2 of the Clayton Act with its Robinson-Patman Act amendments is simply not intelligible unless it is recognized that it was, indeed, *active price competition* that it meant to end. Like the NRA codes, resale price maintenance, and other anticompetitive statutes, Section 2 was designed to restrict and punish free market competition.[12] Since "discriminations" are created and destroyed endlessly in the open market, and since such "discriminations" are, indeed, the essence of price competition, it must be clear that it was price competition that such "antitrust" statutes attempted to legislate out of existence. That they have failed to end all price competition is due more to modest enforcement levels than to any error of intent.

The following is a selective examination of some price discrimination cases from the hundreds of FTC actions over the last forty years. Hopefully the author has chosen some of the more famous and classic antitrust cases in the area of price discrimination. Classic or not, the cases are meant to be illustrative of the real meaning of the law, the FTC enforcement procedures, the attempted "defenses" by the corporations involved, and the various court interpretations of FTC rulings.

THE CORN PRODUCTS CASE (1945)

One of the first important price discrimination cases involved a firm named Corn Products Refining Company, the largest producer of corn syrup (glucose) in the country in the early 1940s.[13] At that time, the Corn Products Company did an estimated 45 percent of the business in the market, with manufacturing facilities located in Argo, Illinois and Kansas City, Missouri. In addition, seven other companies within a 400-mile radius of Chicago sold syrup in competition with the acknowledged industry leader.

[12]Adelman, *op. cit.*, pp. 53, 177.
[13]*Corn Products Refining Company* v. *Federal Trade Commission*, 324 U.S. 726 (1945).

Between 1940 and 1942, the Federal Trade Commission charged seven of the eight glucose manufacturers—including Corn Products—with illegal price discrimination on sales of glucose to different candy makers, and issued cease and desist orders to end the practice. The discriminations allegedly occurred because the firms all sold on a delivered price basis only, with Chicago as the basing point as far as freight charges were concerned. Syrup sellers with no Chicago-area plants apparently "absorbed" freight to sell competitively to candy makers near Chicago. Syrup sellers with a plant, say, twenty miles from a customer—but a hundred miles from Chicago—apparently charged "phantom freight," since they quoted the base price for glucose plus the Chicago freight rate, yet shipped their syrup from the closer plant. Since the candy makers that bought the glucose in the different areas did not pay prices that reflected "true" costs, price discrimination occurred. And since these different candy makers were intensely competitive with each other, the probable effect of the discrimination was to "injure" competition.

The Lower Court Decision

Two glucose manufacturers, Corn Products and A.E. Staley Manufacturing Company, appealed the FTC cease and desist orders.[14] Corn Products, as already mentioned, had manufacturing plants near Chicago and in Kansas City. The Chicago-area plant had been constructed in 1911; the Kansas City facility was built in 1922. District Court Judge Lindley, hearing the case on appeal, stated the conclusions of the FTC on the original cease and desist order:

> The Commission found that a purchaser located nearer freight-wise to Kansas City than Chicago who receives delivery from Kansas City is forced to pay a price which includes an item for delivery not actually incurred; that Chicago purchasers receiving delivery from Kansas City buy at a price which does not include any freight, artificial or real, and that any purchaser located nearer Chicago than Kansas City who receives delivery from the latter point is charged a price which does not include all of the actual freight. Its ultimate finding was that such discrimination results in substantial injury to petitioner's competitors . . . .[15]

[14] *Corn Products Refining Company* v. *Federal Trade Commission.*, 144 f. 2d 211.
[15] *Ibid.*, p. 214.

The substantial injury stemmed from the fact that candy makers in cities other than Chicago had higher costs of production due to higher glucose prices. Consequently the court reasoned that they would either have to increase their prices for candy—and, thus, be noncompetitive with other sellers—or accept lower profits of manufacture. In either case there would be "injury" and competition would probably be lessened.

> We think it irrefutable from the facts that resulting substantial loss is *reasonably likely* to accrue to purchasers in the less favorably located communities. The statute *does not require proof of actual injury.*[16]

As a final note, the Court stated that "several" candy manufacturers had moved closer to Chicago in an effort to decrease their costs of delivery.[17]

The Supreme Court Decision

In 1945 the Supreme Court agreed in all essential respects with both the FTC findings and the District Court decision. Chief Justice Stone stated that Corn Products' pricing system "inevitably" produced "systematic price discriminations" that "created a favored price zone for the purchasers of glucose in Chicago and vicinity."[18] Such discriminations were "unrelated to any proper element of actual cost" and were, therefore, unjustified. Since glucose—a crucial element in candy making—was cheaper in Chicago, the Chicago based candy manufacturers were "in a better position to compete for business" than the more distant manufacturers.[19] There was a "reasonability probability" that the effect of the discriminations may be to lessen competition substantially.[20] And, again, this reasonable probability was illustrated with the FTC finding that "several" candymakers had moved their factories to Chicago.[21]

The Supreme Court rejected Corn Products' argument that there was no discrimination under the basing point system since all buyers at the *same location* paid the same price. Stone argued that the

[16] *Ibid.*, p. 215 (Emphasis added).
[17] *Ibid.*
[18] 324 U.S. pp. 732, 738.
[19] *Ibid.*, p. 738.
[20] *Ibid.*, p. 739.
[21] *Ibid.*

Robinson-Patman Act had made no specific reference to the fact that the buyers had to be at the same location. And besides "the injury to the competition of purchasers in different localities is no less harmful than if they were in the same city."[22]

The court also rejected Corn Products' argument that Congress had sanctioned delivered pricing and basing points since it had not outlawed them specifically when drafting the price discrimination law. The Congressional action, stated Stone, meant only that "Congress was unwilling to require f.o.b. factory pricing, and thus to make all uniform price systems and all basing point systems illegal *per se.*"[23] Whether any *particular* delivered pricing system was legal or illegal rested, however, on a careful examination of that system in light of Section 2 (a) of the Robinson-Patman Act. Since in this case the FTC had "shown" that there were systematic price discriminations that may tend to lessen competition, the company was violating the statute.

THE STALEY CASE (1945)

The companion Staley case, also decided in 1945, is very similar to the Corn Products case.[24] A.E. Staley Manufacturing, a competitor of Corn Products, had a glucose processing plant at Decatur, Illinois. Like its competitors, Staley sold its glucose on a delivered price basis only with Chicago as the basing point. The Circuit Court of Appeals confirmed the FTC charge that there was evidence to indicate that the pricing system was discriminatory and tended to "substantially lessen competition."[25] But Circuit Judge Minton argued for the majority that Staley Manufacturing had rebutted the *prima facie* case of the FTC when the former had demonstrated that their prices had been made in "good faith" to meet the prices of their competitors.

The basing point system had existed before Staley had come into business in 1920. When Staley began selling glucose, it became apparent "that business could be had only by meeting competitors' prices."[26] Thus, Minton concluded, Staley merely followed a system

[22] *Ibid.,* p. 734.
[23] *Ibid.,* p. 737.
[24] *Federal Trade Commission* v. *A. E. Staley Manufacturing Company,* 324 U.S. p. 746.
[25] *A.E. Staley Manufacturing Company* v. *Federal Trade Commission,* 144 f. 2d p. 221.
[26] *Ibid.,* p. 224

established by its competition; "that this was done in good faith is not questioned in the evidence."[27]

Strong dissents were made by Circuit Judges Evans and Major. Evans argued that there was no evidence that Staley was attempting to justify a *lower* price in good faith. It just adopted an existing system so as not to 'stir up the animals' by starting a price war.[28]

Major, on the other hand, argued just as vigorously that:

> . . . there was no evidence in the record to support the finding that the discrimination shown tended substantially to lessen competition or to create a monoply. I am not convinced that we were in error in this respect. In my view, the basing point system has the opposite effect, that is, it has a tendency to preserve competition and prevent monopoly.[29]

Judge Major was concerned less f.o.b. pricing be forced on the defendants and geographic "competition become a thing of the past," with each manufacturer having "a monopoly of the trade in its own area."[30]

Supreme Court Decision

On the same day that the Supreme Court affirmed the Corn Products decision, it reversed the Staley ruling of the Circuit Court of Appeals. Chief Justice Stone argued that the Robinson-Patman Act's "good faith" provision applied only when a seller's lower *price* was "reduced to meet an equally low *price* of a competitor." According to Stone, the Act placed the "emphasis on individual situations, rather than upon a general system of competition."[31] Since Staley apparently had not lowered any particular price to meet a lower competitive price, but had only "slavishly" followed "their competitor's higher prices" and thereby copied a system which resulted in systematic discriminations, they could not avail themselves of the good faith defense.[32] Further,

> . . . the fact that Staley's prices are *lower than those they might have charged, but never did charge,* does not tend to show the

[27] *Ibid.*, p. 225
[28] *Ibid.*
[29] *Ibid.*, p. 230
[30] *Ibid.*, p. 231
[31] 324 U.S. p. 753 (Emphasis added).
[32] *Ibid.*, p. 754.

establishment of a lower price to meet an equally low price of a competitor.[33]

Hence, the original FTC order against Staley to cease and desist its discriminations was sustained.[34]

Comment on the Corn Products and Staley Decisions

Eugene Singer has summarized two important economic difficulties associated with the Corn Products-Staley decisions.[35] He has noted that candy manufacturers located near Kansas City were not necessarily entitled to cost savings when Corn Products built their new glucose plant there. In the short run, Singer argues that the cost savings and resultant profits should, apparently, have gone to the glucose manufacturer. Further Singer emphasizes that it is difficult to understand how the pricing policies of the glucose manufacturers injured competition among the candymakers. *If* candymakers in Kansas City really competed with Chicago-based candymakers (and the Supreme Court accepted that they did), how were the Kansas City candymakers *any worse off* after the construction of Corn Products' Kansas City facility? Lower prices in Kansas City, or f.o.b. prices at the factory in Kansas City would, of course, have allowed Kansas City-based candymakers to extend their marketing area. But how were they injured now *vis-à-vis* the competitive situation that existed *before* the Kansas City glucose facility was constructed? They were not much better off,[36] but they were no worse off, either. If Kansas City candymakers had wanted to sell primarily in Chicago markets, then they should have located there—and not in Kansas City.

Another difficulty with both decisions is that there was no real proof that there had been any serious injury to competition as a result of the "price discriminations." It is hard to believe or accept the idea that "several" candymakers moving closer to a cheap source of supply, and to a potentially larger market (Chicago), is evidence of a substantial lessening of competition or even of a probable lessening. In fact, a movement by candy firms to Chicago would have increased

---

[33] *Ibid.*, p. 755 (Emphasis added).

[34] *Ibid.*, p. 760.

[35] Eugene M. Singer, *Antitrust Economics* (Englewood Cliffs, N.J.: Prentice-Hall, 1968), pp. 231–232.

[36] To the extent, of course, that they received *faster* deliveries than they would have from Chicago, they were better off.

their ability to sell in Chicago and surrounding markets. It would have lowered their glucose costs under the basing point system, and also lowered their freight charges for candy into Chicago markets. Thus, if anything, one would have expected competition among candymakers to have been intensified rather than lessened.

Actually, the movement to Chicago may have been unrelated to basing point pricing. Corwin Edwards reports that one of the greatest advantages of Chicago based candymakers was their ability to purchase sugar at rates based on *water shipment* and ship candy at pool-car rates quoted from Chicago.[37]

The price discriminations calculated by the FTC and accepted unquestioningly by the Courts in both cases are open to serious question. The FTC calculated "phantom freight" by subtracting the actual freight charge from Kansas City—where the goods were actually shipped from—from the freight charge from Chicago, the basing point, with respect to some delivery point. For example, the actual freight charge to Waco, Texas from Kansas City was 63 cents. Since the freight from Chicago actually charged was 85 cents, candy manufacturers paid 22 cents of "phantom freight." And it was this "price discrimination resulting from this systematic inclusion of the freight differential" that was unlawful.[38]

There are two serious issues here. One issue is the magnitude of the freight "absorptions" *vis-à-vis* the "phantom" charges. Although the court did not determine what percentage of business paid phantom freight and what percentage did not, it appears likely that a great percentage of freight was "absorbed" rather than charged as "phantom." Judge Minton stated, for example, that Staley—whose plant was located at Decatur—sold the "bulk" of its glucose in the Chicago area.[39] This would imply that the bulk of Staley's transportation expenses were probably "absorbed." Although absorbing freight is still price discrimination in the eyes of the law, it is surely much less odious to the economist than phantom freight.

An even more serious issue, however, is the fact that the "phantom freight" calculated above on the shipment to Waco, Texas, *is not correct.* The corn syrup producers enjoyed what are termed "freight in-transit" discounts from the railroads on corn and corn syrup shipped various distances. A "back haul" with glucose on the same

---

[37]Corwin D. Edwards, *The Price Discrimination Law* (Washington: Brookings Institution, 1959), p. 395.
[38]324 U.S. p. 733.
[39]144 F. 2d p. 224.

railroad that delivered raw corn to the glucose manufacturer earned a differential freight charge. Hence, the simple FTC calculations that supported their (preconceived) conclusions, and later grounded the decisions of the Circuit Court and the Supreme Court, can hardly be accurate.[40]

Although the basing point-delivered pricing system might create the impression that there was little price competition, and although some authors have stated that the firms "avoided *all rivalry* in their price quotations,"[41] such was just not the case. In fact, an infrequently mentioned part of the case sustained by the Circuit Court and the Supreme Court against Corn Products, was the fact that the firm sold to "favored customers" at old prices long after "old prices" had been increased.[42] Such "booking practices"—which tend to increase competitive pressures among syrup sellers—were regarded as "discriminatory" by the FTC and the courts, and the firms were subsequently ordered to cease the activity. Thus, although the firms publically quoted identical prices in the same geographic area, the terms of the actual exchange might have varied considerably, at least before 1945.

And, finally, the pricing techniques adopted after the 1945 decisions against Corn Products and Staley were still "discriminatory." Although each glucose maker quoted an f.o.b. mill price, freight was still being absorbed to meet prices in distant markets.[43] Final prices still, therefore, did not relate precisely to "costs," and, presumably, candy makers outside of Chicago were still being "injured" attempting to sell candy in competition with Chicago-based firms. It is certainly questionable whether the post-decision pricing system (with tightened booking practices) was significantly "more competitive" than the pre-decision pricing system.

THE MORTON SALT CASE (1948)

On September 18, 1940, the FTC issued a complaint and a cease and desist order against the Morton Salt Company.[44] The complaint alleged that Morton discriminated in price between different pur-

[40]Frederick M. Rowe, *Price Discrimination Under the Robinson-Patman Act* (Boston: Little, Brown and Company, 1962), p. 379.
[41]Joel B. Dirlam and Alfred E. Kahn, *Fair Competition: The Law and Economics of Antitrust Policy* (New York: Cornell University Press, 1954), p. 126 (Emphasis added).
[42]144 F. 2d p. 223
[43]Edwards, *op. cit.*, pp. 391–395.
[44]*Federal Trade Commission* v. *Morton Salt Company*, 334 U.S. p. 37.

chasers of its Blue Label table salt, and that the effect of the discrimination "has been and may be substantially to lessen competition . . . and to injure, destroy and prevent competition between those purchasers receiving the benefit of said discriminatory prices and those to whom they are denied. . . ."[45]

The "discriminatory" prices were a necessary consequence of Morton's volume discount system. As far back as 1922, Morton—like its closest competitors—had granted remittances or rebates to those customers that met particular quantity requirements for salt during the year. Buyers, for example, that bought in less-than-carload lots paid a delivered price of $1.60 per case; the price paid for carload lot purchases was $1.50 per case. In addition, customers that bought as many as 5,000 cases or more paid $1.40 per case, while an additional five-cent discount was available to those customers that bought 50,000 cases or more in any consecutive twelve-month period.

Buyers using this volume discount system could be small single purchasers, wholesalers, or groups of small retailers or wholesalers that combined their salt purchases to take advantage of the cost savings on large volumes. Morton Salt encouraged "combine selling" and "pool car arrangements" and, as a result, few buyers actually paid the highest ($1.60) delivered price for Blue Label salt.[46] As a final point, there were four large chain stores (American Stores Company, National Tea Company, Safeway Stores, Inc., A&P Company) that obtained the lowest rate ($1.35) since they purchased 50,000 or more cases of salt from Morton.

The FTC first charged that Morton Salt's discounts discriminated against certain wholesalers since they

> . . . must either sell at competitive prices and in so doing reduce their possible profits which they might reasonably obtain by the amount of the discriminations against them, or attempt to sell at higher prices than the favored customers of respondent charge for the same product, with the result of inability to secure business and a reduction in the volume of their sales.[47]

In addition the discounts "injured" small retailers in competition with large chain stores since they forced "retail customers of such

---

[45]39 F.T.C. p. 39.

[46]The Supreme Court would admit that "less than $1/10$ of 1 percent" of all salt sold was *not* sold at some discount. See 334 U.S. p. 60.

[47]39 F.T.C. p. 43.

wholesalers to pay prices which *prohibit competition in price* between such small retailers and the large retail chain stores."[48] For
these reasons, the Morton Salt Company was ordered to cease and
desist "discriminating directly or indirectly in the price of such products of like grade and quality as among wholesale or retail dealers
purchasing said salt when the differences in price are not justified by
differences in the cost of manufacture, sale, or delivery...."[49] Morton
had offered a "cost defense," but it had been struck down by an FTC
trial examiner because it was, supposedly, based on "estimates, hypothesis, or mere guesses" and not on facts.[50]

Circuit Court Decision

The Circuit Court of Appeals reviewed, and reversed, the FTC
order against Morton Salt.[51] Judge Briggle (with whom Judge Sparks
concurred) first noted that Morton's discounts were open and available to all on equal terms. There were no secret, personal, or special
discounts to favored customers. In this way, Briggle explained, the
discounts conformed with the normal trade practices of many other
producers and sellers of staple merchandise. If Morton's quantity
discounts were inherently discriminatory, then such illegal discrimination was also inherent in the selling practices of many other
firms.[52]

The judge then sought to distinguish between illegal price discrimination and "harmless differentiation." Drawing "any distinction" produces "discrimination," but the kind of discrimination
outlawed by Section 2 must be unfair, injurious and prejudicial.[53]
Since not all price distinctions "inherently import an adverse effect
upon competition" and since "injury or threat of injury is not infera-
ble from the price structure alone," Judge Briggle argued that the
FTC would have had to prove that the price discriminations were
likely to cause injury forbidden by the law.[54] But this, he concluded,
they had not done.

[48] *Ibid.*, p. 44 (Emphasis added).
[49] *Ibid.*, p. 45.
[50] For a detailed review of Morton's "cost defense," see Herbert F. Taggard, *Cost Justification* (Ann Arbor: University of Michigan School of Business Administration, 1959), pp. 171–185.
[51] *Morton Salt Company* v. *Federal Trade Commission*, 162 F. 2d 949.
[52] *Ibid.*, p. 953.
[53] *Ibid.*, p. 954–955.
[54] *Ibid.*, p. 955.

The FTC had interrogated witnesses as to whether their business would be affected if they had to pay higher prices for Morton's salt than their larger competitors. Fifty-one witnesses were so questioned, and 32 thought that their business *might* be affected. But having one's business "affected" was not enough to infer competitive injury. To quote Judge Briggle:

> Twenty-nine (some of the 32 included) observed that while the competitor enjoying the discount might have an opportunity *to make more profit, there would be no effect on competition,* if, as the record demonstrates to be the fact, the discount was not used to reduce the sale price of the product. This had not occurred in the past.
>
> Any businessman would readily admit that to some degree the price paid by a competitor for a product sold by him affects his business . . . This does not inferentially establish that the competitive position of either of them is being or may be injured, or that competition in the wholesale or retail business in the same line of commerce in general is being or may be injured or that the price differentials in question actually affect or may affect the competitive re-sale fluctuations in the trade.[55]

Contrary to the inferences drawn by the FTC, the judge noted that the evidence in the case demonstrated substantial *increases* in sales of salt to all nondiscount customers.[56] Hence, the actual facts in the case rebutted the FTC suppositions, and rendered "wholly insufficient" the hypothesis of injury or probable injury to competition.[57]

As a final point, Briggle turned to the troublesome issue of whether Morton Salt's volume discounts were related to actual cost differentials. According to the judge, the quantity carload discounts were related by "substantial and uncontroverted evidence to the cost of the sale and delivery of petitioner's product."[58] The other discounts may have been cost related, but it was not up to Morton Salt to have to prove such a relationship. Since Briggle had already deduced that there was no evidence that Morton's prices were "inherently discriminatory," or that they tended to injure competition or even competitors, no cost defense was necessary. As he so curtly put the issue: "One does not justify an

[55] *Ibid.*, p. 956 (Emphasis added).
[56] *Ibid.*, p. 957.
[57] *Ibid.*
[58] *Ibid.*

act which is harmless, inoffensive and legal."[59] The FTC complaint and order against Morton Salt was, therefore, dismissed.

Circuit Judge Minton dissented, arguing that the quantity discounts were discriminatory *per se*, and illegal when the effect *may be* substantially to lessen competition.

> It does *not* have to be shown, and therefore found by the Commission, that such discriminations actually lessened competition. It is sufficient if it is found that there is a *reasonable possibility* that the discriminatory acts "may" have such an effect.[60]

Since the "expert judgement" of the commission had found such a reasonable possibility, Judge Minton thought that the FTC order against Morton Salt should have been sustained.

Supreme Court Decision

A majority of the Supreme Court agreed with Judge Minton's argument and reversed the Circuit Court decision in 1948. They declared that Morton's quantity discounts did result in "price differentials between competing purchasers" and that it was "obvious" and "self-evident" that the competitive opportunities of certain merchants were injured when they had to pay more for salt than their competitors.[61] And since Morton could not demonstrate that the "full amount of the discount was based on . . . actual savings in cost," the discounts were illegally discriminatory.

The court also noted that while Morton Salt's discounts on volume were "theoretically" open and available to all, "functionally" they were not, since no small retailer could purchase at the 50,000 case rate. The implication here, apparently, was that a discount system which purposely "excluded" all but the very large firms from the biggest discount savings was not, in fact, "open and available to all."

Finally (and embarassingly), the court stressed the fact that the Congressional intent of the Robinson-Patman Act was "with protecting small business which were unable to buy in quantities, such as the merchants here who purchased in less-than-carload lots."[62] Since it

[59] *Ibid.*
[60] *Ibid.*, p. 959 (Emphasis added).
[61] 334 U.S. p. 47, 50.
[62] *Ibid.*, p. 49.

was an "evil" that large buyers could secure competitive advantages based only on their purchasing ability, the court ruled that Morton had indeed violated the law regarding price discrimination.[63]

Justices Jackson and Frankfurter dissented *in part* with the majority's interpretation. They argued that the law had always required a "reasonable probability" of injury to competition, rather than a "reasonable *possibility*" as the majority had accepted. "Possibility" was simply to "slender a thread of inference" and the justices felt that it could easily be "translated into a rule which is fatal to *any discount the Commission sees fit to attack.*"[64]

> The law in this case, in a nutshell, is that no quantity discount is valid if the Commission chooses to say it is not. That is not the law which Congress enacted and which this Court has uniformly stated until today.[65]

It was also argued that a distinction should have been made between the discounts condemned by the majority. The 10- and 15-cent discounts to the large purchasers *vis-à-vis* the smaller merchants inevitably accelerated the trend "toward monopoly" (!); it was correct, therefore, that the majority had condemned these. But the 10-cent carload differentials *vis-à-vis* the noncarload purchasers probably did not tend to reduce competition substantially. Since these latter discounts did relate generally to handling and delivery expenses, and since only about one-tenth of 1 percent of Morton's shipments did not contain them, Justices Jackson and Frankfurter thought that they should have been allowed. As a clincher, they maintained (rather unconvincingly) that Morton might have to *raise* prices to its carload customers to eliminate the illegal discrimination.[66]

Comment on the Morton Salt Decision

The Morton Salt decision confirms the suspicion that FTC rulings and Supreme Court "analyses" are made in a kind of misty wonderland, where everything is, apparently, not what it seems. Morton had used a quantity discount system for almost twenty

[63] *Ibid.*, p. 43.
[64] *Ibid.*, p. 58 (Emphasis added).
[65] *Ibid.*
[66] *Ibid.*, pp. 59–61.

years. Surely, if there were "substantial reductions of competition" inherent in such a pricing system, they would have surfaced well before the trials. Yet, as the lower court had underscored, sales of salt to the nondiscount customers had *increased* throughout the period. Even so, the Supreme Court *declared* that it was "self evident" that the "possibility" of such competitive reductions in the future still existed!

But where was one to look for the possible injury to competition, or, more honestly, to "competitors"? Was the fact that the profits or sales of particular wholesalers might be "affected" enough to signify "possible" injury? But why should the government and the courts attempt to preserve particular profit positions for particular competitors when the free market and free competition tended to reduce them? Were any wholesalers or retailers actually driven from the market? Apparently not, but they did not have to be. The mere possibility that they might have their profits or sales influenced by Morton's discount system was quite enough to infer a violation of the law.

Throughout its decision, the Supreme Court tried to convey the impression that the small merchant purchasing salt with no discount, at $1.60 per case, somehow had to compete with firms such as A&P that could purchase salt at $1.35 per case. Actually, as has already been indicated, less than $1/10$ of 1 percent of all salt sold was sold at less than carload lot prices. Thousands of retailers bought through wholesalers that bought 5,000 cases or more and, therefore, enjoyed the $1.40 price per case. The National Retail-Owned Grocers, Inc., for example, with 18,917 retail store members, bought Morton Blue Label salt at $1.40 per case. In the preponderant number of competitive situations, therefore, the cost differential might have been no more than five cents per case or one-fifth of a cent per package. It is impossible to accept the inference that such a discrimination *might* have had any substantial effect upon competition. The evidence in the case bears out the fact that it *did not* have any substantial effect. Thus, the court's statement that it was "almost inevitable" that the discounts would accelerate the trend "toward monopoly" is insulting and absurd.[67]

While the Supreme Court spent little time analyzing "costs," and

[67] *Ibid.*, p. 60.

while Morton's "cost defense" had failed to satisfy the FTC, there was evidence introduced to indicate that there were cost savings associated with the large discount buyers.[68] The savings were directly related to the size of the delivery order and to the fact that there was no "merchandising expense" associated with the largest purchases. Only Morton's ineptly prepared case prevented these real savings from "justifying" their discounts.

Even, of course, if there were no cost advantages associated with the largest customers, the discounts might still have made excellent economic sense. These were *extremely* large orders and Morton could ill afford to lose them. Thus, whether the cost savings precisely covered the discounts was irrelevant; Morton did what it had to in order to secure or retain business that was a substantial percentage of its total volume. Else, why grant any discount at all? If Morton Salt might have done the same volume of business at a nickel *more* a case, why didn't it? Certainly a court order was not necessary to get a firm to *raise* its price—and stop discriminating—when it would have been profitable to do so.

The Morton Salt case confirms the idea expressed in the beginning of this chapter that the Robinson-Patman Act's major purpose was to make price competition and price reductions more difficult. It also substantiates the opinion that the so-called "cost defense" is no defense at all, but is provided only to create the impression that "legitimate" discounts can somehow be distinguished from "illegitimate" ones.

FTC HOSTILITY TO PRICE COMPETITION

The FTC's open hostility to effective price competition—in the name of *saving* competition—has continued to the present day. In many instances the courts have set aside the more ludicrous FTC orders; in some instances they have not. In the Minneapolis-Honeywell case, for example, the FTC held—contrary to the trial examiner's findings—that Minneapolis-Honeywell had tended to reduce competition substantially in the selling of oil burner controls by discriminating in prices to certain oil burner manufacturers. The Circuit Court of Appeals rejected the FTC's case and upheld Honeywell's right to *reduce* prices in an attempt to gain back a declining market share.[69]

[68]Taggard, *op. cit.*, pp. 171–176.
[69] *Minneapolis-Honeywell Regulator Company* v. *Federal Trade Commission*, 191 F. 2d 786 (1951).

Standard Oil of Indiana Cases (1951, 1958)

In the Standard Oil of Indiana cases, the FTC held—contrary to the trial examiner's findings—that *lowering* prices in good faith to meet competition was "immaterial" if such discounts were potentially injurious to competition, i.e., other competitors. Standard Oil had granted one-and-a-half cents per gallon discounts to four jobbers that sold some gasoline at retail in competition with other retail stations that did not receive jobber discounts. Standard had offered an elaborate cost defense[70]—which the FTC rejected— and had argued further that the jobber discounts were necessary to meet rival competition. In 1951, the Supreme Court rejected the FTC version of the "meeting competition" defense,[71] and in 1958 it rejected the FTC rebuttal that the prices Standard Oil was attempting to "meet" were illegal.[72]

Sun Oil Case (1963)

In 1963, the Supreme Court found in favor of the FTC and rejected Sun Oil Company's argument that it had legally *reduced* prices to a particular dealer that was itself attempting to meet competition at the retail level.[73] Such price discrimination, argued the court, was likely to injure other Sunoco dealers that did not receive the Sun Oil discount,[74] and might also injure *independent* petroleum suppliers that might be "the only meaningful source of price competition offered the 'major' oil companies, of which Sun is one."[75] Thus, unfortunately, the FTC's continuing hostility to competition, and especially to the "meeting competition in good faith" provision, was sustained in this case.[76] For a final, and extensive examination of the FTC's hostility to free market competition, we turn to the classic Borden case presented below.

---

[70]Taggard, *op. cit.*, pp. 187–236.
[71]*Standard Oil of Indiana v. Federal Trade Commission*, 340 U.S. 231.
[72]*Federal Trade Commission v. Standard Oil of Indiana*, 355 U.S. 396.
[73]*Sun Oil Company v. Federal Trade Commission*, 371 U.S. 505.
[74]*Ibid.*, p. 519.
[75]*Ibid.*, p. 523.
[76]In 1957, a majority of the FTC commissioners urged the Congress to enact a law that would set aside the right to "meet" a competitor's price under Robinson-Patman!! See C. Lowell Mason, *The Language of Dissent* (New Cannan, Conn.: Long House, 1961), p. 117.

THE BORDEN CASE (1966)

In April, 1958, the Federal Trade Commission issued a complaint against the Borden Company.[77] Borden was accused of selling goods of like grade and quality to different buyers at different prices with the effect that such selling might reduce competition substantially. The goods of "like grade and quality" were Borden's own brand of evaporated milk and some "identical" milk that it made and sold under private label. The price differences between the two milks were substantial.[78] The FTC charged that it was this price difference that violated the Robinson-Patman Act.

The Hearing Examiner's Decision

The hearing examiner for the FTC, Abner E. Lipscomb, offered the initial decision on the complaint in December 1961. Although Lipscomb admitted that there was a decided consumer preference for Borden's evaporated milk vis-à-vis the private brands Borden also made, he argued that this did not tend to prove that "Borden brand and Borden's private label brands are of a different grade or quality of evaporated milk."[79] The raw milk was the same, was all processed in exactly the same manner, and was put into identical cans; "no magic of the market-place thereafter" could change those facts. The different labels that were then affixed, and the different prices that Borden charged did not change the fact that the milk was of "like grade and quality." And since there were different prices for goods of like grade and quality there was prima facie price discrimination within the intent and meaning of antitrust laws.

But had the price discriminations caused a substantial lessening of competition? The hearing examiner explained that Borden had first begun selling private labeled milk as early as 1938. In May, 1957, Borden had been approached by three "orphaned" customers of another creamery that had gone out of business, and they had requested that Borden "pack" milk for them under their private label. Borden agreed and offered them and subsequent customers open and comparable terms.

The evidence shows that all of these new private-label purchasers came to the respondent of their own accord, and were

[77] In the Matter of The Borden Company, 62 F.T.C. 130.
[78] Ibid., p. 132.
[79] Ibid., p. 139.

not solicited by the respondent; that respondent dealt with them in the same manner in which it had dealt with its previous private label customers; and that respondent made no distinction between large and small accounts. Respondent's private label prices were in each instance determined by the use of its cost-plus pricing formula.[80]

It was at this point in the decision that Lipscomb reported that seven small canners of evaporated milk had testified in support of the complaint against the Borden Company. They argued that Borden's willingness to expand its private-label business had "placed severe competitive pressure on the entire unadvertised brand of private label milk structure and that has . . . largely been felt in the way of *lowered market price*."[81] Some of the testifying canners had lost business directly to Borden; some had not. Some were selling more cases of evaporated milk in 1957 than they had been selling in 1950; some were not.[82] But the competition in the market had definitely *increased*, and the small canners did not like that fact one bit. As one witness complained:

The competition has forced our prices down from the level we had previous to that and some of the competition has been selling on a different basis. On an f.o.b. basis and it is made highly competitive because of those factors[83]

The counsel supporting the price discrimination complaint against the Borden Company had argued that there were three factors that Borden employed to restrain trade: 1) Borden's size; 2) the location of Borden's plants; 3) the consequent ability ("power") of Borden to sell its private label milk f.o.b. Borden's size was an important factor in selling because some small canners could not handle the entire business of big potential customers such as Winn-Dixie. Its convenient plant locations were also a factor since Borden sold f.o.b. The FTC examiner estimated that Borden had a clear freight advantage in approximately 86 percent of the new business that it had acquired from its Midwestern competitors.[84] Thus, the advantages that free competition tends to pass along to buyers were the prime factors,

[80] *Ibid.*, p. 143.
[81] *Ibid.*, p. 145 (Emphasis added).
[82] *Ibid.*, pp. 145–149.
[83] *Ibid.*, p. 145.
[84] *Ibid.*, p. 150.

according to council, that "effectively foreclosed the independent packer group from selling to certain of the most desirable private label accounts. . . ."[85] Borden was being accused of possessing and employing the very economic virtues that are the hallmark of the private, competitive market system.

The hearing examiner would not buy the argument that the inherent economies employed by Borden were bad for competition and, hence, had to be condemned. It is best to quote his full statement in this respect:

> These competitive advantages which council supporting the complaint would have us condemn as unlawful are the accumulated benefits of that private initiative, industry and business acumen which our system of free enterprise is designed to foster and reward.
>
> If a supplier is to be penalized because its size enables it to negotiate and fulfill contracts for a product in larger amounts than its competitors can produce, then the efficient conduct of a business, and its resultant growth have become legal detriments.
>
> If a supplier be forbidden to pass on to its customers a saving in transportation costs, made possible by the fact that its plant is more advantageously located than those of its competitors, then the supplier is, in effect, required to add to its selling price a 'phantom freight'—a charge equal to the difference between its cost of transportation and that of its less conveniently located competitors.
>
> Furthermore, if a supplier is to be penalized for selling its product at a lower price f.o.b. its plant, instead of adding thereto the cost of transportation to the customer's plant and selling at a higher delivered price, the supplier's right to conduct its business in the manner it deems most practical is abrogated and its customers are thereby deprived of the legitimate saving in cost which they might otherwise obtain by electing to take delivery at the suppliers plant. Such an edict would injure both the respondent and its customers, by depriving them of what would appear to be a basic right of free business enterprise.
>
> We conclude that the above-described contentions are beyond both the allegations of the complaint and the theory upon which it is predicated. We conclude further that all the above

[85] *Ibid.*, p. 151.

factors, whether considered separately or collectively, constitute lawful commercial advantages of the corporate respondent. Furthermore, we conclude that respondent has made only
lawful use of such lawful advantages, and that the resulting
effect upon the sales of its Midwest competitors has been only
that of the normal give-and-take of healthy competition inherent in the free-enterprise system. Such competition is not unlawful.[86]

The examiner also concluded that the price discrimination had not
substantially lessened competition between wholesale customers or
retail customers of Borden, nor was "there any reasonable probability of such danger to competition in the future."[87]

The hearing examiner then turned to a cost analysis prepared for
Borden by the accounting firm of Haskins & Sells.[88] The analysis
demonstrated to Lipscomb's satisfaction that the lower costs of selling private label milk justified the lower prices charged by Borden
for that milk; in fact the lower costs *more than justified* the price
discrimination.[89] The average cost per case of private label milk was
cheaper because the labels and cartons were cheaper, the freight
charges were nonexistent (Borden sold its private label f.o.b.), there
were no consignment storage fees, advertising expenses or brokerage fees, and the clerical charges were significantly smaller than
Borden's own evaporated milk. In short, once the milk was packed
and labeled for private-brand customers, Borden's responsibility—
and expenses—ended. This was demonstrably *not* the case with its
own nationally branded milk. One would, therefore, have expected
"cost savings" on the former sales, and they were demonstrated to
the hearing examiner's satisfaction.

The examiner next turned to a rebuttal criticism of Borden's cost
defense by a Melvin C. Steele, who had offered a two-plant cost study
allegedly showing that Borden's cost savings could not justify the
price concession they granted. It was noted that his study was not
itself a "correct" cost study(!), but was simply an attempt to show
"distortions" in Borden's own case. The hearing examiner tersely
rejected the criticism:

[86] *Ibid.*, p. 152.
[87] *Ibid.*, p. 155.
[88] Herbert Taggard, professor of accounting at the University of Michigan, served
as advisor in the preparation of the cost analysis. See *Ibid.*, p. 156.
[89] *Ibid.*, p. 159.

The two-plant study presented by council supporting the complaint does, as they suggest, show a distortion, but we believe that the distortion is in the two-plant study itself.[90]

Lipscomb then declared that Borden's cost analysis constituted "full justification" for the price differentials, and ordered the entire complaint dismissed.[91]

The FTC Decision

On November 28, 1962, the Federal Trade Commission[92] *reversed* the hearing examiner's decision and ordered Borden to cease price discriminating on goods of like grade and quality sold to different buyers at different prices. Borden was given sixty days to file a report detailing the manner and form in which it would comply with the cease and desist order.[93]

The FTC decision written by Commissioner Dixon is almost embarrassing to read because of its unbridled sentimentality and confused equivocations. To say that the decision does not accurately relate the facts and logic of the Borden case is to grossly understate the issue.

The implication throughout the Dixon statement is that Borden, because it is a multi-product, larger firm with "broad resources," could and did employ its vast "prestige and power in the market" to the economic detriment of its smaller, "precarious" rivals.[94] The evidence and analysis offered by the hearing examiner that *this was not so, had not happened, and was unlikely to happen* was totally ignored. The fact that Borden's share of the market had climbed less than 1 percent during the period under consideration (9.9 percent to 10.7 percent) was also, apparently, irrelevant. The fact that most (86 percent) of Borden's new business was probably gained because of legitimate freight advantages and the proximity of Borden's plants was summarily rejected as "isolated examples" that proved nothing![95]

It was somehow relevant, however, that a number of companies

[90] *Ibid.*, p. 161.
[91] *Ibid.*, p. 165.
[92] Two members did not participate, and one dissented; thus, only two of the five members concurred in the decision.
[93] *Ibid.*, p. 193.
[94] *Ibid.*, p. 174.
[95] *Ibid.*

had gone out of the evaporated milk business during the 1950s. No argument was offered to indicate that Borden had helped close them out. In fact, a few of the creameries had ceased doing business well before May, 1957, when Borden had begun first to acquire additional private label business. The companies were just listed by Dixon, and the implication was that in some undefined and, perhaps, undefinable way, Borden must have been implicated in their demise.[96] Then after being told for the third time that Borden was a large and "powerful" concern, and that its competitors were small and "precarious," Dixon abruptly concluded:

> In this market setting, respondent's price discrimination is a clear threat to the entire competition provided by the Midwest concerns. If the price discrimination is continued, the elimination or the serious impairment of competition from small competitors in the industry is likely. This is enough to satisfy the injury requirement of the Act.[97]

As a final point, and almost as an afterthought, Borden's extensively prepared and previously accepted cost defense was *declared* to be "inadequate and unacceptable."[98] Without debate or comment, Dixon simply stated that "broad averaging" and the inclusion of investment costs and brokerage costs in the cost defense was completely unacceptable—period! Thus, with no new facts introduced, and no careful analytical rebuttal of the hearing examiner's findings and conclusions even attempted, the Federal Trade Commission issued a cease and desist order against the Borden Company.

Circuit Court Decision

On December 4, 1964, a Circuit Court of Appeals dismissed the FTC's cease and desist order against the Borden Company.[99] Reviewing the "undisputed facts" in the case, Circuit Judge Joseph C. Hutcheson, Jr. argued that the first issue was whether the commission "applied the correct legal test in deciding that the commodities sold at different prices were of 'like grade and quality.' "[100]

Judge Hutcheson indicated that the record clearly showed that

[96] *Ibid.*, p. 187.
[97] *Ibid.*, p. 190.
[98] *Ibid.*, p. 192.
[99] *The Borden Company* v. *Federal Trade Commission*, 339 F. 2d 133.
[100] *Ibid.*, p. 135.

Borden's own brand of evaporated milk *did* command a premium price in the market, and that the Borden product was recognized as a premium product by both consumers and dealers who sold evaporated milk. To support these conclusions, the court quoted the testimony of grocers that had stated that consumers asked for the Borden brand by name, and could not be convinced to accept some other brand. Significant price differentials had to exist, apparently, before dealers would even stock and sell the other brands.[101] That dealers continued to purchase both products at the different prices indicated to the court that one was a "premium line" and one was not.

But was the "demonstrated consumer preference" for the Borden brand to receive *legal* recognition? The Circuit Court thought that it should. Contrary to what the FTC had declared, there was no clear Congressional intent on the matter of "private brands" and price discrimination. In fact, if the intent of the Robinson-Patman Act and the rest of the antitrust statutes generally was to avoid price rigidity and price uniformity, than "commercial factors" had to be considered in pricing.

> An established brand name may have a large following among purchasers. This fact can be of great economic significance in a competitive market. We do not believe it was the intention of Congress that such clearly demonstrable consumer preference should simply be ignored in determining when products may be priced differently. As a practical matter, such preferences may be far more significant in determining the market value of a product than are its physical characteristics.[102]

There was also, according to Hutcheson, no clear court precedent on the matter. The five cases cited by the FTC to support their argument were not at all comparable to the Borden controversy.

> In none of those cases was there any showing that the purchasers paying the higher prices received brand-name products which readily commanded a premium price in the market, while the purchasers paying the lower prices did not. The brand names were not shown to have any effect on the ultimate price the products could command. Here the Borden brand label was clearly of commercial significance. At all levels of distribution it imparted a premium market value to the Borden product which the private label product did not enjoy. That the

[101] *Ibid.*, p. 136.
[102] *Ibid.*, p. 137.

Borden brand product should sell for a higher price than the lesser known private brands came as no surprise to anyone.[103]

Thus, since the commercial value of the Borden brand had clearly been demonstrated, the Court argued that Borden "should be allowed to take it into account in pricing its products."[104] The FTC order against Borden was set aside.

Supreme Court Decision

The Supreme Court, with Justice White delivering the opinion, reversed the Circuit Court of Appeals decision on the issue of "like grade and quality," and remanded the Borden case back to that court so that the remaining matters might be decided.[105] The argument to reverse was a virtual replay of the FTC statements, i.e., that the products under discussion were *chemically the same,* and that the Congressional intent had been to treat national brands and private brands alike if they were chemically the same.[106]

In addition, the Supreme Court hypothesized that *if* a manufacturer sold his branded, higher-priced milk to a retailer, but refused to sell the private label brand to him, then the . . .

> . . . retailer who was permitted to buy and sell only the more expensive brand would have no chance to see to those who always buy the cheaper product or to convince others, by experience or otherwise, of the fact which he and all other dealers already know—that the cheaper product is actually identical with that carrying the more expensive label.[107]

What this particular hypothesis had to do with the Borden Company —which had *never* been charged with such conduct or even the possibility of it—was never explained!

There was a sharply worded dissent in the Borden case written by Justice Stewart, with whom Justice Harlan joined. Justice Stewart argued, *à la* the Circuit Court of Appeals and Edward Chamberlin's *The Theory of Monopolistic Competition,* that goods were not of like grade and quality if consumer preference demonstrated that they were not.[108] Stewart was impressed by the fact that Borden took

[103] *Ibid.*
[104] *Ibid.*, p. 138.
[105] *Federal Trade Commission* v. *The Borden Company,* 383 U.S. 637 (1966).
[106] *Ibid.*, pp. 640–644.
[107] *Ibid.*, p. 644.
[108] *Ibid.*, p. 649.

extra precautions with its own branded product such that a "flawed product" did not reach the consumer; no such precautions were taken with the private brand.[109] To ignore what the majority of the Supreme Court had termed "intangibles," was to ignore the obvious market determination that the products were indeed different, and not to be considered of like grade and quality. And even *if* a relevant "cost determination" could be made,

> . . . the cost ratio between Borden's premium and private label products is hardly the most significant factor in Borden's pricing decision and market return on those products.[110]

Here at last, the inherent conflict between "costs determine prices" and "prices are determined by demand" was made explicit. But, of course, this was a minority opinion endorsed by only two members of the Supreme Court.

Finally, Stewart argued that the supposed threat to competition was unclear. Since there had been *no* allegation that Borden had used its position in "the premium brand market to subsidize predatory price-cutting campaigns in the private label market," and since the consumer of the private brand had been shown to be different from the consumer of the premium brand, "conventional notions of price discrimination under the Robinson-Patman Act may not be applicable."[111] Rather disgustedly the justice concluded:

> In the guise of protecting producers and purchasers from discriminatory price competition, the Court ignores legitimate market preferences and endows the Federal Trade Commission with authority to disrupt price relationships between products whose identity has been measured in the laboratory but rejected in the marketplace. I do not believe that any such power was conferred upon the Commission by Congress . . .[112]

Comment on the Borden Controversy

In many important and embarrassing ways, the Borden controversy is a fitting climax—a climax of absurdity—with respect to price discrimination under the antitrust laws. It is the theoretical dead end

[109] *Ibid.*, p. 651.
[110] *Ibid.*, p. 659.
[111] *Ibid.*, p. 660.
[112] *Ibid.*, p. 662.

to which the mechanistic, demand-ignoring "costs determine prices" theorem can be pushed. The products under discussion were clearly distinguished in the mind, and market actions, of the consumers; the products did not really compete with each other; the products had different brand names, sold in different ways and at different prices to different buyers. Yet they were *declared* by an "expert" regulatory commission and by the highest court in the land to be "equal" and "of like grade and quality." *Declaring it*, apparently, *would make it so.*

What was the Borden Company to do under the circumstances? Were they to adulterate the production of private brand evaporated milk (!) in order to make it "chemically unequal"? Or were they to *raise* the price of the private label milk to the Borden brand "equivalent"? The latter proposal would surely end the alleged "discrimination," although it would also likely bring a huge loss in sales to the Borden Company on its private label accounts. Of course they could *lower* the price of the Borden brand to the private label rates; but this action would surely bring the Justice Department down upon Borden again for attempting to "drive competition from the market"! One would also have to assume, since Borden had not adopted this policy, that such a reduction in price would lower rather than increase Borden's profits. In summation, therefore, Borden was illegally discriminating in price, and *no change in their prices could have*, it appears, *been wholly consistent with the wholly inconsistent antitrust laws.* Any change Borden might have made—other than giving up its private label business altogether—might have tended to "injure" someone in violation of the law.

But what of the supposed reductions in competition in this case; where exactly were they? How precisely was competition being injured? Are we to accept the idea (that the FTC hearing examiner could *not* accept) that there is "injury to competition" within the meaning of the law whenever a firm with production and locational advantages decides to pass along these advantages to buyers? It should be apparent by now that with or without the alleged "price discrimination," the essence of the FTC complaint actually is that Borden's prices for private label milk were attractive enough to draw some business from some smaller rivals. That is what the FTC really objected to. If Borden never sold another ounce of its own brand evaporated milk, the effect of its low prices for private brand milk on "competition" would still have concerned the FTC and the Justice

Department. The price discrimination charge, therefore, was a sham and an absurdity from beginning to end.

Now, finally, what of "cost justification"? If Borden's elaborate defense was unacceptable, then any "defense" can be declared unacceptable. Borden demonstrated beyond a shadow of a reasonable doubt that the costs associated with private brand business were proportional to the prices charged. Herbert Taggard, chairman of the FTC's own Advisory Committee on Cost Justification, had advised in the preparation of the Borden document, and the FTC hearing examiner had analyzed and accepted the report as a "complete justification." Yet the FTC rejected it as "inadequate" without proof, and the courts remained silent on the entire question. Such is the nightmare of antitrust in the public interest under Section 2 of the Clayton Act.[113]

Conclusions on Price Discrimination

Many learned commentators have recognized the economic nonsense inherent in Section 2 of the Clayton Act as amended, and have called for dramatic revisions of the intent and language of the law. The recent "Neal Report,"[114] for example, has suggested that the law be extensively rewritten such that only *substantial* and *persistent* price discriminations be made unlawful, and only when the discrimination had *particular* effects on competition, not competitors. It also would ease the burden of the "cost defense" and do away completely with the competitive-reducing prohibitions on "brokerage" and other services. The companion "Stigler Report"[115] was equally critical although less explicit on proposed changes.

Unhappily, such reports are almost beside the point. Congress has been unmoved by such criticism and is unlikely to revise anything in the Clayton or Robinson-Patman acts. And the reason is perfectly clear. The nightmare that is Robinson-Patman is working out *exactly* as it was designed to back in 1936 when the amendments were

---

[113]As an optimistic postscript to the Borden ordeal, the Circuit Court of Appeals again considered, and again dismissed, the FTC cease and desist order against Borden. It found that "the record does not contain substantial injury to competition at the seller's level." See *The Borden Company* v. *Federal Trade Commission*, 381 F. 2d 175 (1967) especially p. 179. Hopefully the outrage against the Borden Company was over.

[114]Reprinted in BNA *Antitrust and Trade Regulation Report*, No. 411, May 27, 1969, Part 11.

[115]Reprinted in BNA *Antitrust and Trade Regulation Report*, No. 413, June 10, 1969, pp. x–1 to x–8.

carefully drafted. The law, when enforced, can make genuine price competition almost impossible, and that is exactly what Congress intended it to do. After forty frustrating years of price discrimination cases, it would be rather naïve to assume otherwise.

CHAPTER 9

Tying Agreements
in Theory and Practice

THE THEORY OF TYING AGREEMENTS

A conventional tying agreement is said to exist when a buyer
agrees to purchase or lease *one* commodity on the condition that he
also purchase or lease *another* commodity. Such an agreement is
called a "requirements contract" when a buyer agrees to purchase
all his "requirements" of different commodities from some one
seller. And "exclusive dealing" is a tying agreement whereby a buyer
agrees to wholesale or retail only the commodities of some particular
seller or manufacturer. Although different in specifics, the agreements have a substantive common thread; in each instance, a buyer
agrees to restrict his purchase of something from somebody. Under
antitrust law such contracts are illegal under Section 3 of the Clayton
Act when their effect "may be to substantially lessen competition or
tend to create a monopoly." They may also be prosecuted as illegal
restraints of trade under Section 1 of the Sherman Act, or under
Section 5 of the Federal Trade Commission Act of 1914.

It is easy to understand why tying agreements merit special attention under the antitrust laws. Such contracts, in antitrust jargon, are
inherent restraints of trade.[1] Supposedly, a seller with some degree

[1] The literature on tying agreements is vast. For some excellent discussions see,
Eugene M. Singer, "Market Power and Tying Arrangements," *Antitrust Bulletin*, VIII

of "market power" in one commodity (the tying good) is able to "force" buyers of that commodity into purchasing a second commodity or service (the tied good). Buyers are "hurt" because they are required to make a less than optimal purchase in the tied good market. In addition, potential rival sellers of the tied good are "foreclosed" or "excluded" from the market and, therefore, cannot "compete" therein. In this way the tie-in sale acts as a "barrier to entry." Hence the trade-restraining effect of a tying contract injures both buyers and rival sellers and results in an improper and inefficient allocation of economic resources.

As might already be apparent, the original criticism of tying contracts as a restraint of trade stems from the fact that the relationship is not at all consistent with the theory of pure competition. In pure competition, no individual seller would have the power or ability to require or induce a tying agreement. Buyers would be able to acquire all the commodities they wanted at competitive prices from thousands of rival sellers. Tying would thus be both impossible and unnecessary in pure competition.

But as explained in Chapter 2, *all* real sellers in all real market situations have degrees of "monopoly power," and it would be foolish, therefore, to condemn *a priori* all such relationships. Once heterogeneous firms, products, and consumers are recognized, and once the arbitrary welfare assumptions of pure competition are put aside, it becomes difficult to conclude that voluntary market arrangements like tying or exclusive dealing *necessarily* reduce buyer welfare or unfairly exclude potential sellers from the tied good market. To note that tying is a departure from pure competition and contains "monopolistic" elements, is to realize only that it is like every other contract or agreement in a free market system. If tying contracts have some particularly "evil" feature, this particular feature must be demonstrated and explained, rather than simply assumed.

Are Buyers Injured?

The essential objections to tying contracts are that they injure buyers and foreclose rival sellers. It might be appropriate at this point to investigate the idea that buyers are "injured" by tying agree-

(July-August, 1963), 653–657; W.S. Bowman, Jr., "Tying Arrangements and the Leverage Problem," *Yale Law Journal*, LXVII (November, 1957), 19–36; Donald F. Turner, "The Validity of Tying Arrangements Under the Antitrust Laws," *Harvard Law Review*, LXXXII (November, 1958), 50–75.

ments. How, precisely, are they injured? Imagine, for example, a fishing rod manufacturer who offers a rod for sale on condition that a fishing reel—which he manufacturers—also be purchased. If comparable rods are available at lower prices without tied reels, buyers are free to choose the untied—and probably cheaper—rods. If buyers need reels, they are free to purchase untied reels. In this sort of situation, buyers compare the price and quality of the tied package *vis-à-vis* the price and quality of the separate purchases combined. The lowest-priced , highest-quality package—put together by buyers or manufacturers—will be chosen. There is no reason to assume that buyers voluntarily "injure" themselves in such circumstances.

In situations where no fishing reel is desired, buyers can compare the fishing rod under discussion (with its unwanted accessory) against similar rods minus such accessories. Since buyers would place no value on the reel whatever, the price would represent the value of the desired rod only; it is as if the reel never existed. To speak of two "goods" being tied in this instance is ambiguous, since there is only *one good* actually involved—the fishing rod. This rod, as in the former situation, would then have to be compared by buyers with comparable rods, and a choice at the margin would then be exercised. Again, there is no reason to assume that buyers voluntarily injure themselves or would *be* injured under such circumstances.

But what if the fishing rod manufacturer is "dominant" or has "monopoly power" in the rod market? This means, apparently, that consumers prefer these rods over comparable ones, and that they will pay more for the rod, other things equal. Cannot a manufacturer in such a position extend his "monopoly" position into reels? Cannot he use his "leverage" in rods to enlarge his total profits? And will not that policy "injure" buyers? First assume that a superior fishing rod was selling at a premium in the market, and that the manufacturer had priced the rod to yield a maximum profit. Next, assume that the manufacturer realizes that his reel sales could be increased by tying reels to rods. The hope, of course, is that such a move will increase overall profits from rods *and* reels. But will it?

The safest answer must be that there is no guarantee whatever that such a policy will enhance profits, or injure consumers. Everything depends on the reactions of buyers to the tying combination and to the new price for the combination. Potential rod buyers that were prepared to purchase the superior rod at the old profit maximizing price now discover that the price of the rod-reel combination is higher. We must presume that they buy fewer rod-reel combinations. Of course since all the rods that are sold are henceforth sold with reels, reel sales increase somewhat, although the *net* increase will always be in doubt, since some reels would probably have been purchased *without* the tie-in. To realize greater profits than previously, the increase in reel profits must more than compensate for the loss in rod profits. But there is no guarantee that it will; everything will depend on the shift in demand, and the revenues obtainable at the new price. If profits are greater, the same results could probably have been achieved by selective price adjustments on both rods and reels. This suggestion might imply that the manufacturer had not chosen the profit-maximizing prices for the rod and reel in the first place. Hence, the "leverage" in this case, even if profits increase, is not clear at all.

Some tying arrangements may appear to "injure" buyers and involve the use of "leverage," but, in actuality, may only be a unique kind of price discrimination. For example, a superior copying machine might be leased at low rentals on the condition that the paper for the machine be purchased at above market rates from the machine lessor. In this case the machine lessor employs the tied good as a "meter" that registers the intensity of the demand for the leased machines. By tying the relatively expensive paper to the relatively cheap machine, the machine lessor can in effect charge the more intensive machine user a higher rate. The same end could conceivably have been accomplished by attaching a meter to the leased machines, and charging the more intensive users for the additional operations. How has the tie-in inflicted any net injury to the buyers?

In summation, if good substitutes for the tying good are readily available, buyers cannot be injured. And even if the tying good is "relatively superior" and can command a premium in its market, it is very doubtful whether "leverage" in some tied good market can be effective. If the relatively superior commodity was doing as well as it could untied, how is there any "power" left over for "leverage"? Tying may represent an optimal price combination for goods that had been suboptimally priced, or may represent a rather discreet kind of price discrimination. In conclusion, there is no reason to associate tying agreements automatically with consumer or buyer injury.

The longer the time period under consideration, the weaker becomes the argument that buyers are injured by tying agreements.

Certainly, in the long run, if a group of buyers were unhappy with certain tying contracts, sellers of alternative products would arise to offer better terms. Some alternative sellers would offer nontying terms to formerly tied buyers, and over time competition would be expected to force the relatively undesirable practice from the market. If this did not occur, it must be concluded that buyers prefer such arrangements *vis-à-vis* possible alternatives. It would certainly be incorrect and foolish to believe that buyers are victimized by a system that is voluntarily perpetuated—in the face of alternatives—by the very same buyer-victims.

This is not to say, of course, that buyers approve of every aspect of every agreement. No business "agreement" satisfies all desires, and all such agreements are a compromise. In the context of any given market situation, however, a buyer tends to choose that package of commodities that generates the greatest net utility or satisfaction. When a particular agreement is completed in a free market, it must be concluded that the traders find the terms preferable to other arrangements that they could have chosen *but did not*. All aspects of the contract will not be perfect from either's view. But on balance, the agreement must, *ex ante*, be the result of a satisfactory relationship. If the tying agreements are renewed and extended, it must be assumed that the agreements are also satisfactory *ex post*.

Tying agreements may have some obvious, and not so obvious, advantages that make them desirable contracts under certain circumstances. As far as buyers are concerned, tying may provide guaranteed availability of needed materials or services at momentarily favorable terms. The natural desire on the part of a buyer would be to extend a favorable circumstance and attempt to reduce long-term risk and uncertainty with respect to purchasing as much as possible. This would even be true where the combination offered by the seller is "naturally" desirable, i.e., where production and distribution economies make prices attractive. A tying agreement is, therefore, security against uncertain future market conditions.

A corollary set of circumstances exist for the seller. He may be able to provide low-cost terms that enhance his sales and profits *only if* a steady and predictable volume of business is assured. Predictable outputs lower costs, notably inventory expenses. To decrease his economic uncertainty, and to extend a circumstance that he views as favorable, the seller may suggest a tying agreement or arrangement. Hence, for both buyer and seller, tying may be an advantageous arrangement whereby the parties extend favorable terms and decrease long-term risk and uncertainty. It is thus consistent with profit-maximizing behavior on the part of *both* participants.

Foreclosure and Exclusion

Now that we have examined "buyer injury," it might be appropriate to turn briefly to an examination of "foreclosure" and "exclusion." To review, the implication here is that rival sellers of the tied good are unfairly shut out of markets where tying contracts exist. The tying good becomes a "barrier to entry" that effectively forestalls competition in the tied good. Thus, supposedly, economic resources are further misallocated away from some theoretical optimum.

But, of course, the reasonableness of this conclusion will depend on the answer to two important questions: What percentage of the tied good market is tied, and what are the terms of the tying agreement? If the percentage of the tied market that is tied is small, and the tied good is sold under competitive conditions, the effect of the "foreclosure" must certainly be negligible with respect to any "misallocation of resources." And if tying exists because the tied good is offered at cheaper than competitive rates, it is certainly *not obvious* that resources are misallocated or that "exclusion" is unfair.

The concept of "foreclosure" always proves too much. *All* purchases of any commodity or batch of commodities from anyone necessarily "forecloses" and "excludes" other sellers at the moment of sale, and if the particular commodities are relatively durable, the disappointed sellers stay excluded for some period of time. It would be ludicrous, however, to describe such actions as "lessening competition" or "misallocating economic resources." Presumably all sellers "competed" *before* any particular buyer made his specific selection of commodities; competition prior to sale is the only rational manner in which to discuss the level of competition. *All* buyer choice forecloses *less desirable options*, and that indeed, is the necessary consequence of consumer choice in a free market. To inhibit such choices and such contracts would actually be to restrain trade.

It should now be apparent that many of the common criticisms concerning the undesirability of tying arrangements may be misplaced. Tying need not be "exploitative" if it serves to lower prices, reduces market uncertainties, assures regular deliveries of future supplies, or allows effective price discrimination. And buyers need not necessarily be "injured" nor rival sellers be unfairly foreclosed from tied good markets. With these preliminary thoughts in mind, let us turn to an examination of some of the most important "tying cases" in antitrust history.

THE INTERNATIONAL SALT CASE (1947)

The first of the modern classic cases to be examined concerned International Salt.[2] The International Salt Company—one of the leading salt manufacturers in the country—owned two patents on machines that prepared salt for certain industrial processes. The "Lixator" dissolved salt into brine; the "Saltomat" injected salt tablets into cans during the canning process. International leased the machines widely, and had 840 "Lixator" and 73 "Saltomat" leases outstanding at the time of the trial.

The government had brought suit under Section 1 of the Sherman Act and Section 3 of the Clayton Act alleging that International Salt illegally restrained trade by tying the purchase of salt to the lease of its patented machines. In most of the leasing contracts for machines, the following "offensive" phrase appeared:

> . . . that the said Lixate Process Dissolver shall be used for dissolving and converting into brine only those grades of rock salt purchased by the Lessee from the Lessor. . . .[3]

In 1944, the dollar value of salt tied to the patented machines amounted to about $500,000.

Supreme Court Decision

Justice Jackson delivered the opinion of the Supreme Court. He stated that while patents conferred a limited, and legal, monopoly on International's use of its machines, they conferred "no right to restrain use of, or trade in, unpatented salt."[4]

The District Court had issued a summary judgment on the government's charges, and had not taken evidence as to the "reasonableness" of the restraints. Justice Jackson thought this proper since—as with price fixing— "it is unreasonable, *per se*, to foreclose competi-

[2] *International Salt Company* v. *United States*, 332 U.S. 392.
[3] *Ibid.*, p. 394.
[4] *Ibid.*, pp. 395–396.

tors from any substantial market."[5] Since the volume of trade in the tied good (salt) was not "insignificant or insubstantial," the tendency of the agreements to accomplish monopoly appeared obvious. And, the court reminded, the tendency toward monopoly need only be a "creeping one," not necessarily one in "full gallop."[6]

International Salt argued that its contracts were saved from being illegal *per se* by the insertion of the following provision:

> If at any time during the term of this lease a general reduction in prices of grades of salt suitable for use in the said Lixate Process Dissolver shall be made, said Lessee shall give said Lessor an opportunity to provide a competitive grade of salt at any such competitive price quoted, and in case said Lessor shall fail or be unable to do so, said Lessee, upon continued payment of the rental herein agreed upon, shall have the privilege of continued use of the said equipment with salt purchased in the open market, until such time as said Lessor shall furnish a suitable grade of salt at the said competitive price.[7]

Thus, if any lessee could get salt cheaper from another salt seller he was free to do so and still retain International's machines.

The court, however, was not convinced that this particular provision relieved the tying contract of being an illegal restraint of trade. Although the provision made the restraint "less harsh," the agreement still stifled potential competition.

> The appellant [International Salt] had at all times a priority on the business at equal prices. A competitor would have to undercut appellant's price to have any hope of capturing the market, while appellant could hold that market by merely meeting competition.[8]

And, finally, the court dismissed International's argument that the high-quality salt standards of its leased machines necessitated tying. While quality standards might be appropriate, International's machines were surely not "allergic" to the high-quality salt produced by a competitor. International was free to set reasonable quality standards but not free to tie its salt to its leased machines.[9]

[5] *Ibid.*, p. 396.
[6] *Ibid.*
[7] *Ibid.*, p. 394–395.
[8] *Ibid.*, p. 397.
[9] *Ibid.*, p. 398.

Comment

Legally, the International Salt case is famous because it appeared to condemn all exclusive or tying arrangements involving a "not insubstantial" volume of business. Therefore, it established a kind of *per se* rule with respect to tying contracts. But from an economic point of view, the case left a host of relevant questions unasked and, therefore, unanswered.[10]

For example, International Salt had two important machine patents, and patents are a "monopoly" of sorts.[11] But before determining the degree of potential "leverage" in the tied good market (salt), it must be discovered whether there were similar machines—perhaps patented also—that were employed by competitors at relatively competitive rates. The Supreme Court indicated in discussion on a different issue that *there were such machines and such competitors.*[12] Now it must be apparent that the more vigorous the competition in the tying good market, the less significant becomes the issue of leverage. Yet since the Supreme Court treated the tying contract like price fixing, it did not hear, and would not instruct the District Court to hear, arguments relating to the reasonableness of such agreements. Thus, the extent and degree of competition in the tying good remained an unexamined and—as far as the Supreme Court was concerned—an irrelevant issue.

The court never asked, nor was it revealed, whether competition in the market for salt was significantly affected by the tying arrangement between International and its machine customers. How can it be determined whether $500,000 is "not insubstantial" if no determination of the entire market for salt is made? How many firms sell salt, and how many purchase it? Had International's market share been increasing or decreasing over time? What percent of all salt sold was involved in the tying agreements? Since tying was treated as a *per se* offense, these questions—relevant to this inquiry—were never raised. Thus, the court's conclusion that a not insubstantial amount of business was involved must relate to *absolute* figures only, a rather useless guidepost to determining competitive restraint.

Finally, it is possible that International Salt was employing the tied

[10]Joel B. Dirlam and Alfred E. Kahn, *Fair Competition: The Law and Economics of Antitrust Policy* (Ithaca, N.Y.: Cornell University Press, 1954), p. 97.
[11]Patents are a "monopoly" over one's *own* property. They do not prevent anyone else from using *their* own property to compete. See Chapter 2.
[12]332 U.S. 399.

good (salt) as a kind of meter to "discriminate." This presumption is strengthened by International's strong objection to a paragraph in the District Court's summary judgment which directed the sale or lease of the salt machines on "non-discriminatory terms and conditions."[13] Yet this issue, which is of great potential interest, was not explored in this context at court.

THE STANDARD STATIONS CASE (1949)

Standard Stations, Inc. was a wholly owned subsidiary of Standard Oil of California. Prior to 1949, Standard Stations marketed petroleum products and auto supplies through its own retail gasoline stations and through 5,197 "independently owned" stations that were under "exclusive supply" contracts to Standard Stations. The government charged that these contracts violated Section 1 of the Sherman Act and Section 3 of the Clayton Act, and a trial was begun on January 2, 1947.[14]

Judge Yankwich wrote the decision of the District Court in 1948.[15] He admitted that: (1) the dealers voluntarily chose to tie themselves to Standard Stations; (2) the typical contract was for only six months, and did not include additional auto accessories; (3) Standard assisted the dealers financially, expended huge funds for advertising, helped repair and improve independent stations, and generally educated dealers in the handling of its products; (4) Standard's percentage of the gasoline market was only 6.7 percent (1.8 percent in replacement battery sales) and had been declining over the years; and (5) Standard's major competitors employed such a system, had since 1938, and "split pump" retailing represented only 1.6 percent of all gasoline sales.[16] Yet relying heavily on Justice Douglas' opinion in the Socony-Vacuum case,[17] Judge Yankwich was required to conclude that these facts and the resultant economic benefits that might flow from the contracts were quite irrelevant when it came to the legality of exclusive dealing arrangements.

The fact that it may be beneficial *is not material*, if, in effect, it is an unreasonable restraint . . . economic benefits cannot be

[13] *Ibid.*, p. 398.
[14] *Standard Oil of California and Standard Stations, Inc.* v. *United States*, 337 U.S. 293 (1949).
[15] 78 F. Supp. 850.
[16] *Ibid.*, pp. 855, 856, 868, 869.
[17] *United States* v. *Socony-Vacuum Oil Company* 310 U.S. 150 (1940).

taken into consideration if, in fact, there be substantial restriction of commerce.[18]

This did not mean (supposedly) that exclusive supply contracts were illegal *per se*,[19] or that the determination of illegal restraint would rest solely on the fact that certain outlets were "closed" to competitors for the length of the contracts.[20] It would rest on whether an "appreciable" segment of trade had been restrained.[21]

But what *was* an "appreciable segment of trade"? The court's own statistical data—taken from the trial record—demonstrated that Standard Stations was a comparatively *minor* factor in the market. In percentage terms, Standard was certainly not monopolizing, or even tending to monopolize, anything. But the court was not interested in percentages. In one of the most amazing statements in all antitrust history, Judge Yankwich said:

> But while the comparative figures bear on the question, they are not determinate. Substantiality of restraint or tendency to create monopoly is established by (a) the market foreclosed,— here represented by the controlled units—and (b) the volume of controlled business, totalling here in value $68,000,000.
>
> Fractionally speaking, the business done by the competitors with their own outlets or with those under contract is much greater than the business of Standard,—both in volume and in money value. Nevertheless, the business of Standard is considerable. In effect, it amounts to a substantial lessening of competition and a monopoly of a sizeable segment of a line of commerce in a definite area—the seven Western states. What has the *tendency* to achieve such result becomes, *in actual effect*, an unreasonable restraint.[22]

There was a "substantial restraint" because the court said that there was; there is no other way to read the above quotation. The restraint was established by the number of dealers "controlled," and the volume of business accomplished! The volume of business was then declared to be "considerable" and a "sizeable segment" of the market. Hence, the exclusive supply contracts constituted an unreasonable restraint of trade—period. So as to leave no

[18]78 F. Supp. 858.
[19]*Ibid.*, p. 863.
[20]*Ibid.*, p. 864.
[21]*Ibid.*, pp. 865–866.
[22]*Ibid.*, p. 872 (Emphasis in original).

room whatever for doubt, the court summarized its position as follows:

> *Grant* that on a comparative basis and in relation to the entire trade in these products in the area, the restraint is not integral. Admit also that control of distribution results in lessening of costs and that its abandonment might increase costs ... *Concede further*, that the arrangement was entered into in good faith, with the honest belief that control of distribution and consequent concentration of representation were economically beneficial to the industry and to the public, that they have continued for over fifteen years openly, notoriously, and unmolested by the government, and have been practiced by other major oil companies competing with Standard, that the number of Standard outlets so controlled may have decreased, and the quality of products supplied to them may have declined, on a comparative basis.

> ... despite all this, there confronts us the inescapable fact that such "balanced distribution"—as council for the defendants characterized it—calls for concentration of representation, which, in turn, results in an unreasonable restriction of trade, and a substantial lessening of competition, so far as the 5,197 outlets, their independent operators and those who seek to supply them are concerned. As the restriction corners a market of the value of $68,000,000, it is illegal, even considered on a comparative basis.[23]

This is an incredibly revealing statement. While the court grants that the exclusive supply contracts lower costs and benefit the industry and the public, it finds that they restrain trade. How do they restrain trade? *They simply exist. Why* do they exist? Because, apparently, they lower costs and benefit the industry and the public! Thus, in actuality, economic benefits are worse than irrelevant and immaterial in this case; they are positively damaging, since by the court's own "logic," they would not have existed but for their benefits. Firms restrain trade, therefore, when they economize on scarce resources—the exact opposite of the truth. Such is the twisted logic of antitrust in the Standard Stations case.

Supreme Court Decision

The Supreme Court reviewed the Standard Stations case in 1949. Justice Frankfurter suggested that the real issue was whether "the

[23] *Ibid.*, pp. 874–875.

requirement of showing that the effect of the agreements 'may be to substantially lessen competition' may be met simply by proof that a substantial portion of commerce is affected, or whether it must also be demonstrated that competitive activity has actually diminished or probably will diminish."[24] Before 1947, Frankfurter explained, the precedent had been that "domination of the market" was "sufficient in itself to support the inference that competition had been or probably would be lessened."[25] But Standard Stations' position in the market in this case, by Frankfurter's own admission, was "hardly large enough to conclude as a matter of law that it occupies a dominant position, nor did the trial court so find."[26]

The International Salt case, however, changed all the rules in tying cases. That decision "rejected the necessity of demonstrating economic consequences once it has been established that 'the volume of business affected' is not 'insignificant or insubstantial'. . . ."[27] Since tying arrangements "hardly serve any purpose beyond the suppression of competition,"[28] and since the court steadfastly refused to review the economic effects of the contracts,[29] the exclusive supply contracts were illegal because a substantial share of a line of commerce was affected.[30] In a final parting comment the court stated:

> Standard's use of the contracts creates just such a potential clog on competition as it was the purpose of Section 3 to remove wherever, were it to become actual, it would impede a substantial amount of competitive activity.[31]

Thus, the lower court decision and its "reasoning" was affirmed.

Most of Justice Douglas' celebrated dissent in the Standard Stations case is a strange, emotional, and completely unsubstantiated tirade on the rise and effect of "bigness in industry."[32] Yet his point, apparently, was to argue that the majority's decision would force independent gasoline dealers out of business and encourage huge oil companies to "build service-station empires of their own." Thus, in

[24]337 U.S. 299.
[25]Ibid., p. 301.
[26]Ibid., p. 302.
[27]Ibid., p. 304.
[28]Ibid., p. 305.
[29]Ibid., p. 313.
[30]Ibid., p. 314.
[31]Ibid.
[32]Ibid., pp. 315–319.

Douglas' view, the legal medicine in this case was worse than the disease.

> The requirements contract which is displaced is relatively innocuous as compared with the virulent growth of monopoly power which the Court encourages. The Court does not act unwittingly. It consciously pushes the oil industry in that direction. The Court approves what the Anti-Trust Laws were designed to prevent. It helps remake America in the image of the cartels.[33]

Chief Justice Vinson and Justices Jackson and Burton also dissented in a separately written opinion. They argued that the government had not proven that the actual—or even probable—effects of Standard's exclusive supply contracts were to lessen competition substantially or tend to create a monopoly, and that the mere quantity of volume by itself was not sufficient proof of illegal activity.

> . . . proof of their quantity does not prove that they had this forbidden quality; and the assumption that they did without proof, seems to me unwarranted.

> Moreover, the trial court not only made the assumption but did not allow the defendant affirmatively to show that such effects do not flow from this arrangement. Such evidence on the subject as was admitted was not considered in reaching the decision that these contracts are illegal.[34]

Nothing that this author might add could be more devastating than what the court's dissenting justices have stated above. There was no proof of illegal restraint nor—more importantly for our purposes—was the defendant allowed to show that his contracts did *not* do what the government said they did. Evidence that was admitted concerning "beneficial economies" was either immaterial or—as has been previously argued—positively damaging. Thus, the idea of a "defense" in this case was a charade from start to finish: *no defense was possible.*

THE AMERICAN CAN CASE (1949)

In 1947, the American Can Company was the nation's largest maker of "packers cans" and had been since the firm had been

[33] *Ibid.*, p. 321
[34] *Ibid.*, p. 322.

formed in 1902. American sold its cans to food processors through "requirements contracts" that bound the customer to purchase his complete requirement for cans from American. Although there were many different types of contracts, the typical agreement at the time of the trial was a full requirements contract for a period of five years. In addition, machines that completed the can were available on a leasing basis from American.

American Can had been in the courts twice before with respect to its can and can-closing machine business. In 1916 American narrowly escaped divesture under the Sherman Act; in 1924 the FTC prohibited American from formally tying can-closing machine leases to can sales. The Justice Department, however, was not satisfied that "competition" had been restored to the can industry. In 1948, it brought suit under the Sherman and Clayton acts charging that American's requirement contracts for cans and its can-closing machine leases illegally restrained trade.[35] As a remedy, they petitioned the court to end the requirements contracts altogether, and to divest American of its can-closing machine business.[36]

District Court Decision

District Judge Harris delivered the District Court decision in the American Can case on November 10, 1949. The first part of the decision was given over to establishing the fact that although there were approximately 125 competitive canmakers in the United States, American Can led the market with over 40 percent of the business.[37] American's percentage of business had slipped continuously from an estimated 90 percent in 1902, and although the firm was "not in a position of complete monopoly" at the time of the trial, it was still "dominant" in its industry.[38] Thus, adhering to the guidelines set forth in the Standard Stations case, there was no question that a not "insubstantial" volume of business was affected.[39]

But what particular practices had restrained trade? According to the government, the five-year "total requirements contracts" were able, in themselves, to unreasonably "exclude" or "limit competition" from other canmakers. But how had American repeatedly "co-

[35] United States v. American Can Company, 87 F. Supp. 18.
[36] Continental Can (the second largest canmaker in the country), under similar indictment, agreed to accept the decision in the American Can case.
[37] 87 F. Supp. 21–22.
[38] Ibid., p. 23.
[39] Ibid., p. 30.

erced" its customers into such unreasonable restraints? *Why, by offering generous and attractive terms!* The court reported that American offered an attractive discount on quantity purchases, even paid money occasionally to obtain certain business, furnished equipment in addition to closing machines at nominal rates, paid large claims when it appeared good business, and purchased canmaking equipment from customers at "inflated values" in order to secure their can business.[40] In addition, the customers were guaranteed delivery of their requirement of cans regardless of the particular supply conditions. In short, American treated customers to many economies apparently not obtainable from other canmakers, and these customers were generally satisfied with the agreements. Yet the court detected the evil inherent in these economic benefits:

> The incidents, when examined realistically and not as mere abstractions, are deeper than the typical run-of-the-mill, day-to-day business transactions. They represent a studied, methodical and effective method of restraining and acquiring by refined, gentlemanly and suave means, plus an occasional 'commercial massage', the dominant position which American has had and maintained for at least a generation on and over the canning industry. A detailed analysis of this phase of the Government's case convinces that there is little room left in a competitive sense, for the independent small business man. As a competitive influence, he has slowly and sadly been relegated into the limbo of American enterprise.[41]

But were the requirements contracts thus illegal *per se,* or was the court to weigh the merits and demerits of such arrangements? Judge Harris approvingly quoted the Standard Stations decision where it was indicated that any such economic evidence was "immaterial" and "not determinate" with respect to the legal questions involved.[42] Also not determinate were the desires of the consumer of cans!

> In analyzing a contract in terms of its effect on competition, the condition of the consumer should not be completely ignored, although, as it appears, the wishes or desires of the consumer are not determinative in reaching a finding as to whether a monopoly or a tendency to create a monopoly exists.[43]

[40] *Ibid.,* pp. 27–28.
[41] *Ibid.,* p. 28.
[42] *Ibid.,* p. 30.
[43] *Ibid.,* p. 31.

What was to be "determinative" therefore? Why the fact that competition (read "competitors") was being limited by the length of the requirements contract. The five-year length of American's requirement contract was simply *declared* to be "unreasonable," and a one-year requirements contract was approved.[44]

Can-Closing Machine Issue

The same sort of judicial reasoning was employed to condemn American's can-closing machine business. Much was made of the fact that American leased 54 percent of all machines in the industry,[45] leased machines only to customers that bought its cans,[46] and allowed the lease on can machinery and its can requirements contracts to run concurrently. Yet the success of American's leasing policy rested on the quality of the machines manufactured by American, and on the *low rentals* charged for such machines. To quote Judge Harris:

> An important factor which induces canners to lease their machines has been the low rentals charged for such machines. The defendant admits that low rentals provide an effective "sales tool."

> American, over the years, has imposed rentals ranging from purely nominal to a rate sufficient to pay for the cost of the equipment furnished. Recently defendant standardized its charges so that today they represent an amount equivalent to 8.2 percent of the depreciated value of the machines. Such a charge approaches a fair standard, but even present rentals are insufficient to cover the complete cost of furnishing and servicing the machines.[47]

But how can economies "restrain trade"? Why they restrict the market for closing machine manufacturers (there were two independent firms in existence with 12 percent of the business) and, thereby, limit the number of concerns in that business!

> The record disclosed that others would engage in the manufacture of closing machines if there were a free market in which sellers might compete on an equal basis with the canmakers who now lease their machines.[48]

[44] *Ibid.*, p. 23.
[45] *Ibid.*, p. 23.
[46] *Ibid.*, p. 26.
[47] *Ibid.*, p. 23.
[48] *Ibid.*, p. 24.

Reflect on this amazing quotation. The desire (read "wish") of the potential competitor is now, apparently, to be "determinative." We are to pity the poor machinery firms that cannot come into existence because they cannot match the low rentals and terms of American and the other can companies! But if there were only a "free market," laments the court. *Free market?* That is exactly the sort of market that *did* exist, and as a consequence, it kept out the high-cost, high-price, would-be "producers." The pleading for "competition" on an "equal basis" is the familiar refrain of the less efficient organization that wants the government and the courts to push "competition" up to its cost and profit level. Yet instead of exposing this embarrassing uneconomic nonsense for what it was, the District Court enshrined it in legitimate tones that would have the force of law.

The final decree by the District Court (1) prohibited American from offering any annual cumulative volume discounts; (2) lowered the requirements contracts to one year; (3) ordered American to sell its closing machines at extremely low prices for a period of ten years, train buyers in technology and service, and license closing-machine patents *without* royalty; and (4) required that American lease any machine to anyone at rentals that were fully compensatory, including a fair profit. As was the case with United Shoe Machinery,[49] stiff legal measures were required to relegate American Can to the same status as its rivals so that they *all* might compete on an "equal" basis.

The McKie Article

James W. McKie has written the classic defense of the American Can decision.[50] In it, he pointed out some of the advantages of the decision. He noted that (1) "the independent manufacturers of machinery will be able to market closing machines directly to the canning industry"; (2) "small firms are now better able to detach fragments of business which used to be held firmly by the large can suppliers"; (3) "the market position of smaller manufacturers has been greatly strengthened"; and (4) "that large buyers can no longer be pacified with volume discounts."[51] Dissolution of the leading can companies would have, in McKie's view, produced more "spectacu-

---

[49] *United States* v. *United Shoe Machinery Corporation*, 110 F. Supp. 295 (1953).

[50] "The Decline of Monopoly in the Metal Container Industry," *American Economic Review, Papers and Proceedings*, XLV (May, 1955), 499–508.

[51] *Ibid.*, pp. 506–507.

lar" results, but the court decision of 1950 had restored a "workable competition" to the metal container industry.

But certainly there had always been a kind of "workable competition" in the metal container industry even prior to the industry— witness the relative decline of American Can and the number of eager can companies in the industry. How is it to be determined objectively whether the post-decision situation was preferable to the pre-decision situation? The fact that the smaller can companies and independent machinery companies were "stronger" or could do more business proves nothing. For example, as part of the District Court decree, American (and Continental) were ordered to *raise* their leasing rates on closing machines and *end* their volume discount sales on cans. Are we to infer that such actions are automatically in the public interest? Does this action tend to promote a more optimal resource allocation? McKie's concern for the smaller firms involved is no doubt genuine, but it is economically unconvincing. To raise leasing rates by law and then cheer at the sight of "more competition"; to prevent large firms from passing along economies by law and then cheer that smaller rivals are suddenly "more competitive"—these positions reflect ambiguous reasoning, to put it mildly. If this should be sound economic policy, the possibilities for "increasing competiton" in many other areas of the economy would be staggering. The flaws in such an analysis are, hopefully, too obvious for comment.

The same sort of questions can be raised regarding McKie's approval of can-closing machine sales. He claims—much to American and Continental's surprise—that over 75 percent of the machines being leased in 1949 had been sold under the court-established procedures by 1954. Serious competition in can machinery could now begin, and the "commercial leverage" exercised by the large canmakers in the can market could now be ended.

But given the *costs* imposed on the major canmakers, is the outcome so surprising or necessarily an occasion for rejoicing? Purchases of can-closing machinery became popular because the court purposely set "bargain prices" for machines, and because additional court-ordered "gifts" (technical services, patents) made the deal irrational to forego. In short, *machinery buyers were made the beneficiaries of a court-sanctioned expropriation of property.* That this might "increase competition" seems hardly the significant point. No one has ever argued that a competition of sorts could not be "increased" by expropriating the skills, talents, and capital of the more efficient firms, and dividing up the "booty" among the "less fortunate." But this kind of "competition" can hardly be termed "free enterprise."

What acceptable formula would allow us to conclude that competition in 1954 was "more optimal" than competition in 1949? McKie's only suggested method, apparently, is *structural*. But serious objections have been raised to this approach to competition (see Chapter 2). Since McKie had previously admitted that American Can and Continental Can had held their market shares with superior research, customer service, volume discounts, and progressive can-closing machinery,[52] what—besides structural factors—would allow the conclusion that the American Can decision advanced the ever-elusive public interest? McKie's assurances that it did?

There have been many important tying or exclusive dealing cases over the last twenty years, although it is doubtful if any of them approach the significance of the cases already examined. A few of the more significant cases are briefly reviewed below.

THE *TIMES-PICAYUNE* CASE (1953)

In 1953, the Supreme Court reversed a District Court decision that had found the Times-Picayune Publishing Company of New Orleans guilty of illegal tying arrangements.[53] That company's policy had been to sell certain kinds of advertising in its morning newspaper—the *Times-Picayune*—and in its evening newspaper—the *States*—as a unit; it was impossible to purchase add space in one or the other paper separately. The government claimed that such "unit contracts" illegally restrained trade and tended to monopolize in violation of the Sherman Act. After a lengthy trial, the District Court agreed with the government and enjoined the practice. The Supreme Court, however, reversed the order in a five-to-four decision.

Justice Clark delivered the majority opinion of the Supreme Court. Although he admitted that tying contracts "flout the Sherman Act's policy that competition rule the marts of trade,"[54] certain conditions had to be met before such arrangements could be condemned as

[52] *Ibid.*, p. 504.
[53] *Times-Picayune Publishing Company et al.* v. *United States*, 345 U.S. 594.
[54] *Ibid.*, p. 605.

illegal restraints of trade under the Sherman Act. Precedent indicated to Clark that the seller must enjoy a monopolistic position in the market for the tying product, *and* that a substantial volume of commerce in the tied product must be restrained.[55] But in the majority's opinion, *Times-Picayune* was not in a monopolistic or even a "dominant" position in the newspaper advertising market in New Orleans.

There were three newspapers being published in New Orleans at the time of the trial: the *Times-Picayune,* the *States,* and the independently owned *Item.* According to the court, the sales of both general and classified advertising linage for the *Times-Picayune* (the tying good) was about 40 percent of the total in the market. This ruled out "monopoly" according to Clark:

> If each of the New Orleans publications shared equally in the total volume of linage, the *Times-Picayune* would have sold 33½ percent; in the absence of patent or copyright control, the small existing increment in the circumstances where disclosed cannot confer that market "dominance" which, in conjunction with a "not insubstantial" volume of trade in the tied product, would result in a Sherman Act offense. . . .[56]

In addition, the unit arrangements could hardly be compared with standard tying contracts. Under illegal tying, supposedly, a dominant seller uses his "leverage" in the tying good market to suppress competition and inflict economic harm in the tied good market. The *Times-Picayune* situation, however, was quite different.

> Here . . . two newspapers under single ownership at the same place, time and terms, sell indistinguishable products to advertisers; no dominant "tying" product exists (in fact, since space in neither the *Times-Picayune* nor the *States* can be bought alone, one may be viewed as "tying" as the other); no leverage in one market excludes sellers in the second, because for present purposes the products are identical and the market the same.[57]

Hence, it was doubtful whether there was "tying" here at all; apparently, only one product was being sold.

Finally, the court noted approvingly that the *Times-Picayune* ad-

---

[55] *Ibid.,* p. 608.
[56] *Ibid.,* p. 613.
[57] *Ibid.,* p. 614.

vertising rates were significantly lower than the corresponding *Item*'s rates,[58] that many of the nation's publishers (including the *Item*) had switched to the "unit" system,[59] and that the unit system "was viewed as a competitive weapon in the rivalry for national advertising accounts."[60] The Supreme Court could find no Sherman Act violations in any of this.

THE NORTHERN PACIFIC RAILWAY CASE (1958)

In the nineteenth century, the Northern Pacific Railroad—like most of its important transcontinental competitors except the Great Northern—had been gifted with extensive land grants by the federal government. In the case of the Northern Pacific, the grants had totaled almost 40 million acres. By 1949, most of this resource-rich land had been sold or leased off to outside parties on condition that all commodities produced or manufactured on the land be shipped over the Northern Pacific's line, provided that its rates, and in some instances its services, be equal to those of competing carriers. The government charged that these "preferential routing" agreements were unreasonable restraints of trade in violation of Section 1 of the Sherman Act.[61]

Justice Black delivered the majority opinion of the Supreme Court in this case.[62] He stated that there were "certain agreements or practices which because of their pernicious effect on competition and lack of any redeeming virtue are conclusively presumed to be unreasonable and therefore illegal without elaborate inquiry. . . ."[63] He listed price fixing, division of markets, group boycotts, and tying contracts among these *per se* practices. Regarding tying agreements, Black stated:

> They are unreasonable in and of themselves whenever a party has *sufficient economic power* with respect to the tying product to appreciably restrain free competition in the market for the tied product and a "not insubstantial" amount of interstate commerce is affected.[64]

[58] *Ibid.*, p. 622.
[59] *Ibid.*, p. 623.
[60] *Ibid.*, p. 624.
[61] Suit was brought under the Sherman Act since "land" was not included in the Clayton Act, Section 3 prohibition.
[62] *Northern Pacific Railway Company* v. *United States*, 356 U.S. 1 (1958).
[63] *Ibid.*, p. 5.
[64] *Ibid.*, p. 6 (Emphasis added).

But did Northern Pacific have "sufficient economic power" in the tying product market? Black suggested that such "power" could simply be inferred by virtue of Northern Pacific's "extensive land holdings." The fact that there were such "holdings" and the fact that the tying agreements existed was proof enough of that "economic power."

> The very existence of this host of tying arrangements *is itself* compelling evidence of the defendant's great power, at least where, as here, no other explanation has been offered for the existence of these restraints.[65]

Finally, the Supreme Court rejected the defendant's argument that the "preferential routing" clauses did not unreasonably restrain trade since they contained the "escape" provision concerning the matching of a competitor's lower rates. Arguing as in the International Salt decision, the court held that the agreements were still "binding obligations held over the heads of vendees which deny defendant's competitors access to the fenced-off market on the same terms as the defendant."[66] The clauses were, therefore, unreasonable, and the District Court decision to end the restrictive practices was affirmed.

Justice Harlan, with whom Justices Frankfurter and Whittaker joined, wrote a dissenting opinion in the Northern Pacific case. He argued that neither the District Court nor the majority of the Supreme Court had determined whether Northern Pacific was actually "dominant" in the market where the alleged violations occurred. The tying market was land, and there had been no determination of Northern Pacific's relevant market share. The District Court had simply assumed "dominance," or worse, had simply assumed that Northern Pacific dominated "the lands now owned by them and had dominance in the lands formerly owned at the time of sale of such lands."[67] But dominance over *one's own property* was hardly the test of illegality under the Sherman Act!

> The District Court should have taken evidence of the relative strength of appellants' land-holdings *vis-à-vis* that of others in the appropriate market for land of the types now or formerly

---

[65] *Ibid.*, p. 8 (Emphasis added).
[66] *Ibid.*, p. 12.
[67] *Ibid.*, p. 15.

possessed by appellants . . . Short of such an inquiry I do not see how it can be determined whether the appellants occupied such a dominant position in the relevant market as to make these tying clauses illegal per se under the Sherman Act.[68]

Hence, in Harlan's view, Northern Pacific was convicted without positive proof of dominance in the tying-good market, and without, therefore, positive proof of leverage in the tied-good market.

A WORD ON THE TAMPA ELECTRIC (1961) AND LOEW'S (1962) CASES

In the Tampa Electric case,[69] the Supreme Court appeared to modify the extreme position it had taken in the Northern Pacific case. In this instance, the court let stand a long-term requirements contract for coal between the Tampa Electric Company and the Nashville Coal Company. Nashville, at Tampa's request, had agreed to supply one million tons of coal annually for twenty years for Tampa's newly constructed electric power plant. Although the exclusive supply contract involved upwards of $128 million, the Supreme Court ruled that in the relevant market for coal (an eight-state area), the foreclosure of potential suppliers amounted to less than one percent. And less than one percent in 1961 was not enough to make the agreement illegal under Section 3 of the Clayton Act.

In the Loew's case,[70] the Supreme Court reaffirmed a District Court ruling (with some modifications) that ended the "block booking" of films by distributors to television stations. Block booking was a practice whereby distributors sold or leased "desirable" films only on condition that less "desirable" films also be bought or leased. Similar practices had been ended by the Court in the film industry before,[71] but television booking was a new experience.

The distributors argued that (1) "dominance" could not be demonstrated; (2) the "uniqueness" attributed to copyrighted films shown in moviehouses could not be assumed to exist automatically vis-à-vis television; (3) feature films represented only 8 percent of all television programming; and (4) that there was "reasonable interchangeability" of films with other programming shown on television. The

[68] Ibid., p. 16.
[69] Tampa Electric Company v. Nashville Coal Company et al., 365 U.S. 320 (1961).
[70] United States v. Loew's Incorporated et al., 371 U.S. 38 (1962).
[71] United States v. Paramount Pictures, Inc., et al., 334 U.S. 131 (1948).

Supreme Court, in rejecting these notions, agreed with the District Court which had summarized the essential issue in this case:

> There can be no dispute that the evidence showed that *no defendant had market dominance over the feature film market as such*. Each defendant owned its own feature films. There are numerous feature films on the market and there was intense competition among the defendants to market their own films. *However, each film was in itself a unique product*. Each film was copyrighted. Each film was unique in its subject matter and presentation. *Each defendant had market dominance as to its own feature films*.[72]

The copyright created "uniqueness," and the "uniqueness" generated "sufficient economic power" to impose an "appreciable restraint on free competition in the tied product . . . as demanded by the Northern Pacific decision."[73] The "appreciable restraint" may have only tied up as little as $60,800, but that was enough to bring it under the law's prohibition.[74] Hence, to "dominate" one's *own* property—*but not the market for similar property*—and use the "monopolistic advantage" inherent in that dominance to tie one commodity to another violated the antitrust statutes in this case.

It seems safe to say at this point in our discussion that tying arrangements on the part of any firm of appreciable size are illegal, and that information on supposed economic benefits is irrelevant and immaterial with respect to the issue of illegal restraint. Further, illegal restraint will be inferred if the tying agreements exist, since the existence of the contracts themselves evidence "sufficient economic power" on the part of the seller. Finally, the volume of trade "restrained" in the tied-good market can certainly be very small since "not insubstantial" can mean anything the court chooses to have it mean. Therefore, any firm with a patented good, a copyrighted good, or any "unique" product of any sort, that employs that "uniqueness" to tie buyers to another product or service violates the antitrust statutes with respect to tying agreements. No "damage" to the public interest need be demonstrated; it is simply *assumed* to exist. As a final illustration of this thesis, observe the facts and logic of the Supreme Court in the most recent classic tying case discussed below.

[72] *United States* v. *Loew's Incorporated et al.*, 180 F. Supp. 381 (Emphasis added).
[73] 371 U.S. 48.
[74] *Ibid.*, 49.

THE FORTNER ENTERPRISES CASE (1968)

Fortner Enterprises, Inc. had filed an antitrust suit against the U.S. Steel Corporation and its wholly owned subsidiary, U.S. Steel Homes Credit Corporation, claiming that it (Fortner) had been victimized under an illegal tying agreement.[75] The tying agreement consisted of the fact that Fortner, in order to obtain $2 million from the Credit Corporation to purchase and develop lands in Kentucky, had agreed to erect prefabricated homes manufactured by U.S. Steel on the lots purchased with the funds. Subsequently, Fortner experienced financial difficulties—allegedly due to the fact that the prefabricated homes proved to be "defective and unusable"—and sued U.S. Steel for treble damages under the Sherman Act. The suit that reached the Supreme Court in 1968 was over the District Court's decision (affirmed by the Court of Appeals) to enter a summary judgment *for* U.S. Steel, and to dismiss the antitrust charge.

The Supreme Court Decision

Justice Black delivered the majority decision for the Supreme Court on April 7, 1969. He agreed with the District Court that a "traditional" tying arrangement was involved, but he disagreed with the manner in which the District Court had analyzed the legal issues involved. The District Court had held that U.S. Steel did not have "sufficient economic power" over credit, and that the amount of land foreclosed to competing sellers of prefabricated homes was "insubstantial."[76] Thus, according to the precedents set in the Northern Pacific case, the agreements under discussion were not illegal *per se*.

Black noted, however, that while the tying agreements might not be illegal *per se* this did not mean that they were, thus, legal. The failure to meet the *per se* prerequisites of the Northern Pacific decision did not necessarily doom the petitioner's case against U.S. Steel. As Black explained:

> A plaintiff can still prevail on the merits whenever he can prove, on the basis of a more thorough examination of the purposes and practices involved, that the general standards of the Sherman Act have been violated. Accordingly . . . the summary judgment against petitioner still could not be entered without further examination of petitioner's general allegations

[75] *Fortner Enterprises, Inc.* v. *United States Steel Corporation and United States Steel Homes Credit Corporation,* 394 U.S. 495 (1968).
[76] *Ibid.,* p. 499.

that respondents conspired together for the purpose of restraining competition and acquiring a monopoly in the market for prefabricated homes.[77]

Thus, *if necessary*, a detailed examination of the economic issues involved could and should proceed at court, and a summary dismissal prior to such an examination was inappropriate.

Justice Black found further fault with the District Court's analysis. The District Court had determined that the percentage of land foreclosed to competing sellers of prefabricated homes because of the tying agreements involving U.S. Steel was only .00032 percent (!), and had, accordingly, determined that the trade restrained in the tied-good market was "insubstantial."[78] Black noted, however, that a "not insubstantial" volume of trade was not meant to apply to market share in percentage terms, *but to dollar volume of business in absolute terms!* And $190,000 (the annual purchases of homes from U.S. Steel by Fortner) was clearly not "paltry" or insubstantial.[79] In addition, it was the total volume of sales tied by such a policy *with anyone* that was the "determining" amount, and since U.S. Steel did more than $2 million worth of business under such agreements in 1962, the amount "could scarcely be regarded as insubstantial" by the Supreme Court.[80]

The District Court also erred with respect to its examination of "sufficient economic power," according to Black. No monopoly or even dominant position was necessary in the tying good. Quoting the Loew's decision approvingly, Black argued that economic power could simply be inferred "from the tying product's desirability to consumers, or from uniqueness in its attributes."[81] All that was necessary was that the seller be able to "exert *some* power over *some* of the buyers in the market, even if the power is not complete over them and over all other buyers in the market."[82]

The "product" offered by U.S. Steel was, apparently, unique. A.B. Fortner, president of Fortner Enterprises, Inc., testified that he had accepted the tying agreement only because the 100 percent financ-

[77] *Ibid.*, p. 500.
[78] *Ibid.*, p. 501.
[79] *Ibid.*, pp. 501–502.
[80] *Ibid.*, p. 502.
[81] *Ibid.*, p. 503.
[82] *Ibid.*, 503.

ing "was unusually and uniquely advantageous to him."[83] No alternative financing on such cheap and liberal terms was available to his corporation during the 1959–1962 period. No other financial institution in the Louisville, Kentucky area was able to match U.S. Steel's terms and rates of interest. Whether the reason for this "competitive advantage" was "economies resulting from the nationwide character of its operations" or whether state and federal statutes might have prevented such terms from being offered by banks was not clear. But the presence of "market power" was certainly apparent enough to justify a trial on the tying agreements as far as Justice Black was concerned.

Finally, the Supreme Court dismissed the argument that the agreements between U.S. Steel and Fortner were not tying contracts at all, and that only *one* product—the prefabricated homes—was involved. The court admitted that offering credit for the purchase of a product was harmless enough. But this sort of transaction was

> . . . a far cry from the arrangement involved here, where the credit is provided by one corporation on condition that a product be purchased from a separate corporation, and where the borrower contracts to obtain a large sum of money over and above that needed to pay the seller for the physical products purchased.[84]

In Black's view, "credit" was as much a tying good as any other product, and its potential harm was just as great. As an example, he noted that "barriers to entry" had been raised by the tying agreements, since sellers of prefabricated homes in competition with U.S. Steel must also be able to offer credit on comparable terms—and this was probably impossible.[85] Hence, equally efficient, or even more efficient firms, that produce competitive prefabricated homes would be excluded from the market solely because of the economic power of U.S. Steel in the credit market. This, however, was exactly the sort of "evil" that the antitrust laws had been designed to prevent. Therefore, the Supreme Court reversed the order of the Appeals Court, and directed that the Fortner Enterprises suit against U.S. Steel proceed to trial.

[83] *Ibid.*, p. 504.
[84] *Ibid.*, p. 507.
[85] *Ibid.*, p. 509.

Dissent

There were two dissents in the Fortner case, one by Justice White (with whom Justice Harlan joined) and one by Justice Fortas (with whom Justice Stewart joined). White's dissent reviewed the meaning of tying agreements, the historic rationale for making them illegal, and emphasized that it was the existence of "some market power in the tying product" that was the crucial determination in such cases. Without a determination of market power, the economic "distortions" suggested by the theory could not occur. But what proof of "market power" in the tying product—money—was there in this case?[86] The fact that the credit was available at favorable rates and terms from U.S. Steel? Did low prices infer market power? He thought not:

> A low price in the tying product . . . is especially poor proof of market power when untied credit is available elsewhere.[87]

But what of the supposed "barriers to entry" imposed by the tying agreements? They were easily overcome, according to White. The low price of the credit was "functionally equivalent" to a price cut on prefabricated homes. Since buyers could secure untied credit elsewhere, competitors of U.S. Steel could compete by cutting the prices of their homes. There was no good reason why U.S. Steel "should always be required to make the price cut in one form rather than another."[88]

White also argued that if it *were* true that equally available credit terms were not available to Fortner except through U.S. Steel, then the charge that U.S. Steel foreclosed the market had to be incorrect. Who could they be foreclosing the market to? If U.S. Steel assumed risks that *no one* else would assume, then they certainly were not foreclosing any competitor from any market.[89] The Sherman Act could hardly be used against a kind of behavior that, in White's view, it was meant to encourage!

Nor could "market power" simply be inferred from the existence of the tying agreements themselves. Buyers were not "burdened"

---

[86] *Ibid.*, p. 511.
[87] *Ibid.*, p. 515.
[88] *Ibid.*
[89] *Ibid.*, pp. 516–517.

when they could buy tied and untied products elsewhere on "normal" terms. And competing sellers were not foreclosed since they could lower their prices on the tied product and compete. Far from evidencing market power, lower credit rates were

> . . . more likely to reflect a competitive attempt to offset the market power of others in the tied product than it is to reflect existing power in the credit market. Those with real power do not offer uniquely advantageous deals to their customers; they raise prices.[90]

Justice Fortas also wrote a strong dissent in the Fortner case. He argued, quite simply, that the contract between Fortner and U.S. Steel was *not a tying agreement.* U.S. Steel, in Fortas' opinion, was not "selling credit in any general sense." It was selling prefabricated homes with an "incidental provision of financing."[91] Almost all the loaned $2 million was related to the purchase and installation of homes. It was simply "not a sale of one product on condition that the buyer will not deal with competitors for another product or will buy the other product exclusively from the seller."[92] It was, rather, a quite common agreement in the business world whereby a seller extends financing to a purchaser. That such an agreement could violate the Sherman Act was almost inconceivable as far as Fortas was concerned.

> It is hardly conceivable except for today's opinion of the Court, that extension of such credit as a part of a general sale transaction or distribution method could be regarded as "tying" of the seller's goods to the credit, so that where the business man receiving the credit agrees to handle the seller-lender's product, the arrangement is per se unlawful merely because the amount or terms of the credit were more favorable than could be obtained from banking institutions in the area.[93]

To condemn such credit arrangements out of hand was to use, in Fortas' words, the antitrust laws "as an instrument in restraint of competition."[94]

[90] *Ibid.,* p. 519.
[91] *Ibid.,* pp. 521–522.
[92] *Ibid.,* p. 522.
[93] *Ibid.,* p. 524.
[94] *Ibid.,* p. 525.

Comment on the Fortner Case

In an ironical way, the Fortner case is a fitting climax to our discussion of tying theory and practice. It represents the "dead end" to which the *per se* sort of approach can be pushed in this area of antitrust. It also reveals the nonsense of antitrust enforcement that inevitably flows from a theory based on an undefinable concept—monopoly power.

Was the contract between Fortner and U.S. Steel a tying contract of the kind prohibited by the antitrust statutes? Since *all* business contracts tie the participants to certain specific terms and limit their freedom of action, tying contracts must, somehow, be distinguished from "harmless" business relationships. What can distinguish them? One way would be to argue that tying arrangements always provide that one independently identifiable good or service is being sold or leased on condition that some other independently identifiable good or service also be purchased or leased. If *that* is what tying is, then the Fortner case did *not* involve tying contracts. U.S. Steel approached Fortner in an effort to sell them prefabricated homes. The homes were sold *through* financing extended for that purpose. U.S. Steel was not selling homes *and* credit but selling homes through the mechanism of a credit transaction with a subsidiary. Hence the credit was a "conduit" through which the singular product—the prefabricated homes—were sold. It presumably would not have been extended but for the fact that the homes had been sold. If it "restrained trade," it restrained trade like any business contract does when it "forces" the participants to accept certain "restraints" on their freedom of action.

If tying is *not* defined as the linking of two independently identifiable products, then the Fortner arrangements could certainly be "tying." For example, the sale of a product on condition that the product also be serviced by the seller and only by the seller has long been established as tying. Yet the servicing of some product is hardly an independently definable "something." It is inherently linked to that product, and has no "existence" independent of that product. Analogously, the same thing could be said for "credit" in this case; it would not have existed but for the sale of the homes. But, of course, if this is illegal tying then *any* contract with *any* supplemental terms of any sort could be called a tying contract of sorts. Using this definition of tying, therefore, reduces it to the absurd conclusion that all business contracts are tying contracts.

Another curious issue in this case concerns the formalizing of a *double standard* with respect to the relevance of economic evidence. We have already seen in many previous cases that the economic benefits associated with tying contracts are "not determining" and that they are irrelevant with respect to the legal questions involved. Yet, in this case, the Supreme Court makes it perfectly clear that a petitioner—on failure to demonstrate a *per se* violation of the antitrust statutes—can employ such evidence as is necessary to prove a violation of the Sherman or Clayton acts. So while the petitioner can use evidence of economic effects in an attempt to prove illegal restraint of trade, the defense's attempt to use similar kinds of evidence to rebut such accusations is likely to be termed "irrelevant and immaterial."

The determination that the "uniqueness" of U.S. Steel's credit conferred "economic power" on the defendant is the most interesting—though not unprecedented—issue in the Fortner case. The groundwork for such a ruling had been laid before. In sum, the Supreme Court reasoned that U.S. Steel evidenced economic power because it—and only it—could offer superior terms on the financing of purchased prefabricated homes. How it had obtained that particular position was irrelevant. The fact remained that it offered a uniquely advantageous financing arrangement, and that such arrangements "can reflect a creditor's unique economic advantage over his competitors." Thus it again appears—or more exactly, it is confirmed—that the ability to generate unique circumstances for buyers is legally suspect, and that the acceptance of such circumstances is proof positive of economic power. Even more insulting, the court appears to sanction the idea that a buyer may then turn around and sue a seller, claiming that he has been "coerced" into an illegal tying agreement that he has already admitted describing as "uniquely advantageous"!

This open hostility to superior economic performance is the logical and inevitable result of an incorrect economic theory and purposely ambiguous law. But working toward what? Toward a mythical state of pure competition—and pure economic equality —where all firms display an absence of uniqueness of any sort. Under such circumstances, firms would possess zero "economic power" and zero individualism. That this state of "competition" could not be reached in reality, or that most economists shockingly disclaim such policy desires, has absolutely nothing to do with the fact that the Fortner case is a logical progression toward that end result. Such is the *reductio ad absurdum* in tying agreement antitrust cases.

CHAPTER 10

Mergers, Competition, and Antitrust Policy

THE MERGER "CRISIS"

The most exciting area of antitrust law throughout the last decade has been Section 7 of the Clayton Act (as amended) dealing with corporate mergers and acquisitions. That section, it will be remembered, prohibited any corporation from acquiring the stock or assets of any other corporation when the effect of the acquisition might have been "substantially to lessen competition, or tend to create a monopoly." The intent of the amended statute was to prohibit "monopolistic tendencies in their incipiency", i.e., before they matured into Sherman Act transgressions.

The excitement and controversy over Section 7 was ignited and sustained by economic events themselves. The late 1960s witnessed the most spectacular corporate merger movement in all business history. Mergers were spectacular in at least three different respects. In the first place, the number of absolute corporate marriages per year was far higher than it had ever been; the average number of mergers for the 1965–1969 period, for example, was 1,630 per year as against 670 per year for the 1955–1959 period.[1] Secondly, the

---

[1]Calculated from statistics given in Federal Trade Commission, *Current Trends in Merger Activity, 1969*, March, 1970, p. 9.

mergers were larger in dollar value than they had ever been; in 1969 alone, the total value of "large acquired assets"[2] equaled $12.6 billion.[3] And, finally, the mergers increasingly involved firms that bore no obvious economic relationship to each other; an astonishing 82 percent of all recorded mergers between 1966–1968 were classified as "conglomerates."[4] That these developments would cause excitement and controversy among students of antitrust was inevitable.

Mergers and Antitrust Before 1950

The wave of mergers in the 1960s was not, of course, without some precedent in business history. The first great wave of corporate marriages in the 1898–1902 period had produced upward of 2,500 consolidations with an estimated total value of something over $6 billion.[5] Some of America's largest and most prominent industrial giants (U.S. Steel, Standard Oil of New Jersey) were constructed during that active period. Another wave of intense merger activity occurred between 1925 and 1931, when there were a reported 5,846 corporate consolidations.[6] As in the first wave, a considerable percentage of the merger activity was involved with the formation of large "giant" corporations. The merger wave of the late 1960s, however, broke all records for absolute number of consolidations and dollar value of acquired assets.

Although Section 7 of the Clayton Act had been in effect since 1914, the Justice Department and the Federal Trade Commission had not, before the post-World War II period, taken an aggressive antimerger position regarding corporate consolidations. As a general rule, with few exceptions, the giant corporations that had been put together through merger between 1898 and 1950 were left intact. This is not surprising since Section 7 had originally been intended to prevent the formation of holding companies; furthermore, the old statute specifically did not apply to *asset* acquisitions. The law did not (and apparently was not meant to) dampen the enthusiasm of corpo-

[2]Mergers involving acquired firms with assets of $10 million or more. See Federal Trade Commission, *Current Trends in Merger Activity, 1968*, March, 1969, pp. 1–7.
[3]*Ibid.*
[4]Federal Trade Commission, *Economic Report on Corporate Mergers*, Hearings on Economic Concentration, Subcommittee on Antitrust and Monopoly, U.S. Senate, 91st Cong., 1st Sess. (Washington: Government Printing Office, 1969), p. 63.
[5]Ralph L. Nelson, *Merger Movements in American Industry* (Princeton: Princeton University Press, 1959), p. 60.
[6]Samuel R. Reid, *Mergers, Managers, and the Economy* (New York: McGraw-Hill Book Company, 1968), p. 56.

rate combinations generally. The Celler-Kefauver Antimerger Act of 1950, however, clarified the intent of Section 7 and removed the "asset loophole," thereby opening the way for a much *tougher* enforcement policy.[7]

Antitrust Policy Since 1950

Since antitrust policy had been theoretically founded on a market structure approach to competition, it was not difficult to predict or understand the Justice Department's and Federal Trade Commission's new-found concern with the competitive effects of mergers. To review, the structural approach to competition holds pure competition as a welfare ideal and assumes that movements away from a purely competitive market structure imply less competition and, hence, a misallocation of scarce economic resources. Since corporate mergers affect structure *directly*, they are *a priori* a threat to competition and to consumer optimality.

No one has stated the hypothesis concerning mergers, market structure, and competition more exactly than Donald F. Turner, former chief of the Antitrust Department. In 1966, in an article first published in *Fortune*, Turner argued that the fundamental purpose of the antimerger law was to prevent an increase in "market power," and that this could be accomplished by preserving competitively *structured* markets.[8] Turner reminded his readers that economic theory suggested that firms with low market power could be expected to perform better in terms of price, product quality, and innovation, and that the chances for resource "misallocation" would be minimized with competitively *structured* markets. It should not be surprising, therefore, that an antitrust policy firmly rooted in traditional structural considerations would be generally hostile to business merger.

THE THEORY OF MERGER POLICY

It might be appropriate to review the most important theoretical factors underlying antitrust policy with respect to mergers. The following section will explain and analyze critically these factors.

[7] For an excellent review of the legislative history of Section 7, see *Brown Shoe Company* v. *United States*, 370 U.S. 294 (1962) at pp. 311–323.

[8] Turner's article, "The Antitrust Chief Relies," is reprinted in Edwin Mansfield, *Monopoly Power and Economic Performance* (Rev. ed.; New York: W. W. Norton and Company, 1968), p. 202.

Horizontal Merger

When two corporations that sell the same kind of product decide to merge, the consolidation is termed a horizontal merger. A horizontal merger always decreases the *number* of independent competitors by one and may, other things equal, increase the industry *concentration ratio* and the *market share* of the acquiring firm. In simple structural terms, therefore, horizontal mergers would tend to decrease the effectiveness of "competition" and, consequently, tend to lower economic welfare.

As we observed in Chapter 2, however, a simple decrease in the number of competitors or an increase in the concentration ratio does *not* indicate anything significant with respect to the level of competition. Competition in the market *may* be lessened, it may be as vigorous as before the merger, or it may be more vigorous after the merger. Since competition is a process that cannot be cardinally measured, there is no way to proceed from the number of sellers, the change in market shares, or the increase in concentration ratios to specific "degrees" of competition. All previous attempts to quantify competition (or monopoly) in this fashion have failed. To attempt to judge the wisdom of mergers on simple structural factors alone would, therefore, be quite irrational.[9]

It is easy to suggest a situation where a horizontal merger would likely increase competitive pressures even though some structural factors might be "sacrificed." Assume, for example, two beer producers that had not previously marketed their respective products in the same areas to the same customers. A corporate merger between them could economize on management, purchasing, advertising, production, marketing and a host of related expenses, and it could allow their respective local beers to be marketed in different areas increasing competitive pressures on existing sellers in those areas. This merger is particularly competitive if broadening the product line allows a more effective rivalry with, perhaps, some larger more established company. Although there is *one* less independent beer producer, and although market share and concentration ratios would tend to increase, consumers could and probably would be better served by the new arrangement of suppliers.

---

[9]Irrational or not, the present judicial approach to antitrust and particularly to mergers *is* structural. See Richard E. Low, *Modern Economic Organization* (Homewood, Ill.: Richard D. Irwin, 1970), p. 48, Also see Peter Asch, *Economic Theory and the Antitrust Dilemma* (New York: John Wiley and Sons, 1970), pp. 317–321.

It has been argued that such a horizontal merger (or any merger) decreases competition because it forecloses the acquiring firm from the market as an independent competitor. This theory assumes that the acquiring firm *might* have entered the market of the acquired firm by constructing a plant there; that if it had, the number of competitors would have increased instead of decreased, and the market shares and concentration ratios would not have increased; and that therefore, when a firm buys into a market it might have entered on its own, it forecloses some competition and, accordingly, lowers economic welfare.

It has also been argued that a firm on the "brink" of market entry serves as a competitive restraint *vis-à-vis* existing firms in the industry. Existing firms in the market are conscious of the "potential competitor" and conduct themselves accordingly. When that firm purchases an existing competitor, however, "potential" competition is lessened. If the purchasing firm was a "substantial" potential competitor, then competition is "substantially" lessened.

There are many problems with this theory of self-foreclosure. In the first place, it is difficult to believe that a firm can be rationally condemned for something it did *not* do. It was a *potential* competitor, it did *not* construct a plant to compete, *ergo* it decreases competition because it might have but did not enter the market as an independent competitor. Fantastic! Notice that the real issue— whether or not the merger itself reduces competition in some intelligently explainable manner—is conveniently skirted. *Why* is independently entering an economic market *more competitive* than purchasing some existing firm? Because the former procedure produces one more competitor than the latter? Again, it appears that this argument can be reduced to the silly, unprovable *numbers game* inherent in the market structure approach to competition.

Secondly, *why* might a company buy an existing firm rather than build an "independent" facility? One reason for the decision could certainly be that the former investment promised a greater rate of return than the latter, i.e., expected net revenues were greater. If market prices for final products cannot be arbitrarily increased by the corporate marriage (what economic theory would allow us to conclude that this is likely or even possible?), the merger will be *cheaper* than the next best economic alternative. Scarce economic resources are, therefore, being put into an area where they render maximum service to consumers and create the possibility of greater profits for the entrepreneurs. To condemn such allocations of re-sources and to condemn "cheapness" is to condemn economy and consumer welfare.[10] That economies "foreclose" less desirable, i.e., more costly options is always true. But such "foreclosure" is to be applauded, not condemned.

And finally, the potential competition theory always proves or attempts to prove too much. All firms are potential competitors with each other; even firms yet unborn are potentially competitive with existing firms. Are firms never to be allowed to merge because they may someday enter some market and produce some product? Such a theory could be used to stop all merging anywhere with anyone. But that, perhaps, is the major thrust of the theory anyway.

The "domino" theory of mergers suggests that one merger could spawn other mergers and that the effect, ultimately, would be to weaken competition. Through such a process, supposedly, "competi-tive" industries deteriorate into "oligopolies"; the wisest public policy would be to stop the merger process in its incipiency. Cer-tainly it is more rational to *prevent* competition from declining than to attempt to restore competition after the process is well along.

This argument suffers from a number of fatal flaws. The primary flaw is, again, a repeat of the unprovable assumption that mergers somehow automatically lower consumer welfare. If they do not, then preventing a merger movement in an industry is not *a priori* benefi-cial. *What is the optimal number of independent business units in a market place at any given period of time?* If the market structure enthusiasts could supply that information we would know how many mergers to allow and how many to prohibit. Lacking that informa-tion there is no sound basis for concluding that many mergers are somehow less optimal than fewer mergers or no mergers. Mergers may be dangerous, but that danger must be carefully demonstrated rather than simply assumed.

A secondary flaw can be illustrated by asking: *Why* do mergers encourage other mergers? Are the subsequent mergers consum-mated in order to be better able to compete with previous corporate combinations? Did the first consolidation realize economies and profit opportunities that other firms desire to imitate and indeed

---

[10]Yet such "cheapness" *has* been explicitly condemned. See the discussions in *Brown Shoe Company* v. *United States*, 370 U.S. 294; and of *Federal Trade Commis-sion* v. *Procter & Gamble Company*, 386 U.S. 568 that will follow in this chapter.

must imitate to stay competitive? But low-cost operations should be imitated and the sooner the better. If cheaper methods of production and distribution are discovered, it is imperative that rival firms and the consumers that they ultimately serve be able to enjoy these same economies, whatever the structural sacrifices. To impede such a process on the pretext that antitrust policy is vitally concerned with "consumer welfare" is almost ludicrous.

Vertical Merger

When a manufacturing firm merges with a supplier or with a distributor, the merger is termed vertical integration or a "vertical merger." The manufacturing firm is combining one or more of the stages of production in the product line from raw material to the final delivered product in the hands of some buyer. Since such mergers are not between direct competitors—or even potential competitors—the antitrust issues are more subtle than with horizontal combinations. Nevertheless, such mergers are reputed threats to competition.

The major concern over vertical integration centers around the concept of foreclosure, a rather familiar issue in our discussion at this point. According to this concept, to purchase a supplier would be to "preempt" or "foreclose" some rivals from sources of supply; to purchase a retailer would be to preempt or foreclose some competitors from channels of distribution. In either case, supposedly, nonintegrated competitors would find it more difficult to compete since their access to certain markets had been made more difficult. The tendency would be to "substantially reduce competition or tend to create a monopoly."

But how exactly are competitors foreclosed from markets? Assume, for example, that a firm that makes steel ingot buys a coal producing firm. Certainly the steel firm can and probably will increase its own purchases of coal from its own firm (assuming that its own firm is at least competitive), but this action will hardly foreclose rivals from significant coal purchasing opportunities. Why should there be less opportunities after the merger than before the merger? Economic activity is emphatically *not* a zero-sum game where increased purchases by one firm necessarily imply that other firms must purchase less. If the steel company is interested in operating the coal subsidiary profitably, that firm will be interested in selling *additional* units of output. What would prevent other coal firms, especially the ones that have lost orders for coal, from doing additional business? In short, why should anyone be foreclosed from anything?

The same question applies to a vertical merger involving a distributor. The natural tendency is to conclude that the manufacturer will increase his own requirements of his own product thereby excluding some of the products of his competitors. But consider the situation just prior to the merger. The distributor is attempting to sell that batch of commodities that render the greatest total profit. Assuming that the merger has just been completed, where does the distributor get the "power" to "force" more of one supplier's product on the public than before and, thereby, foreclose rival manufacturers from markets? If it had been profitable to sell more Brand-X and preempt competitors prior to the consolidation, why hadn't the firm done so? Precisely how does the merger alter *demand* conditions in the final market?

It has also been argued that particular nonintegrated competitors will be put in a disadvantageous position if a vertical merger realizes certain economies for the firms involved. It may, for example, be easier, more convenient and certainly cheaper to retail goods through subsidiaries than through "independent" distributors. If this allows lower prices or greater profits, then nonintegrated firms are at a "disadvantage" in the competitive market. But, of course, such "disadvantages" are *absolutely desirable* and are the essence of competitive pressure in a free market. They are the particular business practices that insure that scarce economic resources will be channeled toward their most productive employment. Notice that the disadvantage arises only because final consumers prefer "cheapness" and tend to reward sellers that curb expenses. If they did not, then the merger could not and would not create any "disadvantages" for any rivals. To condemn the creation of such situations is, therefore, to strike at the heart of consumer tastes and preferences. And to do so in the name of "protecting consumers" would be the ultimate irony and hypocrisy of antitrust policy.

The foreclosure or preemption of certain competitors by companies that realize certain economies of production and selling might also be termed a "barrier to entry." As already explained, the fact that some manufacturers are vertically integrated can make competition with them more difficult. If consumers reward integration, for example, a kind of "barrier" is created *vis-à-vis* firms that do not offer consumers similar advantages. But, again, it would be ironical to blame consumers for the welfare reductions supposedly associated with such barriers when they are produced and sustained by consumer preference itself! It is to be observed that all such "barriers" are in reality *economies* that some firms have achieved and others have not achieved. Such economies are barriers to entry; they keep out firms that cannot organize their scarce economic resources in a manner that is pleasing to the consumer. Those who argue that such a condition is "unfair," or unfairly limits competition, do not really understand the free market system.

The most interesting element in vertical merger theory is the concept of "subsidization" and its corollary, "squeezing." Subsidization implies that vertically integrated firms have competitive advantages since certain stages of production can be used to support or finance other stages. A steel firm, for example, might "buy" its own coal from itself "at cost," and use this price "advantage" to depress the final price of steel ingot. Nonintegrated ingot-producing rivals purchasing relatively more expensive coal would be "squeezed" between higher coal prices and relatively low steel ingot prices. The evil tendency, supposedly, would be to reduce competition substantially and to create a monopoly in ingot production.

There are many objections to this line of reasoning. In the first place, it would appear that successful "squeezing" depends upon a near monopoly in the supply of the resource under discussion. Nonintegrated manufacturers that can turn to alternative suppliers cannot be so squeezed. Therefore squeezing depends upon monopolization and extreme barriers to entry in resource markets—an extremely unlikely occurrence in a free market, as this volume has argued and demonstrated.

Secondly, if there were no monopoly over the resource, and "squeezing" occurred, it would *not* necessarily be condemnable. The essence of the process of squeezing is to *cheapen* the stages of production such that final goods prices will be as low as possible. Properly understood, what is being squeezed is *cost*. Nothing would or should prevent other firms from making similar mergers to enjoy the same "advantages" of vertical integration. Such mergers and such competition between firms that squeeze costs are to be encouraged.

In the third place, it must be realized that "subsidization" can occur only at the sacrifice of some profit at that particular stage of production.[11] To use resources at cost or below cost is to sacrifice the return on that investment. Capital can, of course, be temporarily consumed. But since the integrated firm has already made a substantially larger investment than its nonintegrated rivals, it must (eventually) secure a greater profit on its investment. If it voluntarily foregoes that profit in one stage of production it will have to recoup it in another.

But where will it be able to recoup that profit? If final product markets are competitive, how will the integrated firm be able to earn a higher than normal rate of return there? Will the lower ingot prices bring a volume and a profit sufficient to cover subsidization through the stages of production? Perhaps, but in no way can this be guaranteed or assured. If it occurred, of course, it would be a delightful development as far as the consumer of ingot is concerned. Such low price-high volume operations are the very thrust of competitive markets.

If final markets for ingot are not competitive, *higher* prices would allow classic recoupment in the spirit of a true monopoly. But why is "subsidization" necessary before final goods prices can be *increased?* If prices can be increased, they can be increased with or without any subsidization. The advantages of vertical integration, therefore, would have nothing at all to do with that "problem."

To summarize, the "competitive problems" associated with vertical integration are illusionary. There is no sound theoretical reason for accepting the proposition that such mergers—employing foreclosure, subsidization, and squeezing—will work a serious injury to consumers. They may, as indicated, be a serious threat to relatively inefficient nonintegrated rivals, and they may certainly upset status quo market structures; however, their danger to the competitive process in a free market is not obvious.

Conglomerate Merger

There is no generally accepted definition of the term conglomerate nor, accordingly, of the mergers that should be classified as conglomerate.[12] In our discussion, mergers that are not clearly

[11]For an excellent discussion of this issue see Eugene Singer, *Antitrust Economics* (Englewood Cliffs, N.J.: Prentice-Hall, 1968), pp. 262–266.

[12]For three different views on this issue of definitions, see Betty Bock, *Antitrust Issues in Conglomerate Acquisitions* (The National Industrial Conference Board, Studies in Business Economics, No. 110, 1969), p. 8.; Donald F. Turner, "Conglomerate

horizontal or vertical will be classified as conglomerate: the term will refer to corporate marriages between firms that are not direct competitors, suppliers, or distributors. Some conglomerate mergers may involve firms in related but not identical product lines; some may involve firms whose product lines are complementary rather than strictly competitive or "unrelated." Some conglomerate mergers may involve firms with high degrees of "concentricity" or a "mutuality of interest." Although these latter terms defy precise definition, the general impression is that the acquired firm acts as a kind of catalyst to the potential market performance of the acquiring firm. The term "synergy" has also been used to describe the effects of such mergers on the acquiring firm.[13] And, finally, the term conglomerate may apply to any "free form" merger where no "concentricity" or "synergy" is obvious.

Since conglomerate mergers do not directly involve competitors, suppliers or distributors, the conventional market structure approach would not appear immediately applicable. At first it would appear that conglomerate mergers could not endanger competition in any meaningful or measurable way. Yet the belief that "large conglomerate enterprises possess kinds of power that may involve jeopardy to competition" is certainly widespread in key governmental as well as some academic circles.[14] We will explore how these "kinds of power" might, supposedly, endanger the competitive system.

It would be incorrect to create the impression that there is a separate body of conglomerate theory apart from the general market structure approach to competition already outlined—and criticized —in this volume. Actually almost all the arguments about the "dangers" of such mergers involve theoretical factors that we have already discussed at length, and rejected. For example, it has been maintained that conglomerate mergers are a threat to competition since they eliminate *potential* competitors, create the potential for *subsidization* and *predatory price cutting, foreclose* smaller firms

Mergers and Section 7 of the Clayton Act," *Harvard Law Review*, LXXVIII (May, 1965), 1315; and John C. Narver, *Conglomerate Mergers and Market Competition* (Berkeley: University of California Press, 1967).

[13]Editors of Fortune, *The Conglomerate Commotion* (New York: Viking Press, 1970), p. 81.

[14]Corwin Edwards, "The Large Conglomerate Firm: A Critical Appraisal," Mansfield, *op. cit.*, p. 121. The Federal Trade Commission has held this position since at least 1949. See Narver, *op. cit.*, p. 39.

from entering markets, increase *concentration ratios* in the economy, and generally entrench "market power." But these are all familiar issues, and any further comment on them would only be redundant.

One theoretical factor that may appear to be new—but that actually is not—is the concept of "reciprocity." Reciprocity is the practice of buying from those that buy from you or, to put the concept in antitrust jargon, to exert market power on suppliers such that they also purchase from you. The effect, as might be guessed, is to foreclose competitors from certain markets and to reduce competition.

Certainly reciprocal dealings predate conglomerate mergers, and there is no question that purchasing agents have always been keenly aware of potential reciprocal arrangements. An article in *Fortune* once reported that of the top 500 companies, over 60 percent used trade relations men that conducted reciprocal dealings.[15] The antitrust issue, however, is not the existence of reciprocal dealing, but the idea that situations are created where suppliers are forced to deal in some *noncompetitive* fashion or on some *noncompetitive* terms with certain buyers.

Imagine a situation with no reciprocal agreements where a buyer —even a large buyer—is purchasing materials from some seller. The buyer, presumably, is doing the best that he can with that seller: he is obtaining the best product at the lowest possible price. One must presume that he is employing all his supposed "market power" to obtain the optimal factor package. Under such circumstances, where does that buyer suddenly obtain the *additional* power to dictate a reciprocal agreement? As was the case in our analysis of tying agreements, the reciprocity issue is a clear example of economic double-counting.[16]

It is possible, of course, that the buyer may make the reciprocal purchase so *attractive* to the supplier that a reciprocal agreement is established. Suppliers may, for example, accept a slightly lower price for their supplies in exchange for a slightly better reciprocal purchase. Or certain economies on the part of the conglomerate buyer may allow attractive reciprocal purchases without any price concessions. But these developments are hardly anticompetitive; they tend

[15]Edward McCreary, Jr. and Walter Guzzardi, Jr., "Reciprocity: A Customer is a Co.'s Best Friend," *Fortune*, LXXI (June, 1965), 180.
[16]Robert H. Bork, "Antitrust in Dubious Battle," *Fortune*, LXXX (September, 1969), 160.

to lower costs and increase competitive pressures. They are, therefore, desirable and to be encouraged. Reciprocity, like the rest of
antitrust theory, is an illusionary "hobgoblin"; it is either harmless or
beneficial in a free market.

It has also been argued that conglomerates can reduce competition
in an industry into which they have merged by effecting the price-
making calculus of the smaller independent competitors.[17] This argument holds that independents facing conglomerates would be
more reluctant to reduce prices for fear of "retaliation" by the multi-
product giant. Thus "rigid pricing," supposedly familiar in oligopolistic industries, would prevail in an industry that was formerly "competitive." The net effect, of course, would be to reduce economic
welfare.

There are many familiar difficulties here. In the first place, inter-
dependence is a factor in *all* real markets; its appearance is not
unique with conglomeration. Even "small" firms in "competitive"
industries must integrate the likely reactions of rivals into their pricing decisions. Since competition is never "pure," all firms *have* a
pricing policy and all pricing decisions are "affected" by competitors.
Conglomerates, therefore, do not spoil some purely competitive
wonderland.

Secondly, the entire business about "retaliation" and "predatory"
practices is becoming a bit tedious at this point. Where is the documented empirical evidence—even the smallest shred of it—that real
firms in real markets engage in such practices?[18] This "theory," like
the rest of antitrust theory, is just so much idle daydreaming; it has
never been confirmed in the marketplace. Since it is a daydream, and
since firms (unlike economists) understand it to be a daydream, it can
not realistically play any role in "pricing." Even if it *did* exist, it
might just as logically prevent prices from going *up* as well as down!
And any theory that can as easily lead to two completely opposite
conclusions cannot possibly be sound.

[17]See John M. Blair, "Conglomerate Mergers—Theory and Congressional Intent",
J. Fred Weston and Sam Peltzman, *Public Policy Toward Mergers* (Englewood Cliffs,
N.J.: Goodyear Publishing Company, 1969), pp. 186–188.
[18]Even Donald F. Turner has admitted that there is no empirical evidence to verify
the thesis that large firms, particularly conglomerates, engage in predatory pricing
practices. See Turner, "Conglomerate Mergers and Section 7 of the Clayton Act," *op.
cit.*, p. 1340. See also Ronald H. Koller II, "The Myths of Predatory Pricing: An
Empirical Study," *Antitrust Law and Economics Review*, IV (Summer 1971), 105–123.

The Dead End of Antitrust

Lacking a rational and consistent theory to explain the anticompetitive effects of mergers, the arguments against mergers have deteriorated into irrelevant concerns. For instance, it has been stated that an important reason for mergers is to gain the tax advantages and promoters' profits associated with some consolidations. Perhaps. But what has this to do with competition or more specifically, *with a threat to competition?* Whether or not it would be wise to legislate on tax advantages and stock promotions is a completely different issue from the one that is under examination in this chapter. Do mergers restrain trade, lessen competition, and tend to subvert consumer sovereignty and consumer welfare? If they do, *how* do they? Tax advantages and stock promotions are only relevant if it can *first* be demonstrated that mergers are destructive of competition. Lacking such a demonstration, discussions of tax advantages and stock promotions are beside the point.

The same argument applies to the "human dislocations" that may accompany mergers, particularly where small sleepy firms are acquired by growth-oriented conglomerates. Although such issues might be relevant in "sociology" and "management," they are *bogus* antitrust issues. They do, however, ironically serve to demonstrate the almost *total bankruptcy* of antitrust theory with respect to mergers.

The first part of this chapter has attempted to outline and criticize some popular merger theories. The second part of this chapter will be devoted to an examination of some of the most famous merger cases in recent antitrust history.[19] If mergers actually restrain trade, tend toward monopoly, foreclose substantial amounts of competition, encourage noncompetitive reciprocity and generally reduce consumer welfare, an examination of the leading merger cases should reveal such activity.

THE BROWN SHOE CASE (1962)

The Brown Shoe case involved the legality of a 1956 merger between the Brown Shoe Company and the G.R. Kinney Company.[20] Before the merger Brown was the nation's fourth largest shoe

[19]For reasons of time and space, the following discussion will only treat some of the classic merger cases of the 1960s. For some information on merger cases prior to the 1960s, see Irwin Stelzer, *Selected Antitrust Cases: Landmark Decisions* (3rd ed.; Homewood, Ill.: Richard D. Irwin, 1966), pp. 56–74.

[20]*Brown Shoe Company* v. *United States*, 370 U.S. 294 (1962).

manufacturer with about 4 percent of total domestic manufactured shoe output; in addition, Brown owned 845 retail shoe outlets, all of which had been acquired between 1950 and 1955. Kinney, an almost insignificant shoe manufacturer (½ percent of industry output), was the nation's largest family-style shoe store chain with over 400 stores in 270 cities. Although there were a reported 1,048 shoe manufacturing plants in the United States in 1956, and over 70,000 retail outlets that sold shoes, the government charged that the pending merger between one of the nation's largest shoe manufacturers and the nation's largest family-owned chain of shoe stores violated the amended Section 7 of the Clayton Act. And after failing in an attempt to obtain a permanent injunction to stop the merger in 1955, the Justice Department sued for divesture in 1956.

District Court Decision

The District Court with Judge Weber presiding, found against the Brown-Kinney merger on November 20, 1959.[21] In summary it stated that the merger would (1) increase manufacturing and retailing concentration in the shoe industry; (2) eliminate competition between Kinney and Brown at the retail level; and (3) "establish a manufacturer-retailer relationship that would foreclose other firms from a fair opportunity to compete for Kinney's business."[22]

There can be little doubt that concentration, and trends in concentration, were the decisive issues in the District Court decision. Judge Weber emphasized that it had been the Congressional intent in passing the Antimerger Act of 1950 to "encompass minute acquisitions which tend toward monopoly and to do so in their incipiency."[23] Even though the share of the shoe market held by Brown —or even by Brown-Kinney—might be small in percentage terms, that was *not* to be the determining issue:

> We are not so much concerned with percentages as such, but with what these percentages mean in examination under the light of the fact of the case and the economic realities involved.[24]

[21] *United States* v. *Brown Shoe Company*, 179 F. Supp. 721.
[22] *Ibid.*, p. 741.
[23] *Ibid.*, p. 737.
[24] *Ibid.*

The "economic realities" demonstrated, according to Weber, that there was a "definite trend" toward concentration in the shoe industry. The most important phase of the concentration took the form of leading manufacturers obtaining additional retail outlets. The court record showed that many of the large shoe manufacturers had acquired over a thousand independent retail shoe stores between 1950 and 1956; in fact, the 13 largest shoe manufacturers operated 21 percent of all shoe outlets in 1956.[25] And this trend, coupled with the declining number of shoe manufacturers, was the very sort of thing that Congress had meant to "arrest in its incipiency" when it amended Section 7.

The concentration trend was not just important for its own sake. When shoe manufacturers acquired shoe retailers they "definitely increased the sale of their own manufactured product to these retail outlets," thus "drying up the available outlets for independent manufacturers."[26] Judge Weber held that the smaller manufacturers were "losing that market" through foreclosure, and that this "substantially lessens competition between manufacturers."[27] Therefore, the tendency in the shoe industry was toward the elimination of small manufacturers and small independent retailers.[28]

The Brown-Kinney merger might also lessen competition at the retail level since there might be substantial economies associated with vertical integration in the shoe industry. Weber admitted that company-owned retail outlets had "advantages" in advertising, insurance, inventory control, and price control. These advantages would likely be reflected "in lower prices or in higher quality at the same prices." But, of course, the independents would have a much harder time competing with company-owned stores under such conditions.

And finally, after much discussion, the court admitted that competition was likely to be lessened in the "men's," "women's" and "children's" shoe market. There were at least 141 cities of over 10,000 people where Brown and Kinney retail outlets competed directly.[29] The merger would eliminate Kinney as an independent competitive factor and simply make them an "adoptive child" of a larger shoe

[25] Ibid., pp. 737–738.
[26] Ibid., p. 738.
[27] Ibid., p. 739.
[28] Ibid., p. 740.
[29] Ibid., p. 735.

family.[30] For all these reasons, therefore, Weber ordered Brown to divest themselves of Kinney.

Supreme Court Decision

The Supreme Court decision written by Chief Justice Warren affirmed the decision against Brown.[31] The Chief Justice first reviewed the lower court's findings and the legislative history of Section 7 of the Clayton Act as amended. He agreed that the "relevant market" in the case was the market for "men's, women's and children's" shoes. These were lines of commerce easily recognized by the public, typically manufactured in separate plants, not directly competitive, and clearly directed at different classes of consumers.[32] An analysis of whether the "vertical" aspects of the Brown-Kinney merger reduced competition substantially in those lines of commerce was now required.

The Supreme Court first convinced itself that the issue of foreclosure in this case was somewhat akin to foreclosure in tying contract clauses.[33] They then went on to argue that the foreclosure in the *Brown* case was not just "*de minimus* since no merger between a manufacturer and an independent retailer could involve a larger potential market foreclosure."[34] And since there was a trend toward vertical integration in this industry, and since the District Court had found a "tendency of the acquiring manufacturers to become increasingly important sources of supply for their acquired outlets," the tendency must be "the foreclosure of independent manufacturers from markets otherwise open to them."[35] But this tendency was against the clear Congressional intent in passing the Celler-Kefauver Act:

> Congress was desirous of preventing the formation of further oligopolies with their attendant adverse effects upon local control of industry and upon small business. Where an industry was composed of numerous independent units, Congress appeared anxious to preserve this structure.[36]

[30] *Ibid.*, p. 741.
[31] 370 U.S. p. 294.
[32] *Ibid.*, 326.
[33] *Ibid.*, pp. 330–331.
[34] *Ibid.*, p. 332.
[35] *Ibid.*
[36] *Ibid.*, p. 333.

Hence the court found that the vertical aspects of the merger might foreclose competition from a substantial share of the relevant market, and that there were no "countervailing competitive, economic or social advantages" associated with the merger. Strangely, there had been *no discussion* whatever of such advantages until that point in the decision when they were suddenly declared *not to exist!*[37]

Warren then moved to the horizontal aspects of the merger. He accepted the District Court's finding—over Brown's strong objection —that the relevant markets under consideration were men's, women's, and children's shoes in cities of over 10,000 people. He also agreed that the District Court had taken enough of a sample to estimate the competitive consequences of the merger in those markets.[38] In 118 cities, for example, the court estimated that the combined Brown-Kinney share of the relevant market exceeded 5 percent. But was market share to be directly related to a lessening of competition, and was 5 percent a "substantial" volume of trade? Warren answered "yes" on both counts:

> In an industry as fragmented as shoe retailing, the control of substantial shares of the trade in a city may have important effects on competition. If a merger achieving 5 percent control were now approved, we might be required to approve further merger effort by Brown's competitors seeking similar market shares. The oligopoly Congress sought to avoid would then be furthered and it would be difficult to dissolve the combinations previously approved. Furthermore, in this fragmented industry, even if the combination controls but a small share of a particular market, the fact that this share is held by a large national chain can adversely affect competition.[39]

But how would competition (read "competitors") be adversely affected? Why through certain economies and efficiencies realizable from the merger! Integrated national chains could alter styles in footwear quickly, eliminate wholesalers, and "market their own brands at prices below those of competing independent retailers."[40] And this type of process was to be condemned if it endangered the economy of "numerous independent units" envisioned by Congress. In one of the most amazing and revealing statements of all antitrust rulings, Warren declared:

[37] *Ibid.*, p. 334.
[38] *Ibid.*, pp. 334–343.
[39] *Ibid.*, pp. 343–344.
[40] *Ibid.*, p. 344.

Of course, some of the results of large integrated or chain operations are beneficial to consumers. Their expansion is not rendered unlawful by the mere fact that small independent stores
may be adversely affected. It is competition, not competitors,
which the Act protects. But we cannot fail to recognize Congress' desire to promote competition through protection of viable, small, locally owned businesses. Congress appreciated that
occasional higher costs and prices might result from the maintenance of fragmented industries and markets. It resolved these
competing considerations in favor of decentralization. We must
give effect to that decision.[41]

This is classic antitrust double-talk; moreover, it exposes the antitrust
hoax. The act protects competition, not competitors, by protecting
competitors! Economies that adversely affect small, independent
businesses are not to be condemned unless they adversely affect
small, independent businesses! No amount of economic or legal ra-
tionalization can possibly put this antitrust house back together
again.

Justice Harlan wrote a separate decision in which he dissented in
part and concurred with the majority in part. Harlan dissented because he would have dismissed the case for lack of jurisdiction.[42]
More importantly, he dissented because he felt that the District
Court's conclusions on the vertical aspects of the merger were sufficient to condemn the merger without regard to any examination of
the horizontal issues.[43] Since "Brown's merger with Kinney potentially withdraws a share of the market previously available to the
independent shoe manufacturers" and since these manufacturers
would have to "enter some other market or go out of business," the
Brown-Kinney consolidation was condemnable on vertical foreclosure grounds alone.[44] Harlan concluded by admitting that the economies of integration would also tend to work a competitive
disadvantage to nonintegrated retailers.[45]

Comment
Much of the argument in the Brown Shoe case was premised
on the assumption of increasing concentration in the shoe industry. The District Court had stated, and the Supreme Court had

[41] *Ibid.*
[42] *Ibid.*, p. 357.
[43] *Ibid.*, p. 366.
[44] *Ibid.*, p. 372.
[45] *Ibid.*, p. 372–373.

agreed, that there was a "definite trend" toward concentration in shoe manufacturing and shoe retailing and that it was the Congressional intent to halt such movements in their incipiency. Without even restating the argument made in Chapter 2 that changes in concentration prove nothing *a priori* about competition, it might suffice to note that the court-observed "trends" are open to serious question. It is true that there had been an absolute decline in the number of shoe manufacturers between 1947 and 1956,[46] but concentration ratios for the largest group of firms had actually *declined* during the same period. Harlan had noted in a footnote that while the four, eight, and fifteen largest shoe firms had accounted for 25.9 percent, 31.4 percent and 36.2 percent of industry output in 1947, they accounted for 22 percent, 27 percent and 32.5 percent of industry output in 1955.[47] Was this the legendary tendency toward oligopoly that Congress had supposedly legislated against?[48]

Even stronger doubts linger over the inference that there was increasing concentration in retail outlets, or in the percentage of retail outlets owned by manufacturers or chains. Although the *absolute number* of such outlets purchased by the larger shoe manufacturers undoubtedly increased throughout the period, Brown introduced data that indicated that retail sales by chains with eleven or more stores stood at a constant 19.5 percent of national dollar volume in both 1948 and 1954.[49] In addition, there were unquestionably more shoe retailers in 1955 than there had been in 1948. Any talk of concentration in an industry with nearly 100,000 units and such ease of entry must not be taken seriously unless it can be supported with inconvertible fact. There was no such fact in this case. Yet a good part of the case against the Brown-Kinney merger rested on such "evidence."

Even more importantly, the entire argument concerning "substantial foreclosure" and the supposed "drying up of available outlets for independent manufacturers" depends upon and is logically derived from the "concentration" myth just exposed. Obviously out-

[46]There were, however, almost 500 *more* shoe manufacturers in 1947 than there had been in 1937; the Court failed to mention this! See *United States* v. *United Shoe Machinery Corporation*, 110 F. Supp. 295, (1953), at p. 301.
[47]370 U.S. 374.
[48]It should also be remembered that no account was taken of *foreign manufacturers*.
[49]370 U.S. 374.

THE MYTHS OF ANTITRUST

lets could *not* be "drying up" if the retail shoe markets were *not* becoming increasingly concentrated, if the number of retail outlets was growing, and if the volume of business done by these shoe stores was increasing. Even if Brown switched some of its shoe business to its own stores, the old outlets *from* which Brown had switched were "opened" to independent shoe manufacturers. While particular independent manufacturers may have been foreclosed from particular outlets, therefore, they would not in any sense be foreclosed from the retail shoe market.

But even admitting this is admitting too much. Both the District Court and the Supreme Court noted the fact that Kinney's purchases of shoes from Brown had gone from zero prior to the merger to 7.8 percent after the merger.[50] Information supplied from other Brown acquisitions indicated that Brown had a habit of increasing its shoe requirements at outlets which it owned or franchised. The clear impression conveyed by the court decisions is that the independent shoe manufacturers must have sold fewer shoes to Brown retail outlets and particularly to Kinney after the merger, and that the independents were "losing that market" as the purchases of Brown shoes by Kinney increased.[51] But the impression is a wholly inaccurate impression since *independent sales to Kinney did not decrease.* The trial record indicates that independents sold just as many shoes to Kinney after the merger as they had before.[52] In fact, even the Supreme Court admitted at one point that "the dollar volume of Kinney's outside shoe purchases in 1955 was between 16 and 17 million dollars, and this amount *has increased to 19.4 million by 1957.*"[53] Thus the court's mistakenly inferred consequences concerning foreclosure that *had not happened* from concentration assumptions that *were not accurate.* Such are the dreams (nightmares?) of which an almost religious faith in antitrust is composed.

Finally and briefly, the Supreme Court's open hostility to the economies of vertical integration has to be the most embarrassing part of the decision against the merger. Again, we are told by the highest tribunal in the land that economies and efficiencies restrain trade and tend to reduce competition—the very opposite of the

[50]179 F. Supp. 738 and 370 U.S. 304.
[51]179 F. Supp. 739.
[52]See "Proceedings of Section 7, Subcommittee A.B.A.", *The Antitrust Bulletin,* VIII (March-April, 1963), 249.
[53]370 U.S. 371 (Emphasis added).

truth. When it is demonstrated that competitors with admittedly "higher costs and prices" have to be "preserved" and vertically integrated firms that would pass economies on to consumers have to be dissolved, antitrust stands naked stripped of all pretense. That antitrust can still find substantial intellectual support is, in a way, the most incomprehensible aspect of the entire charade.

THE CONTINENTAL CAN AND ALCOA CASES (1964)

An increasing hostility to mergers became more pronounced in the Continental Can[54] and Alcoa[55] cases, both decided by the Supreme Court in 1964. In the Continental case the court struck down a merger between the nation's second largest canmaker (Continental) and the third largest producer of glass containers (Hazel-Atlas). Although the Court admitted that the "products" of the two companies were different and certainly not as interchangeable as they might be, they ruled that there was sufficient inter-industry competition to permit rational discussion of a "glass and metal container market" as a separate line of commerce! Since in *that* market the share of the combination was high (25 percent), and since a dominant, multiproduct firm would hold "advantages" over single-product smaller rivals and, perhaps, tend to trigger additional mergers, the Continental-Hazel-Atlas merger could not be permitted. In addition Continental and Hazel were *potential competitors* in the future, and to allow this merger would reduce potential competition. Although Justice Harlan's strong dissent argued that the court's "bizarre" calculations of a "nonexistent" market had enabled them to dispense with any elaborate proof that competition had been substantially reduced, it was apparently to no avail.[56]

In the Alcoa case, a majority of the Supreme Court overturned a lower court decision that had allowed the merger between the Aluminum Company of America and the Rome Cable Company. Justice Douglas held that aluminum and copper conductor cable were different enough to form their own submarkets, and that in the aluminum conductor market, Alcoa held 27.8 percent of "industry" sales, Rome 1.3 percent, and the nine largest firms over 95 percent. Since the "market" was already highly concentrated, and since

[54] *United States* v. *Continental Can Company et al.*, 378 U.S. 441.
[55] *United States* v. *Aluminum Company of America*, 377 U.S. 271.
[56] 378 U.S. pp. 470–477.

Rome was a "substantial" and "aggressive competitor," the merger violated Section 7.[57]

Justices Stewart, Harlan, and Goldberg joined in a vehement dissent in the Alcoa case. The essence of the dissent was that the Supreme Court majority had "clearly failed to prove its line of commerce claims." The District Court's long (3,500-page trial record) and careful analysis demonstrated to these justices that insulated aluminum conductors and insulated copper conductors were part of the *same* relevant market; the Supreme Court majority was mistaken on that crucial point.[58] And the District Court's opinion that the merger was a " 'combination of an aluminum and an essentially copper manufacturing company' undertaken by Alcoa in the face of its declining market for the purpose of obtaining insulating know-how and diversification needed 'to overcome a market disadvantage rather than to obtain a captive market. . . . or to eliminate a competitor' " was more nearly accurate than the Supreme Court majority's opinion.[59] But, as usual, the findings and conclusions of a District Court were not determining.

THE CONSOLIDATED FOODS CASE (1965)

In 1965 the Supreme Court reversed the Court of Appeals and found that Consolidated Foods should divest itself of Gentry as the FTC had ordered in 1961.[60] Consolidated Foods, a large, diversified food processor and wholesaler had purchased Gentry, Inc., a manufacturer of dehydrated onion and garlic in 1951. The FTC alleged that the acquisition violated Section 7 of the Clayton Act since the threat of reciprocal purchasing might create "for Gentry a protected market which others cannot penetrate despite superiority of price, quality or service."[61] Supposedly, Consolidated could (and did) pressure some of its suppliers to deal with Gentry, thus foreclosing some competition. Since "the share of the market that might be insulated from the effective interplay of fair competition" was substantial (25 percent of all Consolidated's suppliers required onion and garlic), a "substantial" lessening of competition was probable and the FTC ordered divesture.

[57] 377 U.S. p. 281.
[58] *Ibid.*, pp. 285–286.
[59] *Ibid.*, p. 287.
[60] *Federal Trade Commission* v. *Consolidated Foods Corporation*, 380 U.S. p. 592.
[61] 62 FTC 960.

Circuit Court of Appeals Decision

The Circuit Court of Appeals reversed the FTC divesture order in 1964.[62] Although Judge Castle (speaking for Judges Knoch and Mercer) admitted that Consolidated Foods had "overtly *attempted* to use its purchasing power as a devise to obtain business for its Gentry division," the trial record indicated that (1) it was not apparently a consistent company policy and (2) it was completely ineffective in a number of instances.[63] Most importantly for the Circuit Court

> ... ten years of post-acquisition experience—during which Consolidated attempted overt enforcement of reciprocal buying practice where it deemed it might be successful—serves to demonstrate that neither the acquisition of Gentry, in and of itself, nor the overt attempts to use buying power to influence sellers to Consolidated to purchase from Gentry resulted in substantial anticompetitive effect. No substantial impact on the relevant market occurred, and . . . we are of the view that the experience reflected by this post-acquisition period must weigh heavily in appraising future probabilities.[64]

Between 1951 and 1958, Gentry's share of the market in dehydrated onion sales rose from 28 percent to 35 percent while its dehydrated garlic sales declined from 51 percent to 39 percent. Since the industry as a whole was growing rapidly, Gentry's "slight gain" in onion and "significant loss" in garlic demonstrated that reciprocity—implied or overt—was *completely ineffectual* and of no concern as far as competition was concerned.[65]

Supreme Court Decision

The Supreme Court reversed the Appeals Court decision on April 28, 1965.[66] Justice Douglas was sympathetic to the FTC argument that in an "industry" that was already extremely concentrated (the industry leader Basic and second-ranking Gentry combined for 85 percent of all sales), anticompetitive obstacles like potential reciprocity should be removed. The fact that reciprocity had been tried repeatedly was sufficient cause to infer that a substantial lessening of competition was probable.[67] And the post-acquisition evidence,

[62] *Consolidated Foods Corporation v. Federal Trade Commission*, 329 F. 2d 623.
[63] *Ibid.*, pp. 625–626.
[64] *Ibid.*, p. 626.
[65] *Ibid.*, pp. 626–627.
[66] 380 U.S. 592.
[67] *Ibid.*, pp. 596–597.

Douglas argued, tended to confirm the FTC allegations regarding the potential anticompetitive effects of the merger.[68]

Mr. Justice Harlan and Stewart concurred in the majority opinion although both expressed some disagreement with Douglas' particular opinion. Stewart argued that neither the "mere effort at reciprocity" nor the peculiar structure of the industry would be sufficient for a finding of a substantial lessening of competition.[69] In fact, he hypothesized, it was perfectly possible that the merger intensified competition between Basic and Gentry; certainly the outputs and qualities of product were more impressive in 1958 than in 1951.[70] Moreover, there was no evidence to indicate—contrary to the FTC implications—that barriers to entry were particularly severe in this industry.[71]

Stewart would have placed much more weight on the post-acquisition evidence than did the Supreme Court. For it was here, he said, that Consolidated's probable effect on competition was evidenced. Stewart maintained that while Consolidated was not able to wield reciprocal pressure against large, brand-name food processors like Armour and Swift, it could and did strong-arm smaller, private-label food processors.[72] Since these "independents" were substantial purchasers in the dehydrated onion and garlic market, the FTC was right to order divesture on the probable effects of reciprocity.

Comment

Stewart's criticism of the Supreme Court decision is certainly well taken. We can easily agree with the argument that simple market structure and concentration statistics combined with a few mostly unsuccessful efforts at reciprocity are not enough to infer substantial competitive restraint. But neither, of course, is Stewart's suggestion that certain small independents were pressured to deal with Gentry evidence of substantial competitive restraint. What is crucial and completely unexamined in this case is the nature of the wholesale market for foods. If this market is reasonably competitive (and there is every reason to believe that it is) then it becomes difficult to accept

[68] *Ibid.*, p. 598.
[69] *Ibid.*, p. 604.
[70] *Ibid.*
[71] *Ibid.*, p. 605. (A firm by the name of Gilroy Foods, Inc. had entered the industry in 1959.)
[72] *Ibid.*, p. 608.

the idea that any sellers were "injured" by Consolidated's actions.[73] A competitive wholesale market would make effective anticompetitive reciprocity extremely unlikely with anyone, and completely undermine the justice's interesting opinion. But since the Supreme Court's decision was based on the fact that the structural organization of the market gave rise to potential reciprocity and that actual reciprocity had been attempted, such an examination and analysis was beside the point.

THE VON'S GROCERY CASE (1966)

The mistaken inference that certain structural factors lead to substantial competitive restraint reached a climax of absurdity in the Von's Grocery case decided by the Supreme Court in 1966.[74] In that decision, Black concluded—contrary to the District Court—that the merger between the Von's Grocery Company and Shopping Bag Food Stores would tend to restrain competition substantially in the retail grocery market in the Los Angeles area.

Black's conclusion was based completely on structural factors and suppositions: the merger combined the third and sixth largest retail grocery sellers; their combined sales represent 7.5 percent of total grocery sales in the Los Angeles market in 1960; the number of owner-operated single grocery stores had decreased from 5,365 in 1950 to 3,590 in 1964; and the grocery business was falling into fewer and fewer hands.[75] Since Congress was anxious "to prevent economic concentration in the American economy by keeping a large number of small competitors in business," and since mergers and acquisitions had continued at a rapid pace since the Von's merger, it was logical to conclude that competition might have been substantially reduced by the Von's-Shopping Bag consolidation.[76] Thus, in the most completely mechanistic approach to antitrust yet applied, the Supreme Court ordered divesture.

As some sort of consolation, there was a long, careful, and devastating dissent by Justice Stewart in the Von's Grocery case. The following exerpt will set the tone and the context of his criticism:

> The Court makes no effort to appraise the competitive effects of this acquisition in terms of the contemporary economy of the

---

[73]See discussion in Eugene Singer's *Antitrust Economics*, p. 223.
[74]*United States* v. *Von's Grocery Company*, 384 U.S. p. 270.
[75]*Ibid.*, pp. 272–273.
[76]*Ibid.*, pp. 274–275.

retail food industry in the Los Angeles area. Instead, through a simple exercise in sums, it finds that the number of individual competitors in the market has decreased over the years, and, apparently on the theory the degree of competition is invariably proportional to the number of competitors, it holds that this historic reduction in the number of competing units is enough under Section 7 to invalidate a merger within the market, with no need to examine the economic concentration of the market, the level of competition in the market, or the potential adverse effect of the merger on that competition. This startling *per se* rule is contrary not only to our previous decisions, but contrary to the language of Section 7, contrary to the legislative history of the 1950 amendment, and contrary to economic reality.[77]

Stewart offered rebuttal on every phase of the brief Supreme Court decision. He first argued that there was no incipient trend toward a lessening of competition in the grocery business in Los Angeles. The simple "counting-of-heads game" played by the court majority could not rationally be equated with a lessening of competition. In fact, the grocery markets in Los Angeles were competitive to a fault with intense rivalry among chain stores and between chains and single grocery stores.[78] An exploding population and the buying and selling of cooperatives made entry into the industry easy, and made competition between all sizes of stores possible.[79]

The numerical decline in single-store units was only the result of a "transcending social and technological change" in consumer tastes and retailing techniques; there could be no reasonable inference that competition had suffered because of the "attrition" of some smaller stores. Yet, Stewart added bitterly, the Supreme Court's decision was "hardly more than a requiem for the so-called 'Mom and Pop' grocery stores," and an indirect attempt "to roll back the supermarket revolution."[80]

Even more crucial to the opinion in this case, the justice maintained that the court erred when it implied that concentration in the Los Angeles grocery business was increasing. Between 1948 and 1958, the leading grocery chain's percentage of total market sales *declined* from 14 percent to 8 percent; the top two chains percentage declined from 21 percent to 14 percent.[81] Although the com-

[77] *Ibid.*, pp. 282–283.
[78] *Ibid.*, p. 287.
[79] *Ibid.*, p. 288.
[80] *Ibid.*
[81] *Ibid.*, p. 290.

bined share of the top twenty stores had increased from 44 percent to 57 percent, the substantial turnover in the membership of the top twenty made that concentration ratio an unreliable measure of concentration and, most assuredly, of competition in the market place.[82] Further, the empirical evidence that the court relied upon to prove that the bigger firms were buying out the smaller firms and, therefore, increasing concentration in the retail market, did not appear to substantiate its allegations.[83]

Stewart also noted that a "great majority" of the post-Von's Grocery mergers in the grocery market were market-extension mergers that neither eliminated direct competitors nor increased concentration. In fact, the District Court had documented the fact that the Von's-Shopping Bag consolidation itself involved firms that competed in *different* areas of Los Angeles.[84] Stewart suggested that that particular merger was three-parts product extension and only one-part horizontal; with this interpretation, less than 1 percent of total grocery sales could have been foreclosed![85] Yet the Supreme Court majority had not even mentioned this important aspect of the merger controversy.

Finally, Stewart noted that the supposed victims in this case—the small independent firms—were aggressive, able, and efficient competitors; the District Court had "found *not a shred of evidence* that competition had been in any way impaired by the merger."[86] The defendants, therefore, were being punished for "the sin of aggressive competition," and not for any lessening or probable lessening of competition.[87] Certainly any additional comment by the author concerning the irrationality of the Supreme Court decision would be superfluous.

THE PROCTER & GAMBLE-CLOROX CASE (1967)

Because the history of the Procter & Gamble-Clorox affair[88] is extremely complicated, a short summary of the major legal issues might be helpful. Procter & Gamble (referred to as Procter, hereafter) purchased Clorox in August 1957; the FTC issued a complaint

[82] *Ibid.*, 290.
[83] *Ibid.*, pp. 292–294.
[84] *Ibid.*, p. 295.
[85] *Ibid.*, p. 296.
[86] *Ibid.*, pp. 298–300 (Emphasis added).
[87] *Ibid.*, p. 297.
[88] *Federal Trade Commission* v. *Procter & Gamble Company*, 386 U.S. 568.

against the merger in September 1957; after 14 months of hearings, an FTC examiner found that the merger violated Section 7 of the Clayton and Celler-Kefauver acts and ordered divesture on June 17, 1960; the FTC, on appeal by Procter, set aside the hearing examiner's original opinion because it was based on "treacherous conjecture"; a second hearing examiner's report of February 28, 1962 found against Procter and ordered divesture of Clorox; the FTC agreed with the second examiner's report, and issued a formal divesture order on November 26, 1963; a Federal Appeals Court dismissed the FTC complaint against Procter in 1966 because the FTC decision was "not supported by substantial evidence"; and finally, on April 13, 1967—almost ten years after the case had begun—the U.S. Supreme Court reversed the Appeals Court and ordered Procter to divest itself of Clorox.

Second Opinion of the FTC (1963)

Commissioner Elman wrote the FTC decision[89] and summarized some of the undisputed facts in the Procter case. Procter was one of the nation's fifty largest manufacturers with net sales of over one billion dollars in 1957. More importantly, Procter was the nation's largest advertiser in 1957, when they had spent $80 million on mostly television advertising. Before its purchase of Clorox, Procter had sold soaps, packaged detergents, and household cleaning agents, and many other low-priced, high-turnover consumer products—but it had not sold liquid bleach. A stock exchange valued at over $30 million with the Clorox Chemical Company in the summer of 1957 changed all that, however.

Before 1957, the Clorox Chemical Company was a relatively small firm ($12 million assets, $40 million sales) but one that had come to dominate the nation's production and sale of liquid bleach. Although liquid bleach was a standardized commodity (5¼ percent sodium hypochlorite, 94¾ percent water), unprotected by patent and made by upward of 200 different firms, Clorox brand bleach represented almost 50 percent of industry sales by 1957. More importantly, Clorox was the only bleach selling on a *national* basis; with the exception of the Purex Company (Purex had about 15 percent of the national market), almost all Clorox's competitors were smaller, regional, "down-cellar" producers. Thus, the Procter merger united the na-

---

[89] *In The Matter of the Procter & Gamble Company*, 63 FTC 1465.

tion's largest advertiser and the nation's largest liquid bleach firm. That this spelled antitrust problems should come as no surprise at this point.

The market structure of the liquid bleach market *before* the merger first interested Commissioner Elman. That market was "highly concentrated and oligopolistic" and one firm, Clorox, had almost half of all industry sales. Clorox had created, probably through advertising, a "definite consumer preference" for its brand of bleach that allowed it to be sold at prices equal to or greater than competitive products.[90] It would be extremely difficult for a new firm to compete with Clorox since:

> A new entrant into the bleach industry would have to advertise and operate from the outset on at least a broad regional scale, and consequently incur a very heavy initial investment for advertising.[91]

But even if a competitor was somehow able to accomplish the initial thrust, Clorox could not afford to "remain passive in the face of a significant encroachment upon its market position"; in the resulting "competitive struggle," Clorox, by reason of its substantial accumulated consumer preference, would undoubtedly have a "great advantage." Therefore Clorox, even *before* merging with Procter, was a "significant impediment to new entry" and "an effective barrier to the growth or expansion . . . of existing rivals in the bleach industry, and thus an inhibitor of vigorous competitive activity."[92] Even without Procter, the bleach industry was concentrated "to a degree inconsistent with effectively competitive conditions."[93]

According to Elman, the merger of Procter and Clorox would undoubtedly worsen competitive conditions in the bleach industry because "substantial cost savings and other advantages in advertising and sales promotion, especially in television advertising," were available to Procter-Clorox.[94] Supposedly the maximum volume discounts were 25 percent to 30 percent for network television; magazine, newspaper and radio volume discounts were also substantial. Even worse for competition (again, read "competitors"), the Clorox adver-

[90] *Ibid.*, p. 1562.
[91] *Ibid.*
[92] *Ibid.*, p. 1563.
[93] *Ibid.*
[94] *Ibid.*

tising could be placed in better time slots and selectively shown in areas of the country where Clorox faced particularly intense competition.[95] In addition, the economies obtainable from joint promotions and the more efficient use of Procter's large sales force "would in all likelihood substantially increase Clorox's already great market power."[96] This market power could presumably be applied against retailers to obtain more valuable shelf space and might even support tie-in and full-line forcing agreements with other Procter products. Thus, the overall effect of Procter in the bleach market would be to enhance the already considerable "power" of Clorox.

Procter's size advantages were crucial in another area—pricing. Elman stated that only a firm with "ample reserves" could offer merchants the "price concessions" needed to gain increased shelf space.[97] And since Procter was a multiproduct firm, it might be able to offer such concessions and engage in "systematic underpricing" to the detriment of its single product rivals. Even worse, if local price cutting flared, the smaller single-product rivals, short on reserves, would be in a precarious position:

> In a price fight to the finish, Procter, whose aggregate scale of operations and fiscal resources dwarf the entire liquid bleach industry, can hardly be bested.[98]

Since the "appropriate standpoint for appraising the merger is, then, *that of Clorox's rivals* and of the firms that *might* contemplate entering the liquid bleach industry," the FTC was forced to conclude that the Procter-Clorox merger had "increased the power of Clorox, by dominating its competitors . . . discouraging new entry . . . and foreclosing effective competition in the industry."[99]

Elman granted that the merger restrained competition in the bleach industry; but was a *substantial* lessening of competition probable? He noted that the Procter-Clorox merger was not horizontal or vertical and that the "ready crutch of percentages" common to all such cases was not to be available in this one. Therefore, other methods that were "non-percentile and non-quantitiative—of roughly, but fairly, estimating the substantiality of a merger's probable ad-

[95] *Ibid.*, p. 1564.
[96] *Ibid.*, p. 1566.
[97] *Ibid.*, pp. 1566–1567.
[98] *Ibid.*, p. 1567.
[99] *Ibid.*, p. 1569 (Emphasis added).

verse effect on competition in the relevant market" had to be discovered.[100] He then went on to suggest five criteria that would take the place of "percentage ratios" in this product-extension or conglomerate-like merger case:

> (1) the relative disparity in size and strength as between Procter and the largest firms in the bleach industry; (2) the excessive concentration in the industry at the time of the merger, and Clorox's dominant position in the industry; (3) the elimination, brought about by merger, of Procter as a potential competitor of Clorox; (4) the position of Procter in other markets; and (5) the nature of the "economies" enabled by the merger.[101]

Most of Commissioner Elman's discussion of the "size disparity" issue is a virtual replay of his previous comments on the effects of the Procter-Clorox merger on competition; the *only* difference is the inclusion of the word "substantial" in his remarks. For example, we are told that Procter's size would realize *"substantial* cost savings which impart a *substantial* competitive advantage to the acquired firm."[102] The most important effect of the size disparity, however, would be on the merger activity of the smaller firms:

> ... the remaining firms may now be motivated to seek affiliation by merger with giant companies. The practical tendency of the instant merger, then, is to transform the liquid bleach industry into an arena of big business competition only, with the few small firms that have not disappeared through merger eventually falling by the wayside, unable to compete with their giant rivals.[103]

But this "transformation" was the essence of Congressional concern in amending the Clayton Act in 1950. Nothing, therefore, could be more relevant than the likely effect of this merger on concentration in the bleach industry generally. Although bigness was not to be condemned *per se,* and although disparity of size was not to be relevant in every merger case, it was certainly condemnable and relevant in this one.[104] It would "eliminate virtually all possibility of an eventual movement toward deconcentration in the liquid bleach

[100] *Ibid.,* pp. 1570–1571.
[101] *Ibid.,* p. 1571.
[102] *Ibid.,* p. 1572 (Emphasis added).
[103] *Ibid.,* p. 1573.
[104] *Ibid.,* p. 1574.

industry" and that was sufficient to find against this particular merger.[105]

Another crucial and somewhat novel factor to be considered in this case was the fact that the merger eliminated Procter as a potential competitor of Clorox in the bleach industry. Before the merger, Elman declared, "Procter was not only a likely prospect for new entry into the bleach market, it was virtually the *only such prospect*": the merger, therefore, removed a substantial competitive threat.[106] It destroyed one of the "last factors tending to preserve a modicum of competitive pricing . . . in the liquid bleach industry." Since Procter's potential effect on Clorox's pricing policies no longer existed, the merger tended to reduce competition substantially.

Procter's "market power" in related markets and industries was also a legitimate factor in appraising the competitive effects of the merger, according to Commissioner Elman. Procter was unquestionably able to subsidize Clorox's activities if it chose to do so;[107] but even if it did not, the "psychological response" of Clorox's competitors to Procter's "prowess as a competitor gains an added, *even sinister dimension*" in terms of the impact of the merger on competitive activity.[108] Procter, by its very presence, could literally scare off competition; certainly no smaller bleach firms would dare do battle with such a powerful combination.

Finally, a merger "so productive of efficiencies" would undoubtedly heighten the barriers to new entry into the bleach industry.[109] Since the explicit concern of Congress was with the competitive effects of merger, *and not necessarily with efficiency,* economies and efficiencies were certainly not to be determining factors in any merger case. In fact, to the extent that "economies and efficiencies" made it difficult for other firms to compete, they would actually reduce competition and not, therefore, be in the real consumer interest. Elman stated the matter as follows:

> A merger that results in increased efficiency of production, distribution or marketing may, in certain cases, increase the vigor of competition in the relevant market. But the cost savings made possible by the instant merger serve, we have seen,

[105] *Ibid.*, p. 1575.
[106] *Ibid.*, p. 1578 (Emphasis added).
[107] *Ibid.*, p. 1578.
[108] *Ibid.*, p. 1579 (Emphasis added).
[109] *Ibid.*, p. 1580.

not to promote competition, but only to increase the barriers to new entry into the relevant market, and thereby impair competition . . . while we do not doubt that marketing economies including those of advertising and sales promotion, are as socially desirable as economies in production and physical distribution, there does come a point "at which product differentiation ceases to promote welfare and becomes wasteful, or mass advertising loses its informative aspect and merely entrenches market leaders." We think that point has been reached in the household liquid bleach industry. In short, *the kind of "efficiency" and "economy" produced by this merger is precisely the kind that*—in the short as well as the long run—*hurts, not helps, a competitive economy and burdens, not benefits the consuming public.*[110]

Although the post-acquisition evidence was "entitled to little weight," it tended to confirm, in Elman's view, the FTC's analysis. Clorox's share of the liquid bleach market had increased from 48.8 percent in 1957 to 51.5 percent in 1961.[111] To remove the anticompetitive effects of the merger on the bleach industry, a divesture of Clorox from Procter was necessary; it was so ordered.[112]

Comment on the FTC Statement

Since the Appeals Court and U.S. Supreme Court decisions to follow are based almost completely on this Federal Trade Commission decision, it might be appropriate to re-examine and critically analyze some of the arguments made above. Commissioner Elman's first significant point in this case was to argue that advertising created "barriers to entry" in the bleach industry and that this would deter new entrants. He strongly emphasized that Clorox was the only truly *national* producer, and that it would be difficult for any firm, particularly any new firm, to compete with Clorox on a national scale since advertising expenditures were so crucial to success in this industry. Since Clorox, even before the merger, outadvertised everyone, and since a Procter-Clorox combination was the largest potential advertising combination in the economy, it was clear to Elman that "the industry was barricaded to new entry."[113]

But logic and the facts in the case belie this FTC approach completely. Household bleach was a fairly standardized item, easily pro-

[110]*Ibid.*, pp. 1580–1581 (Footnote omitted; emphasis added).
[111]*Ibid.*, p. 1583.
[112]*Ibid.*, p. 1585.
[113]*Ibid.*, p. 1563.

duced, and unprotected by patent. Since it was a relatively heavy product and had a relatively low price per unit weight, effective "competition" was always limited to about a 300-mile area from the point of actual production. One did *not* have to be some sort of "national" seller to be able to compete with Clorox or anyone else in this industry. Competition always takes place in *particular* markets for *particular* customers, and bleach markets were actively competitive with over 200 firms vying for the consumer dollar. In addition, there was a high percentage of liquid bleach sold in supermarkets under the store's own label. Unless Clorox was required to have the *same* competitor in *different* markets, whether one was a "national" producer had nothing at all to do with competition in the actual marketplace.

Elman also made the usual market structure error regarding competition in the bleach industry. He moved directly from the fact that concentration ratios were high in the bleach industry, to some negative and rather dismal conclusions about competition in that industry. But where is the slightest bit of empirical information that would allow us to conclude that competition in the bleach industry was, say, less vigorous in 1957 than it had been in 1951? Or in 1941? Had prices for bleach been rising quickly? Had the number of competitors been falling dramatically? Had Clorox engaged in successful predatory price cutting in the bleach market? Was Clorox in fact suppressing competitors or consumers? What information, beside raw structural concentration ratios, would allow the conclusion that competition in the liquid bleach industry had all but been extinguished, as the FTC inferred, and that the Procter merger would be the last nail in the competitive coffin? Since absolutely *no proof* that competition was in fact dying was offered by the FTC (or anyone else), is it reasonable to assume that no such proof existed? Apparently the "inevitable inferences" of the market structure approach to competition worked their mysterious hocus-pocus in still another antitrust case.

The Federal Trade Commission could never really make up its mind on the pricing dangers inherent in the merger of Procter and Clorox. On the one hand, they argued that the substitution of Procter for Clorox would lend further *rigidities* to an already oligopolistic industry and would tend to eliminate what little competition remained in that industry;[114] on the other hand, however, they argued that the substitution of Procter for Clorox would tend to create a situation of "extreme pricing *flexibility* available only to a firm with ample reserves."[115] With typical consistency, the FTC argued that *both* practices were likely, and that both would tend to reduce competition substantially!

The latter pricing policy, as might be expected, was the greater competitive danger. It would allow "cross-subsidization" from Procter's other product markets and allow Procter to subsidize Clorox's activities in the bleach industry. As explained earlier in the chapter, however, such inferences depend on crucially important assumptions. Where, for example, did Procter possess the "monopolistic advantage" to fund such subsidization? The FTC assumed, again mistakenly, that its off-handed reference to the fact that Procter was a "large" firm, and possessed high "market shares" in other product lines or industries, would be enough to demonstrate that they earned monopoly profits that might fund subsidization.[116] It should be apparent, however, that if simple market structure assumptions do not allow accurate inferences about competition in the bleach industry (where at least *some* additional information was provided), they can hardly allow accurate inferences with respect to competition in Procter's *other* markets (where *no* information at all was provided). Again, the FTC's inferences were based on unproven structural assumptions.

One of the most novel and telling aspects of the FTC decision was the "potential competition" thesis: Procter lessened competition in the bleach industry since its merger with Clorox removed itself as an independent competitive threat. Since we have already commented upon this issue earlier in this chapter, it will suffice to indicate here that it was *not* established that Procter was a likely entrant into the bleach business nor—as the FTC boldly stated—"virtually the only such prospect" for entry. There was no evidence whatever in the FTC account that would lead inevitably to the conclusion that Procter was a likely entrant. The only mention of Procter's plans was a statement to the effect that Procter, after a two-year study, had decided *not* to enter the bleach industry.[117] Are we to infer that

[114] *Ibid.*, p. 1575.
[115] *Ibid.*, p. 1567 (Emphasis added).
[116] *Ibid.*, p. 1579.
[117] *Ibid.* p. 1541.

they were a potential competitor because they decided *not* to enter the bleach industry?

Why the FTC believed Procter to be virtually the *only* prospect for entry was never explained. Why weren't Colgate-Palmolive, Lever Brothers, B.T. Babbit, or any number of large firms making related household products considered as potential competitors? Weren't these firms as likely—or as unlikely—to enter the bleach industry as Procter? In fact, why weren't any of America's industrial giants considered potential competitors? Weren't they "potential" enough? Since the FTC decided to play it "deuces wild" when they introduced *one* "potential" competitor, Procter, they should have been prepared to admit that there could have been many other potential competitors. That the number of potential competitors was reduced by one (and that one became an active competitor in the bleach industry), therefore, certainly cannot lead to the FTC conclusion that competition in the bleach industry was substantially lessened because Procter bought Clorox.

The most embarrassing part of the FTC decision concerns Commissioner Elman's discussion of the trade-restraining possibilities of "economies and efficiencies." Repeatedly we are told that cost savings achievable from the consolidation will only increase the bleach industry's barriers and thus impair competition. Relying heavily on Dirlam's notion that product differentiation and advertising beyond a certain point is "wasteful" and merely entrenches market leaders,[118] and the FTC's belief that it had discovered that certain point, Commissioner Elman boldly asserted that any further "economy" and "efficiency" would burden not benefit the consuming public.[119]

But how had the FTC arrived at its decision? What was that "certain point," and how did the Commission know that it had been reached or exceeded? Was the FTC to be the judge of what product differentiation was "wasteful"? In a free market, the concept "wasteful" is only relevant to voluntary consumer choice. Since consumer demand determines the priorities for the use of scarce economic resources, consumers always determine what product differentiation they consider wasteful. If they have free choice, they will support just that degree of product differentiation that they desire, and the market will faithfully reflect that choice. *To assert that product differen-*

[118] *Ibid.*, p. 1580.
[119] *Ibid.*, p. 1581.

tiation is wasteful despite apparent consumer preference is to substitute one's own preferences for those of the consumer's in the marketplace. Dirlam and the Federal Trade Commission should at least be honest enough to admit that they are speaking *for themselves* and not for the consumers.

Seen in this light, economies and efficiencies in production, distribution or marketing are never to be regretted, and product differentiation is never "wasteful." The thrust of economic activity in a free market—as explained in Chapter 1 of this volume—is to produce greater outputs at lower costs and to economize on scarce factors of production. To legislate against that thrust because certain competitors might find the resulting competition more difficult, or because certain economic experts are confident that economies or differentiations past some point are "wasteful," is to strike at the heart of consumer welfare in the name of defending and protecting it—such confident paternalism is the common thread in all noncapitalist economic systems.

The entire FTC decision is the logical culmination of a long series of cases where economies and efficiencies have been "suspect." Here, of course, they are more than just suspect; they are blatantly condemned since they will create regrettable burdens that the consuming public will have to bear should the merger be allowed. No hypothetical decision that this author might invent could better illustrate the argument of this volume that antitrust theory and policy is a complete hoax.

Finally, the most ironical part of the issue regarding economies, particularly advertising economies, is that they may not have been achievable after all. The essence of the FTC arguments concerning "barriers to entry" was that the smaller bleach firms (even Purex) would be at a severe disadvantage in purchasing network advertising time as compared with Procter-Clorox. Yet David Blank has argued that in reality no such disadvantages actually existed.[120] He has charged that the FTC—like other scholars in other similar studies—unquestionably accepted the "book prices" for advertising time, rather than the *prices actually paid* in the market for such advertising time. From Blank's analysis it is clear that there was little if any

---

[120]David M. Blank, "Television Advertising: The Great Discount Illusion, or Tony-pandy Revisited," *Journal of Business*, XXXXI (January 1968), 10–38. See also John L. Peterman, "The Clorox Case and the Television Rate Structures," *Journal of Law and Economics*, XI (October 1968), 321–432.

price advantage for the large buyers; if anything, the larger buyers may have had to pay *higher* rates per unit of time than smaller buyers. Thus still another FTC case has been built around some fundamental assumptions that turn out, upon analysis, to be incorrect. Is there any salvagable theory or fact left in this case?

Court of Appeals Decision

Much of the criticism related above concerning the FTC's decision in the Procter case is certainly not new or original. A good share of it can be found in a reading of the Appeals Court decision of 1966 which reversed the FTC divesture order.[121]

Chief Judge Weick of the Appeals Court first reviewed the circumstances of the FTC proceedings. He emphasized the fact that the first FTC ruling on the Procter matter had set aside an initial hearing examiner's decision because "the evidence was insufficient to support a finding of illegality"; the remand and rehearing was for the sole purpose of taking postacquisition evidence in the matter.[122] Yet, surprisingly, the second FTC decision (Commissioner Elman's decision), while admitting that there had been no dramatic change in market structure or behavior in the postmerger market, dismissed the relevance of such information and found against Procter's purchase of Clorox. The second FTC decision, therefore, was based solely on a record that the first FTC decision "had ruled insufficient to support a finding of illegality."

But was there "substantial" evidence to support the FTC's second decision? Judge Weick thought not. In the first place, he argued, there was just *no* evidence that Procter planned to engage in the manufacture or distribution of liquid bleach prior to the Clorox merger as the FTC had assumed.[123] The "potential competitor" hypothesis was based on "mere possibility and conjecture" and not on any supportable facts.

> Household liquid bleach is an old product; Procter is an old company. If Procter were on the brink it is surprising that it never lost its balance and fell in during the many years in which such bleach was on the market. It had never threatened to enter the market.[124]

[121] *Procter & Gamble* v. *Federal Trade Commission* 358 F. 2d 74.
[122] *Ibid.*, p. 78.
[123] *Ibid.*, p. 80.
[124] *Ibid.*, p. 83.

Secondly, the court rejected the FTC notion that Procter was virtually the only potential competitor, and that the barriers to entry surrounding the liquid bleach industry made new entry impossible. Certainly a moderately sized firm like Clorox would not deter

> large companies like Lever Brothers and Colgate-Palmolive Peet Co. (Procter's largest competitors) from entering the field on a national basis if they concluded that the *profits were sufficiently attractive to justify the expenditure required.*[125]

In addition, there were several other large firms (Monsanto Chemical, Diamond Alkali Company) that might have either entered the industry independently or combined in a conglomerate merger to produce bleach. And, finally, the fact that there were upward of two hundred smaller producers "would not seem to indicate anything unhealthy about the market conditions."[126]

Judge Weick next turned to the issue of possible "economies" that were likely to accrue from the merger. There certainly were possible cost savings in marketing and advertising, but the court was not overly impressed with their size, nor with their probable effect on competition in the bleach industry. That some economies might be effectuated from a merger *otherwise lawful* was no reason to condemn such a consolidation.

The court was also not impressed with the "sinister" aspects of Clorox's market power, nor with the market power of the Procter-Clorox combination. Clorox brand bleach was an excellent product with a high degree of quality control; its ability to get "shelf-space" was clearly a function of the corresponding "great consumer demand" for the product. Procter, on the other hand, had never engaged in predatory practices, and the singular example of a "price war" offered by the FTC only proved that the Procter-Clorox combination would retaliate to *meet* the competitive price thrusts of other firms.[127] Nothing in either the history of Clorox or Procter, therefore, could substantiate the "sinister" market power assumptions of the FTC.

And finally, all the FTC's conjecture on what *might* happen to competitors and consumers was belied by the post-acquisition evi-

---

[125] *Ibid.*, p. 80 (Emphasis added).
[126] *Ibid.*
[127] *Ibid.*, p. 82

dence on what *did* happen. There had been no important change in market shares and Clorox's rivals were selling "substantially *more bleach* for more money than prior" to the merger.[128] Certainly such evidence, virtually ignored by the Commission, "does not prove the anticompetitive effects of the merger." The Appeals Court then set aside the FTC's divesture order and remanded the case with instructions to dismiss the entire matter. The FTC however, appealed the decision to the Supreme Court.

Supreme Court Decision

Justice Douglas delivered the unanimous opinion of the Supreme Court in the Procter case on April 11, 1967.[129] After sympathetically reviewing the FTC's major hypothesis, Douglas concluded that the Court of Appeals had "misapprehended the standards for its review."[130] That court, it will be remembered, had noted (but as a *final* point only) that the post-acquisition evidence did not prove that the Procter-Clorox merger had anticompetitive effects. But, Douglas pointed out, no such *proof* of anticompetitive effects was required in the section 7 cases. Since the act dealt with "probabilities" and "not with certainties," no "manifestation" of anticompetitive power was necessary for conviction.[131]

But was it even *probable* that competition would be substantially lessened because of the merger? The Supreme Court thought that it was for, apparently, the same reasons as the FTC had suggested—and the Appeals Court had rejected. Douglas merely repeated the unsubstantiated FTC arguments that Procter's advertising economies would raise entry barriers, and that Procter's size would "dissuade the smaller firms from aggressively competing."[132] He also drearily repeated the "potential competition" hypothesis that Procter was the most likely entrant, that FTC evidence supported such a conclusion(!), and that the merger, therefore, eliminated the potential competition of the acquiring firm.[133] Accordingly, the Court of Appeals decision was

---

[128] *Ibid.* (Emphasis added).
[129] 386 U.S. 568
[130] *Ibid.*, p. 576.
[131] *Ibid.*, p. 577.
[132] *Ibid.*, pp. 578–579.
[133] *Ibid.*, pp. 580–581.

reversed and the original FTC order to divest was ordered enforced.

Justice Harlan's concurring opinion in the Procter case was a careful, serious, attempt to formulate some standards for judging the legality of product-extension and conglomerate style mergers. Unfortunately, most of Harlan's suggested standards are founded on traditional market structure assumptions; however, he maintained a healthy skepticism about "the state of our economic knowledge" and two of his standards certainly bear out this skepticism. His four suggested standards are reproduced below:

> First, the decision can rest on analysis of *market structure* without resort to evidence of postmerger anticompetitive behavior. Second, the operation of the premerger market must be understood as the foundation of successful analysis. The responsible agency may presume that the market operates in accord with *generally accepted principles of economic theory*, but the presumption must be open to the challenge of alternative operational formulations. Third, if it is reasonably probable that there will be a *change in structure* which will allow the exercise of substantially greater market power, then a *prima facie* case has been made out under Section 7. Fourth, where the case against the merger rests on the probability of increased market power, the merging companies may attempt to prove that there are countervailing economies reasonably probable which should be weighted against the adverse effects.[134]

Harlan's standards are simply a rehash and a rework of very familiar criteria. The sum and substance of these criteria is a heavy reliance on "generally accepted principles of economic theory," i.e., on the market structure approach to competition. Market structure or probable changes in market structure create "market power" and, therefore, a *prima facie* case against any merger; countervailing economies may only be introduced as a last resort. Thus, Harlan would strap conglomerates with the same sort of simplistic structural approach that had already proved economically irrational in horizontal and vertical merger cases. So ended the famous Procter case.

A Note on Conglomerate Cases

The applicability of Section 7 to divergent conglomerate mergers remains in doubt. In 1969 the Justice Department filed five major complaints involving mergers of this type.[135] In addition to the famil-

---

[134] *Ibid.*, pp. 598–599 (Emphasis added).
[135] The five complaints are: *United States* v. *Ling-Temco-Vought, Inc., Jones and*

iar sorts of charges, these complaints dealt with the newer "potential competition," "potential reciprocity" and "aggregate concentration" theories already explored in the first part of this chapter. Finally, in the first court test of its full arsenal of conglomerate theories, the Justice Department was reported to have been "resoundingly defeated."[136] Since the Supreme Court has yet to hear a divergent conglomerate case, however, the issues discussed above are far from being settled.[137]

Summary and Conclusions

An examination of some of the most famous merger cases in antitrust history has demonstrated—not surprisingly—that antitrust makes no more economic sense here than it had elsewhere in this volume. The firms involved in the cases examined were not restraining trade, foreclosing competition, accomplishing reciprocity, engaging in predatory practices. Nor, for that matter, were they generally abusing consumers or competitors. In fact, the more likely inference from all the cases is that the mergers would have intensified competitive pressures, realized certain economies, and would have increased consumer welfare. Since the courts have accepted the assumptions of the market structure approach to competition, however, and since they have been convinced that "economies" and "efficiencies" endanger competition because they might injure some competitors, such mergers had to be condemned.[138] As explained in Chapters 8

Laughlin Steel Corporation, and Jones and Laughlin Industries Inc.; United States v. International Telephone and Telegraph Corporation (Canteen Corporation); United States v. International Telephone and Telegraph Corporation and Grinnell Corporation; United States v. International Telephone and Telegraph Corporation and the Hartford Fire Insurance Company; United States v. Northwest Industries, Inc. and The B.F. Goodrich Company.

[136]District Court Judge Timbers ruled that ITT's purchase of the Grinnell Corporation did not violate Section 7. See United States v. International Telephone and Telegraph, 306, F. Supp. 766. (1970).

Most recently, ITT's purchase of the Canteen Corporation has been successfully defended at court; District Court Judge Richard B. Austin ruled that the government's charges pertainint to "reciporcity" and the "forecosure of potential competition" were completely without foundation. See the Wall Street Journal, July 6, 1971, p. 3.

[137]As this manuscript goes to press the Justice Department and ITT are in the process of formalizing a bazaar consent decree whereby ITT would divest itself of Canteen Corporation, the fire protection division of Grinnell Corporation, and either Hartford Fire Insurance Company or the following group of companies: Avis Rent-A-Car; ITT-Levitt & Sons Inc. and its subsidiaries; ITT Hamilton Life Insurance Company and ITT Life Insurance Company of New York. See the Wall Street Journal, August 2, 1971, p. 2.

[138]The reader should be reminded that the author has not just picked those antitrust

and 9, such decisions are not a mistake but the inevitable logic of a public policy based on ambiguous law and incorrect economic theory.

cases that "prove" his general arguments. The cases reported in this chapter and in the entire volume are the most famous cases in antitrust history. Thus, in the most famous cases in antitrust history, trade was *not* being restrained and competition was *not* being lessened.

CHAPTER **11**

Antitrust: A Final Word

THE CRITICS OF ANTITRUST

Many academic scholars and practicing professionals in the area of antitrust, with a much less extreme position on these issues than the author's, have recently been voicing skepticism and criticism concerning present antitrust policy.[1] However, none of these critics has as yet called for the wholesale abandonment of antitrust. But the rumblings and stirrings are interesting and even, perhaps, encouraging. For example, Robert H. Bork and Ward S. Bowman have written one of the most scalding attacks on antitrust theory and policy ever published.[2] Morris A. Adelman has always been in the forefront of scholarly criticism with respect to antitrust.[3] Likewise, Donald Dewey has never been much of an antitrust enthusiast.[4] George J.

[1]The following discussion does *not* apply, of course, to the very few economists and critics that have *always* opposed antitrust in theory as well as practice. See Murray N. Rothbard, *Power and Market* (Menlo Park, Calif.: Institute for Humane Studies, 1970), pp. 44–47; Sylvester Petro, "The Growing Threat of Antitrust," *Fortune*, LXVI (November, 1962), 128–138+; and Alan Greenspan, "Antitrust," in Ayn Rand, *Capitalism: The Unknown Ideal* (New York: New American Library, 1966), pp. 63–71.

[2]"The Crisis in Antitrust", *Fortune*, LXVIII (December, 1963), 138.

[3]"Problems and Prospects in Antitrust policy—11", in Almarin Phillips, ed., *Prespectives on Antitrust Policy* (Princeton-Princeton University Press, 1965), p. 32.

[4]"The Economics of Antitrust: Science or Religion," Richard Low, ed., *The Economics of Antitrust* (Englewood Cliffs, N.J.: Prentice-Hall, 1968), pp. 61-73.

Stigler and Simon N. Whitney have eloquently warned of the economic consequences of present antitrust policies.[5] Betty Bock of the National Industrial Conference Board has challenged the applicability of present antitrust policy in rapidly changing market structures with complex firms and undefinable "markets."[6] Frederick M. Rowe has emphatically echoed the same kind of thinking.[7] Peter Asch has written the first textbook in this area that makes the problems and criticisms of antitrust theory (and occasionally policy) *primary* instead of secondary.[8] And even Lee Loevinger, former chief of the Antitrust Division of the Justice Department, has severely criticized current antitrust policies warning that such policies—particularly the "potential abuse" theories—threaten the very existence of the free enterprise system.[9]

In many important ways, however, the academic and professional criticism is extremely disappointing. In the first place, the critics (excepting the "libertarian" critics) have not objected to antitrust *in principle;* rather, they are unhappy about the consequences or potential consequences of specific enforcement policies. Apparently there would be *some* sort of enforcement policy that would satisfy the various critics, although it might be different, even radically different, from the present policies. Unwilling to make an explicit value judgment concerning the very existence of antitrust in a free society, they accept the existence of antitrust by default as if *that* decision did not, somehow, involve a value judgment.

Secondly, almost all the critics assume that antitrust *did* make sense and *did* have relevance in the past, but that it is the increasingly complexity of the modern business world and the increasing difficulty of measuring competition and monopoly that makes pre-

---

[5]George J. Stigler, "The Economic Effects of Antitrust Laws," *Journal of Law and Economics,* IX (October 1966), 225–258; and Simon N. Whitney, "Antitrust Threats to the Market Economy," *The Intercollegiate Review,* IV (January-February 1968), 70–77.

[6]See, for example, her *Antitrust Issues in Conglomerate Acquisitions,* Studies in Business Economics, No. 110, published by the National Industrial Conference Board.

[7]"Antitrust and Vanishing Boundaries," *New Technologies, Competition, and Antitrust,* Ninth Conference on Antitrust Issues in Today's Economy (Washington, D.C.: National Industrial Conference Board, 1970).

[8]*Economic Theory and the Antitrust Dilemma* (New York: John Wiley and Sons, 1970).

[9]Mr. Loevinger's speech titled "How to Succeed in Business without Being Tried," was given January 13, 1971, and published by the Bureau of National Affairs, Washington, D.C. It is reprinted in *Antitrust and Trade Regulation Report* (January 19, 1971), pp. D1–D23.

sent antitrust policies uncertain and even dangerous. Times change, the critics argue; policies that might have been rational and relevant a hundred years ago may no longer be rational and relevant today. Consequently, of course, one could not be sure what *new* governmental policies might be necessary to cope with the new complexities of monopoly and monopoly power in the future.

In glorifying the past rationality and relevance of antitrust, however, the critics knowingly or unknowlingly ignore the information brought to light in this volume. There was no "golden age" when monopolistic abuse was running rampant in the free market and when, accordingly, antitrust was magnificently relevant. Antitrust law has *always* been ambiguous, the theoretical foundations of antitrust theory have *always* been faulty, and the empirical "evidence" has *always* been nonexistent. Although the belief in some golden age of antitrust might be emotionally satisfying, and although it is consistent with the critics' position that antitrust *is* acceptable in principle, it is the ultimate in naïveté and deserves no support whatever.

Thirdly, most of the criticism of antitrust has not been directed at the fundamental assumption of antitrust theory, i.e., the market structure approach to competition and its corollary, the concept of pure competition. Almost all the critics admit that present policies, particularly in the area of mergers, go too far and that potentially competitive situations that would realize economies for consumers are prevented by antitrust policy and court decision. But how far would the critics go with antitrust, how would they rationally tell how *far* to go, and what would they be going *toward?* What tests to "measure" competition would they devise? What is their idea of an ideally competitive market, or of an "optimal allocation of resources"? Would they really give up the idea of pure competition as some sort of welfare ideal, or would they simply attempt to make pure competition "more realistic" and market structure tests "more practical"? To refine and modify policies is to "work within the system" of antitrust and to *accept its premises.* But it is the *premises themselves* that need challenging.

The present criticisms of antitrust theory and policy are interesting, therefore, but they are not fundamental. They all accept government intervention in a free market system; they criticize the particular form of the intervention. They all accept the antitrust laws (primarily the Sherman Act) as a legal bulwark against actual or potential monopolistic abuse; they criticize present interpretations of "monopolistic abuse," particularly in the area of corporate mergers. They accept the idea that antitrust was relevant historically; yet they ignore the fact that there is little or no documentation to support that thesis. And finally, they refuse to challenge seriously the essence of antitrust theory: the concept of pure competition. Apparently they realize that to challenge such a concept would mean to destroy antitrust theory and the entire intellectual rationale for antitrust policy. And this the critics will not or cannot do.

THE "OTHER" CRITICS OF ANTITRUST

While a few economists have begun to doubt the wisdom of recent antitrust policy, another far more substantial group of economists is vigorously pressing for more forceful enforcement of existing laws or, alternatively, new laws that would deconcentrate oligopolistic industries. Many leading economists have been arguing for years that oligopolistic concentration breeds costly product differentiation, retards innovation, dampens enthusiasm for price competition, and summarily costs the American consumer upwards of $50 billion dollars a year in "overcharge."[10] Although we have noted that such "arguments" depend on crucial assumptions that are not valid, such views are easily the conventional wisdom among the antitrust "intellectuals." Spectacular divesture suits against major American firms in concentrated industries would not be at all surprising. Indeed, this may be the major thrust of antitrust in the 70s.

Capitalism is a viable economic system or it is not. An active policy of government intervention in a free market business system is a contradiction in terms. Trades of private property are either voluntary or they are not; one cannot legislate the free market or create competition. To have a free market the government must leave the markets alone; to have the state *make* markets "free" is again a contradiction in terms. Critics of antitrust policy who pretend to be concerned with the free enterprise system have either not realized, or have refused to realize, this fundamental issue.

Is there business monopoly in the present economic system? Of course there is. Government favors, privileges, patents, subsidies, tariffs, and franchises can and do allow certain corporations to hold and employ "monopoly power," i.e., *governmental power for eco-*

---

[10]Such views are echoed consistently in the *Antitrust Law & Economics Review.* See any issue or, more specifically, IV (Summer 1971).

nomic advantage. Such "plutocratic" devices (as William Graham Sumner termed them) are the essence of monopoly and they are absolutely improper in a free market system and should be ended. The "monopolies" that the FCC, CAB, and ICC maintain could not last a day without governmental support.

But this kind of "monopoly" has nothing directly to do with the mission of antitrust. Antitrust, supposedly, was aimed at free market monopoly problems and the marginal competitive problems that would arise when business was left free to pursue its own self-interest. Yet, ironically, the essence of the monopoly in the market place is *governmental.* In this light, antitrust may be seen as a diversionary tactic to draw attention away from the real monopolistic problems —the developing plutocratic relationship between business and government. Certain elements of the business community have never desired "free competition" and the uncertainties and "irrationalities" often associated with it. They have sought and gained economic subsidy and protection through the political system. They have been anxious to use the government to "regulate competition" because it was, supposedly, tending toward monopoly.[11] Antitrust, therefore, may be an even bigger hoax than anyone has imagined.

Anyone who has agonized over the antitrust cases discussed in this volume does not need to be reminded that antitrust is a hoax. And a hoax, no matter how sacred, does not deserve a future. Yet the antitrust laws and the antitrust mystique are part of the conventional wisdom of a mixed enterprise system. Neither the laws nor the mystique are about to be "repealed." In fact no laws could be a safer part of the existing business regulatory system than antitrust. And the business community, as explained above, has *never* opposed the laws in principle, and never will.

Yet the political economy of an issue or of an economic system can be turned around. It is hoped that this book provides some leverage for that effort.

[11]Again, for the best treatment of this issue see, Gabriel Kolko, *The Triumph of Conservatism: A Reinterpretation of American History, 1900–1916* (New York: Free Press of Glencoe, 1963).

Index